The Musical Human

To the memory of
Professor John Anthony Randall Blacking
(1928–1990)

The Musical Human

Rethinking John Blacking's Enthnomusicology in the Twenty-First Century

Edited by

SUZEL ANA REILY

ASHGATE

Published by
Ashgate Publishing Limited
Gower House
Croft Road
Aldershot
Hampshire GU11 3HR
England

Ashgate Publishing Company
Suite 420
101 Cherry Street
Burlington, VT 05401-4405
USA

Ashgate website: http://www.ashgate.com

British Library Cataloguing in Publication Data
European Seminar in Ethnomusicology (16th : 2000 : Belfast, Northern Ireland)
   The musical human : rethinking John Blacking's
   ethnomusicology in the twenty-first century. – (SOAS)
   musicological series)
   Blacking, John – Congresses 2. Ethnomusicology –
   Congresses
   I. Title II. Reily, Suzel Ana, 1955–
   780.8'9

Library of Congress Cataloging-in-Publication Data
The musical human : rethinking John Blacking's ethnomusicology in the twenty-first century / edited by Suzel Ana Reily.
       p. cm.—(SOAS musicology series)
    ISBN 0-7546-5138-X (alk. paper)
   1. Ethnomusicology. 2. Blacking, John. I. Reily, Suzel Ana, 1955– II. Series.

   ML3799.M85 2005
   780'.89—dc22

2005005330

ISBN-10: 0 7546 5138 X

Typeset in Times by IML Typographers, Birkenhead and
printed in Great Britain by T.J. International, Padstow, Cornwall.

Contents

List of Figures and Table

Figures

Table

Notes on Contributors

John Baily is Professor of Ethnomusicology at Goldsmiths University of London and has completed doctorates in experimental psychology at the University of Sussex and in social anthropology (ethnomusicology) at Queen's University Belfast; he also holds a postgraduate degree in documentary film from the National Film and Television School. Formerly Associate Professor of Music at Columbia University, New York, he has conducted ethnomusicological fieldwork in Afghanistan, Iran, Nepal, Pakistan and amongst South Asian communities in Britain. His many publications include *Music of Afghanistan: Professional Musicians in the City of Herat* (Cambridge University Press, 1988) and articles on musical cognition, music and the human body and ethnographic film-making.

Fumiko Fujita holds an MA in Music from Kunitachi College of Music (1975) and a PhD from Queen's University Belfast (1988), where she was supervised by John Blacking. Now she works as Professor and Doctor of Music Education in the School of Music at the Nagoya University of Arts in Shikatsu, Japan. She is the author of *Problems of Language, Culture and the Appropriateness of Musical Expression in Japanese Children's Performance* (Academia Music, 1989), and her research interests focus on the study of Japanese music-making in the sociocultural setting.

Keith Howard is Reader in Music at SOAS (School of Oriental and African Studies), University of London, and Director, AHRC Research Centre for Cross-Cultural Music and Dance Performance. Keith studied under John Blacking from 1981, receiving his PhD in Social Anthropology (Ethnomusicology) in 1986. His books include: *Korean Musical Instruments: A Practical Guide* (Se-kwang Music Publishers, 1988), *Bands, Songs, and Shamanistic Rituals: Folk Music in Korean Society* (Royal Asiatic Society, 1989), *True Stories of the Korean Comfort Women* (Cassell, 1995), *Korean Musical Instruments* (Oxford University Press, 1995), *Korean Shamanism: Revivals, Survivals, and Change* (Royal Asiatic Society, 1998), *Korean Musical Instruments: A Listening Guide* (Oxford University Press, 1999), and the official book for Her Majesty Queen Elizabeth's 1999 state visit to Korea. He is currently completing two volumes entitled *Preserving Korea* and *Creating Korea* for Ashgate and editing a volume on Korean pop music.

Deborah James studied anthropology at Witswatersrand University, where she first met John Blacking and read his writings on Venda music. His work, alongside that of Andrew Tracey, provided guidance and inspiration in the writing of her PhD, which was later published as a book: *Songs of the Women Migrants: Performance and Identity in South Africa* (Columbia University Press, 1999). She is currently Reader in Anthropology at the London School of Economics. Her research interests include migration, ethnomusicology, ethnicity, property relations and the politics of land reform in South Africa.

Jaco Kruger holds a PhD (1993) from Rhodes University. He has been researching Venda music since 1983, taking particular interest in processes of change and the application of research findings in the music education curriculum. He is currently Associate Professor in ethnomusicology in the School of Music at North-West University, Potchefstroom, South Africa.

Suzel Ana Reily is Reader in Ethnomusicology at Queen's University Belfast. She completed her doctoral degree at the University of São Paulo in 1990, during which she spent a year in Belfast receiving special supervision from John Blacking. Her publications include *Voices of the Magi: Enchanted Vision in Southeast Brazil* (University of Chicago Press, 2002) and *Brazilian Musics, Brazilian Identities* (Special Issue of the *British Journal of Ethnomusicology*, 2000). She has also prepared a website based on John Blacking's ethnographic material of Venda girls' initiation schools, which drew her attention to the potential ethnomusicological applications of hypermedia.

Rebecca Sager holds an MM (1993) and PhD (2002) in Ethnomusicology from the University of Texas at Austin. Following a period teaching in the Department of Music at Istanbul Bilgi University (2000–2001), she works as an independent scholar in Tallahassee, FL, and holds a Rockefeller Fellowship through the Center for Black Music Research (2004–2005). She has authored entries on Caribbean musics and Haitian communities in the United States, another book chapter on Blacking's theory of music and identity, and co-authored a volume about entrainment – processes of rhythmic synchronization. Sager conducted archival research in John Blacking's papers at Queen's University Belfast in September, 2001.

Britta Sweers is Junior Professor of Ethnomusicology at the Hochschule für Musik und Theater, Rostock (Germany). Having also worked as online editor for *Folk/World Music*, she is interested in the transformation of traditional music and has undertaken research in various Anglo-American regions and in north-eastern Europe. Her publications include *Lontano – 'Aus weiter Ferne': zur Musiksprache György Ligetis* (von Bockel, 1997) and *Electric Folk: The Changing Face of English Traditional Music* (Oxford University Press, 2004).

She was also guest editor of *The World of Music*, 46 (1), titled *Contemporary British Music Traditions* (2004).

Helena Wulff has a PhD in Social Anthropology from Stockholm University, where she is Associate Professor. Among her publications are *Twenty Girls: Growing Up, Ethnicity and Excitement in a South London Microculture* (Almqvist & Wiksell International, 1988), *Ballet across Borders: Career and Culture in the World of Dancers* (Berg, 1998), *Youth Cultures: A Cross-Cultural Perspective* (co-edited with Vered Amit-Talai, Routledge, 1995), *New Technologies at Work: People, Screens and Social Virtuality* (co-edited with Christina Garsten, Berg, 2003) and 40 articles for volumes and journals. Her current research focuses on the anthropology of dance, the arts, visual culture, transnationality and Ireland.

Acknowledgements

No volume can be put together without the help of many people, and I wouldn't even presume to be able to name them all. The book is made up of a selection of papers presented at the Sixteenth Annual Meeting of the European Seminar for Ethnomusicology (ESEM), in 2000, so I want to begin by thanking the then president, Ruediger Schumacher, and secretary-general, Udo Will, for having invited me to organize the event in Belfast. The conference could not have been a success without the help of fellow members of the Programme and Local Organizing Committees, which included Martin Clayton, Kevin Dawe, Hastings Donnan and Tina Ramnarine; my sincerest thanks to them. I also thank the British Academy and Queen's University Belfast for the financial support they provided for the conference, as this assistance was critical in enriching the debate at the event as well as its aftermath. I also take this opportunity to express my gratitude to everyone who attended the conference, and especially to those who presented papers. But, above all, this volume could not have come into existence without the support of the contributors, whom I also thank for their patience throughout the long period of preparation.

This project has been made especially worthwhile because of the support I have received from John Blacking's family. My thanks, therefore, to Zureena Desai and to daughters Leila, Talia, Munira and Deena Blacking.

I am also grateful to the anonymous referees, whose judicious comments and suggestions have made a significant impact on the content of the volume. Furthermore, I must also express my gratitude to Linda Cayford for her careful copy-editing and also to the Ashgate team and to the Board of the SOAS Musicology Series for their enthusiastic support of the project since its inception.

Suzel Ana Reily

CHAPTER ONE

John Blacking in the Twenty-First Century: An Introduction

Suzel Ana Reily

The musical human: without a doubt, this vision of the human species as naturally musical has become the most enduring legacy that John Blacking bequeathed to ethnomusicology. The image aptly embodies his preoccupations, which integrated theoretical and methodological issues within the discipline with a deep concern for the physical and psychological well-being of humanity. Blacking sincerely believed in the power of music and he contended that people's general health depended on the musical opportunities made available to them. For this reason, he placed great importance on ethnomusicology, the discipline that investigates the way in which different societies around the world organize their musical activities and the impact of these diverse alternatives on the people involved in them.

My first personal encounter with John occurred as he was proclaiming his vision of how ethnomusicology should confront the twenty-first century. This took place at the Society for Ethnomusicology meeting in Bloomington, Indiana, in 1980, where he presented a paper titled: 'Purpose, Theory and Practice for the Next Twenty-Five Years in Ethnomusicology'. Blacking began his talk by arguing that colonialist mentalities still lingered in the discipline: ethnomusicologists were continuing to plunder the musical raw materials of the Third World, returning them in the processed form of their own ethnocentrically-biased publications. In his view they needed instead to turn their attention to the notions about music held by egalitarian peoples amongst whom music-making is central to social life. Such an emphasis would allow researchers to better assess the potential (progressive) political implications of musical performance in other contexts.

The full force of his argument emerged when he situated it in terms of his own personal experience:

As an anthropologist and as a music-maker and devotee of the performing arts, I find myself constantly torn between concern for the world as it is and as it might be. ... I am appalled by the contrast between our technical ingenuity and our inability to organize peaceful, co-operative societies, harmonious families, and equitable political systems, and to develop the full intellectual potential and sensibilities of every individual human being. And yet, when I perform or listen to music, I often enter a world of sensuous beauty that is noble and uplifting and which compels people to be gentle and loving, as long as they are involved (Blacking, 1980a: 8).

What Blacking was advocating at the Bloomington conference was that ethnomusicologists acquire consciousness of their political role in the world. He saw ethnomusicology as having the methods to show that music can be *part* of life, not separate from it. If the distinction between producers and consumers of music could be abolished, everyone would regain the 'ownership of their senses' and the means to develop their intellect to its full potential, ultimately generating more harmonious coexistence amongst humans in the world.

As we confront the new millennium, in which ethnic conflicts are dividing communities, nations and continents, this message gains special urgency. While few of us would be so naïve as to believe that ethnomusicology could save the world, most of us probably do agree with Blacking that music can have the power to motivate people to action. It is precisely because we believe that ethnomusicology can make a difference in the world that the discipline has relevance to us. Throughout his career Blacking, with messianic vigour, made sure that we sustained this conviction.

This message underpins the work for which he is probably best remembered, *How Musical is Man?* (1973). Written in a fluid and accessible style, it continues to provide a stimulating introduction to the concerns of ethnomusicology, especially for undergraduates and non-specialist readers. However, as Reginald Byron has pointed out, '*How Musical is Man?*, very much in the character of [Blacking's] exhilarating and provocative lecturing style, made bold and sweeping assertions on sometimes rather slender evidence, and occasionally none at all, about the innate musical capacities of humankind' (1995: 17–18).

Undoubtedly, an image of Blacking that lingers amongst many of us is that of the inspirational man of ideas. It is worth noting, however, that this image masks another one, that of the meticulous ethnographer. It was because Blacking held such a vast body of ethnographic data on the Venda that he was able to draw on this material throughout his academic life, and to use it to engage in practically every debate that emerged in the field of ethnomusicological inquiry during his career. And he had a long career, one that spanned over 40 years, during which he witnessed and accompanied several theoretical advances and major paradigm shifts.

To celebrate his vision for ethnomusicology and to assess the impact of his academic contributions a decade after his death, in September, 2000, the European Seminar for Ethnomusicology (ESEM) held its Sixteenth Annual Meeting in Belfast around the theme of 'John Blacking's Legacy'. The response to the call for papers was extremely enthusiastic, drawing well over 100 abstracts from all over the world – a clear indication of the great respect that Blacking's work still commands within ethnomusicology internationally. Over 30 nationalities were present at the meeting, coming from six different continents. Among the participants there were several former students and associates, but there were also many scholars, especially young ones, who had never met John personally yet had been deeply inspired by his writing, his larger-than-life presence and the unwavering optimism that shone through the words on the page. The contributions in this volume all began life as papers at the ESEM Belfast conference, and their authors were invited to further develop their presentations for the collection. As editor, my aim was to bring together a selection of articles that covered Blacking's varied academic interests in ways that fully engaged with his contributions and placed them within current debates.

John Blacking, the man[1]

John Anthony Randall Blacking was born in Guildford, Surrey, in 1928, but, while he was still a toddler, his family moved to Salisbury, Wiltshire, where his father worked as an Anglican ecclesiastical architect. He received a cathedral choir school education (1934–1942), where he began his studies of music, before going on to Sherborne School (1942–1947), which had a good reputation for music, allowing him to continue to pursue his musical interests. He became an accomplished pianist and, for a time entertained the idea of becoming a professional musician. Although his career subsequently took a different path, the piano remained a companion throughout his life, and he frequently played in public.

On completing his studies Blacking joined the army, and was sent to Malaya, where he developed a fascination for the country's musical traditions and religious diversity and engaged in independent studies of Malay culture and language. When he returned to England in 1949 he decided to read social anthropology, with the intention of returning to Malaya to pursue these new interests. He took his degree from King's College, Cambridge (1950–1953), under Meyer Fortes who encouraged him to combine his interests in music with his anthropological studies, and during his final year at Cambridge he spent a summer in Paris with André Schaeffner at the Musée de l'Homme, receiving basic training in musical ethnology.

After graduation he found employment under army command as a civilian assistant adviser on aboriginal affairs, which took him back to Malaya where he intended to begin field research as part of the job. Almost as soon as he took up the post, however, he lost it as a result of objecting to army plans to displace the native peoples of the forest. Still hoping to conduct fieldwork in Malaya, he moved to Singapore, taking a teaching post, but lack of research funds made it impossible for him to pursue his aims. In a letter from Fortes, he was told that

Hugh Tracey had received a large Nuffield Foundation grant and was searching for someone to assist him in making recordings of African music. Blacking wrote to Tracey, who offered him a job at the International Library of African Music in Roodeport, South Africa. He immediately packed his bags and set off for South Africa where he remained for 15 years (1953–1969) until he was declared *persona non grata*, on account of his anti-apartheid views and activities.

Shortly after his arrival in South Africa Blacking accompanied Tracey on short recording expeditions to Kwazulu and Mozambique. Although this type of documentation was the common practice in ethnomusicology at the time, these experiences made him acutely aware of the limitations of such field methods in contradistinction to the extended field methods common to anthropology with which he had become familiar in Cambridge. Having persuaded Tracey to allow him to undertake such extended research, he embarked on his now famous expedition to the Venda which lasted from May 1956 to December 1958. He began by learning to speak Tshivenda, and, throughout his stay, he participated in music and dance activities with his hosts, keeping careful records of all aspects of Venda culture – the political structure, the economic system, kinship and marriage patterns and ritual life, as well as Venda history and the vast Venda repertoire of expressive forms. He returned from the field with extensive notes, recordings, photographs and film footage – arguably the most complete record of a single non-Western musical culture ever amassed up until that time. The primary data collected during those 22 months provided the basis for his publications for the remainder of his professional career, and at the time of his death he was working on a collection of three volumes dedicated to the music and culture of the Venda.

Before embarking on his extended field expedition, Blacking married Brenda Grebers, with whom he had five children, although two of them died in childhood. Immediately after he returned from the field he took up his first lectureship at the University of Witwatersrand. In 1965 he was awarded a PhD from that university for his work on Venda children's songs, and in the same year he was made professor and head of the department of Social Anthropology. During his time at Witwatersrand, Blacking wrote extensively, his most notable publications of the time being *Venda Children's Songs* (1967), in which he introduced his approach to the 'cultural analysis of music' (discussed below), and a series of papers published in *African Studies* entitled 'Songs, Dances, Mimes and Symbolism of Venda Girls' Initiation Schools (Parts 1–4)' (Blacking, 1969c–f), which contain the bulk of his ethnographic data on the *domba* initiation cycle.

Blacking left South Africa with Zureena Desai, who would become his second wife, with whom he had four daughters. He was offered a professorship at Western Michigan University, in Kalamazoo, but while he waited for his visa he was offered another professorship at Queen's University Belfast, which he took up in 1970 on the condition that he be allowed to spend the first year in America. Although Blacking never lectured in ethnomusicology at any of the institutions at which he held permanent employment, he played a leading role in the establishment of the discipline in the United Kingdom, Europe and further afield. He founded the degree programme in ethnomusicology at Queen's, with both undergraduate and postgraduate levels of study, for which two permanent posts were established. He attracted students to Belfast from all over the world, playing a significant role in the training of professional ethnomusicologists in many parts of the globe. Moreover, he not only founded the ESEM, but also played an active role within the UK branch of the International Council for Traditional Music (ICTM), now known as the British Forum for Ethnomusicology. He was also the president of the Society for Ethnomusicology (SEM) from 1982 to 1983 – the only president to date not based in a North American academic institution.

After *How Musical is Man?* (1973), Blacking produced only one other single-authored book, *'A Common-sense View of all Music': Reflections on Percy Grainger's Writings on Ethnomusicology and Music Education* (1987), but he edited two other volumes, *The Anthropology of the Body* (1977) and *The Performing Arts: Music and Dance* (with Keali'inohomoku 1979) and was a prolific writer, producing numerous scholarly articles for a wide range of journals and collected volumes for readerships in a number of disciplines.[2] Furthermore, he was the general editor of the Cambridge Series in Ethnomusicology, and he also produced a series of six programmes called *Dancing* for Ulster Television, broadcast in 1988.

Since Blacking's death there have been at least three major publications aiming to make his work more widely available. The first of these is Reginald Byron's collection, *Music, Culture and Experience: Selected Papers of John Blacking*, which appeared in 1995; along with well-chosen representative pieces covering Blacking's major interests, Byron's introductory chapter provides an excellent overview of Blacking's intellectual trajectory. Second, the website, *Venda Girls' Initiation Schools* (1998), produced by Suzel Ana Reily and Lev Weinstock, brings together Blacking's ethnographic material on the *domba* initiation, including published texts, photographs, moving images and sound recordings. Finally, in 2001 the SEM launched its production of Blacking's 1980 film, *Domba: A Personal Record of Venda Initiation Rites, Songs and Dances*, a project that was overseen by John Baily who, together with Andrée Grau, produced a study guide to accompany the production (Baily and Grau, 2001).

To date there has only been one collection of writings in tribute of John Blacking's contributions to scholarship, and this is the 1995 issue of *The World of Music*, 37 (2), titled *Working with Blacking: The Belfast Years*; edited by John Baily, the contributions were written by former colleagues and students of Blacking's in Belfast. With this collection we hope to add to the efforts that have been made in drawing attention to Blacking's work, highlighting in particular his vision of the musical human – a vision constructed through his encounter with the Venda.

Blacking's representations of the Venda

When one thinks of John Blacking, the Venda of the Northern Transvaal in South Africa also come instantly to mind. Indeed, one could say that, through Blacking's work, the Venda have become to ethnomusicology what the Nuer are to anthropology. But the significance of the Venda to ethnomusicology does not reside only in the fact that Blacking used his Venda ethnography to substantiate practically every academic argument he made, but rather on the fact that the Venda have been heralded as a group that exemplifies the power of music to generate a healthy society.

Blacking's encounter with the Venda confronted him with a people amonsgt whom his social ideals seemed to be realized, but it was also through this encounter that the ideals themselves took shape. Amongst the Venda, Blacking found a group whose aim, he claimed, was 'human contentment rather than competition and conflict' (1964a: 37): 'success in Venda society', he noted, '[was] measured in terms of a [person's] ability to get on well with people, rather than to exploit them' (1964a: 57). By participating in their musical activities, he 'began to understand how music can become an intricate part of the development of mind, body, and harmonious social relations' (1973: vii–viii). Thus he came to see the Venda as holding out hope for humanity, and in their music and music-making he saw the makings of a potential utopia.

To highlight their messianic potential, Blacking frequently employed the mechanism of systematically comparing Venda musical life to the musical practices of the West, especially in *How Musical is Man?*. In Venda society, he claimed, everyone engaged in music-making, while in the West only a limited number of people are considered musical. Rather than accepting that this difference could be explained in terms of a fundamental difference in the level of complexity of the two musical systems, Blacking argued that musicality is an innate human capacity present in all humans, but in some societies – such as the Venda – it is nurtured in everyone, whereas in others – as in the West – it is only encouraged amongst those who belong to 'the right social class' or who happen to 'show evidence of what people have learned to regard as talent' (1973: 9). The apparent 'complexity' of Western music, he contended, was the result of the development of literacy and the division of labour in industrial societies, in which individuals have to learn more about less, whereas the full repertoire of skills required of a hunter-gather, for instance, involves knowing less about more.

Although the overt manifestation of the musicality of all Venda people convinced Blacking of the biological foundation of music, it was the social consequences of nurturing this latent ability that he viewed as crucial: in making music together, the Venda constructed shared experiences which made 'them more aware of themselves and of their responsibilities toward each other'; their music-making enacted their saying that 'man is man because of his associations with other men' (1973: 28).

The style that best epitomized this ideal was *tshikona*, the Venda 'national' dance. According to Blacking:

> The music of *tshikona* expresses the value of the largest social group to which a Venda can really feel [s]he belongs. Its performance involves the largest number of people, and its music incorporates the largest number of tones in any single piece of Venda music involving more than one or two players ... *Tshikona* is valuable and beautiful to the Venda, not only because of the quantity of people and tones involved, but because of the quality of the relationships that must be established between people and tones whenever it is performed. *Tshikona* music can be produced only when twenty or more men blow differently tuned end-blown reed-pipes with a precision that depends on holding one's own part as well as blending with others, and at least four women play different drums in polyrhythmic harmony. Furthermore, *tshikona* is not complete unless the men also perform in unison the different steps which the dance master directs from time to time.
>
> The effectiveness of *tshikona* is not a case of MORE = BETTER: it is an example of the production of the maximum of available human energy in a situation that generates the highest degree of individuality in the largest possible community of individuals ... Of all shared experiences in Venda society, a performance of *tshikona* is said to be the most highly valued: the dance is connected with ancestor worship and state occasions, incorporates the living and the dead, and is the most universal of Venda music. (Blacking, 1973: 50–51)

Blacking's idealization of the Venda led him to play down the hierarchical structure of the society, with its crucial division between nobles and commoners and its system of seniority. Although Blacking recognized that the Venda were 'by no means a thoroughly democratic society', he claimed that 'in many respects they [were] nearer this ideal than most western societies' (1964a: 57). Undoubtedly the power of the noble class during Blacking's fieldwork period was tempered by the limitations available to them in the use of force or in the threat of the use of force, obliging them to construct alliances with commoners.[3]

But Blacking was content to avoid discussing tensions between the differently positioned hierarchical groups because he believed that they were mediated through ritual, in consonance with the structural–functionalist orientation of the time. Thus, with ritual as a safety-valve, the system itself absorbed the tensions before they could erupt into full-blown conflict. In his introduction to *Black Background*, for example, Blacking stated: 'The Venda method of reducing an individual's nuisance value is to encourage him to acquire a new skill, which will involve new social commitments, and in Venda culture the skill may consist of a series of rituals' (1964a: 53). And he went on to say:

> [The Venda] appreciate the dependence of the individual on [her] society, and they have directed their energy toward the perpetuation of harmonious social relations by the cultural technique of ritualizing them in a way that is acceptable to, and easily acquired by, almost every member of their society. (Blacking, 1964a: 57)

It is not surprising, therefore, that many of his early publications focused on rituals and ritualized activity, particularly those involving the socialization of children and young people. Indeed, his first major publications – namely *Black Background* (1964a), *Venda Children's Songs* (1967), 'Songs, Dances, Mimes and Symbolism of Venda Girls' Initiation Schools (Parts 1–4)' (1969c–f) – deal with this issue. Blacking's understanding of socialization through ritual is perhaps best represented in the *African Studies* papers even though the series is not structured as an explicit argument but more as a description of initiation premised on how it *should* take place. In other words, it provides an extended inventory of what the girls undergoing initiation were expected to learn through their participation in the rituals of the three phases of the *domba* cycle.

The very organization of the material on girls' initiation suggests that, at the time, Blacking held a prescriptive orientation towards ritual as a documentable item (or collection of documentable items) embodying culture. Both *Venda Children's Songs* and the *African Studies* papers include extensive collections of musical 'items', each carefully annotated and numbered: there are 56 Venda children's songs, 63 *vhusha* songs,[4] 322 'laws' of initiation (*milayo*),[5] 460 great *domba* song lines[6] and so on. Accompanying the items there are recordings, photographs, moving images, song texts and explanations of their meaning. Similarly, each 'item' in his main collection of recordings of Venda music is individually numbered: there are 190 of them, and many have an a, b and c subdivision to generate a total of around 550 distinct pieces.

Blacking's orientation towards fixed items is linked to the development of his methodology in the 'cultural analysis of music' which is explicated in *Venda Children's Songs* and other publications of the late 1960s and early 1970s. In its broadest sense, the cultural analysis of music involved looking at how 'musical structures grow out of the cultural patterns of which they are a part' (1967: 191). The practical exemplification of the approach in *Venda Children's Songs* focused on the detailed analysis of his collection of 56 songs, through which he extracted the 'principles' of Venda music – a list he would further refine and extend in 'Part 4' (1969f: 259–62) of the *African Studies* papers and in 'Tonal Organization in the Music of Two Venda Girls' Initiation

Schools' (1970b). Ultimately, then, the analytic procedures were designed to generate the full 'grammar', so to speak, of Venda music, defining its Venda-ness – in other words, that which distinguished the Venda musical culture from other cultures.

While the methodology involved in such 'cultural analysis' required a fairly large body of independent items, the very breadth of data Blacking held on each item may also have contributed towards the suggestion of an entirely different – and far less essentialist – analytic route which he also pursued. It is perhaps precisely because he was so meticulous about documenting each item as fully as possible that he came to realize that the meaning of expressive forms to participants is not necessarily based on their referential content. In fact, he frequently claimed that performers often had no idea of the meaning of their songs and, even when they could interpret them, the content was not what they cherished most about their music and dances. Of Venda childern's songs, for example, Blacking argued that their value to the children resided in their ability to perform them. Indeed, he claimed, '*Knowledge of the children's songs is a social asset, and in some cases a social necessity for any child who wishes to be an accepted member of his own age group*, and hence a potential member of adult society' (1967: 31, emphasis in the original).

Similarly, he noted that girls in Venda initiation schools were less concerned with the meaning of the texts of their songs and dances than with the experience they generated in performance:

> Women who had forgotten most of what they might have learnt about the associated symbolism [of the dances of initiation] had not forgotten the experience of dancing: they talked of problems of co-ordinating movements and music, the closeness of others' bodies, the excitement when the dance went well, the transcendence of altered time schedules and the sense of transformation from the physical to the social body that was experienced through contrasting movement styles. (Blacking, 1985a: 86-87)

This observation would become central to his arguments regarding the political dimension of music and music-making, which even led him to claim that: 'I spent too much time collecting the wrong kind of data!' (1985a: 89; see also Blacking 1982: 98–99). This shift in perspective led him to:

> ... explore the notion that ideas and feelings can be expressed collectively through dance and music before they are articulated in speech, although the associated ideology and verbal explanations of ritual action may express a false consciousness. That is, ritual may be enacted in the service of conservative and even oppressive institutions ...; but the experience of performing the nonverbal movements and sounds may ultimately liberate the actors. (Blacking, 1985a: 65)

This, he felt, applied to the repertoire of the girls' initiation, but also to *tshikona*. The performance of *tshikona* was generally sponsored by chiefs and headmen, and it was often used as an expression of their political power. Yet 'the experience stimulated individuality as much as a strong sense of community, and people talked more of the refreshment that it brought to their lives rather than of the adherence to a political order that it was supposed to consolidate' (1985: 87). Thus, the very effectiveness of the forms which political leaders employed to mark their social position may have been compromised by the power of the experiences they generated amongst participants.

Although, in his published work, Blacking tended to refer to 'the Venda' – an abstraction derived from the observation of 'real people' in 'real situations' – one does here and there come across descriptions of Venda people in actual events, and, perhaps not surprisingly, things rarely go according to plan. This type of narrative, however, is far more common to his earliest publications, and some of the best examples can be found in 'Musical Expeditions of the Venda', published in 1962. The *tshigombela* group[7] that set out from Magidi to Tshivhambe in 1957 arrived at their destination without the one pound they were supposed to take to the chief they were visiting, so last-minute arrangements had to be made for someone to go back and get it; because of this oversight, there was no beer for the dance team, and they still received none even after the gift had been presented to the chief; furthermore, the fourth day of the visit was marred by an unfortunate incident in which the girls were (falsely) accused of stealing someone's oranges. Yet, despite all the mishaps, Blacking claimed that: 'all said they had greatly enjoyed the expedition, and nobody complained about the disappointing lack of beer' (1962: 19). The cynic might add, 'Perhaps not to him!'

But things really went pear-shaped the following year, when some girls decided to organize another *tshigombela* team, a project that ultimately had to be abandoned altogether. Although the original passage is quite long, it is worth reproducing it in an edited version, since it contrasts so considerably with Blacking's more well-known representations of the Venda.

> In the middle of February 1958, several girls asked if they could dance *tshigombela* … The senior girls were not very keen on the idea, because they wanted to attend the *domba* initiation which was being held for Mphaphuli's people at Malamangwa. However, daily practices began on March 3. …
>
> In 1957, the Magidi girls had invited girls from Mbaleni to join their team, because they only had an acting headman. In 1958, the Mbaleni girls came to watch the dancing at Magidi, and complained that they had not been invited: 'Why don't the Magidi girls ask us to join them? They are showing off too much this year, and if they go on being so full of themselves, we will ask to have our own team. Tshidavhula and her friend Tshidaho are particularly full of themselves; and they are just doing it to attract the boys'. … On the seventh day, Tshidavhula and two senior girls asked headman Magidi's permission to invite the girls from Mbaleni, and he agreed. They called their team together and took

their drumsticks (*tshiombo*) with them, in order to call the Mbaleni girls. ...
When they said that they had come to invite the Mbaleni girls to join them, one
woman suggested that *tshigombela* should rather be held at Mbaleni, as it had
been held at Magidi the previous year; but this suggestion was overruled. The
Mbaleni girls then played the drums and the Magidi girls sang and danced again.
It was getting dark, and so the Magidi girls stopped playing and left without even
putting the drums away or saying good-bye. One old woman was cross and said,
'What about our drums? You had better not leave them out again! Besides, we
had some *mukumbi* beer made of marula fruit for you, and now that you have
gone away without saying good-bye, we cannot give you any'. ...

On the next day, when the Mbaleni girls came along to dance, Tshidavhula
showed off and annoyed everyone. She knew that they relied too much on her,
and that when she was not there the alternative soloists were ineffectual. She
arrived late, made rude remarks about the performance, took over the playing of
the *thungwa* drum[8] and confused the dancers by mixing the rhythms: 'I am
making mistakes on purpose', she said, 'in order to teach you a lesson. You're not
dancing properly.' The Mbaleni girls and several Magidi girls were fed up and
went home, but a few stayed on and performed under Tshidavhula's direction. At
ensuing practices the girls from Mbaleni and the juniors from Magidi were much
more enthusiastic than Tshidavhula and her contemporaries. The result was that
the Mbaleni girls often found that they were the only seniors present, and they
resented the indifference of the senior Magidi girls. ...

Eventually the Mbaleni girls said that they would not come, because they had
to do all the work while Tshidavhula and her friends flirted with boys and played
cards, or merely tapped the *murumba* drums[9] in an idle fashion. ... (Blacking,
1962: 19–20)

Not surprisingly, it was not long after that that rehearsals ceased to take place
altogether that year.

While such episodes may come as a relief to us, demonstrating that perhaps
the Venda are, after all, 'real' people like the rest of us, Blacking rarely drew on
actual events as the basis for his theoretical arguments, preferring the
generality of the norm. One explanation for this is that the structural–
functionalist paradigm that dominated his anthropological training was not
exactly well suited to reconciling everyday negotiations with the norms of an
underlying system. But Blacking's dilemma may have hinged also on the
problem of reconciling petty politicking with his vision of the great persuasive
power of musical performance experience, and his personal messianic agenda
led him to focus on the latter. Furthermore, to have drawn attention to the
pettiness that often accompanies face-to-face negotiations would surely have
detracted from the image of the Venda that Blacking wished to memorialize.

Yet it was not so much the Venda as Venda that were the focus of Blacking's
academic concerns, but rather the Venda as a cultural group other than his own.
By demarcating difference, the Venda became the means of forging a space for
the encounter between 'us' and 'them'. Through this encounter cultural

differences could be highlighted, but so too could commonalities. Ultimately, therefore, the Venda fulfilled a paradigmatic role for Blacking, operating as a counterpoint through which he strove to dissolve the 'other' into a common humanity. But the commonalities he highlighted were not the trivialities of everyday life, but the fullness of human potential, the sum total of human capabilities that can be documented across the globe and over time, ultimately allowing humans to live 'beyond culture' (Blacking,1973: 7).

Rethinking Blacking's ethnomusicology

John Blacking is one of the few scholars within ethnomusicology to have provided the discipline with both an extensive body of field data as well as a wide range of readings of the material. However bold many of his propositions may seem, they stand as testament to just how often he was well ahead of his time, anticipating the trends and directions that ethnomusicology would take in the following decades. By trusting his instincts in ways not generally encouraged within academia, he broadened the scope of ethnomusicological inquiry into new realms of exploration which still remain a challenge to the discipline. In an effort to confront this challenge, each chapter in this volume addresses a distinct theoretical and/or methodological issue raised through Blacking's work. Several authors draw on Blacking's Venda material as a counterpoint to their own field data. And, not surprisingly, many of the contributions point out how the musical materials under investigation can be seen as specific cultural manifestations of the humanity of their research subjects.

The volume opens with Keith Howard's piece, 'Memories of Fieldwork: Understanding "Humanly Organized Sound" through the Venda', as it extends my discussion of the centrality of the Venda in Blacking's work, moving it into the realm of the post-colonial critique of anthropological 'othering'. As Howard points out, Blacking frequently compared Venda musical practices to those of the West, and he notes that the systematic observational techniques that Blacking used in the collection of data amongst the Venda were distinctly absent in his commentaries on the Western musical universe, often resulting in clumsy generalities or rather idiosyncratic illustrations. Although Blacking's focus on the understanding of the Venda as a clearly defined cultural 'other' challenges us to reconsider the role of fieldwork within ethnomusicology, Howard claims that the postmodern, 'reflexive' way in which Blacking drew upon his experiences as a Western musician placed him ahead of his time in terms of ethnographic practice. Thus, Howard argues, Blacking's work was not 'Vendacentric' but 'Venda-grounded'; by establishing the Venda as an anchor, he was able to challenge concepts of otherness, even as he undertook the kind of fieldwork that privileges the exotic.

The next two chapters deal with South African ethnographic material, both of which address Blacking's concerns with the political dimensions of music and musical performance. Although the authors draw on quite distinct sources from Blacking's writings, they demonstrate how, despite his general focus on precolonial repertoires, Blacking's incursions into the study of post-colonial genres anticipated the concerns of the next generation of South African scholars, whose interests have been directed toward forms of subaltern expression and their strategic role for the performers.

In 'Tracks of the Mouse: Tonal Reinterpretation in Venda Guitar Songs', Jaco Kruger, who succeeded Blacking in Venda, focuses on musical analysis to construct his argument and therefore draws heavily on Blacking's musico-logical studies of the traditional Venda repertoire. Approaching the material following Blacking's 'cultural analysis of music', Kruger shows how Venda guitarists have creatively adapted Western musical codes, generating new musical alternatives that remain firmly grounded in traditional aesthetic patterns. Such tonal resilience, Kruger argues, turns a symbol of domination into a dynamic force of transcendence.

'Black Background: Life History and Migrant Women's Music in South Africa', by Deborah James, was inspired by Blacking's interest in the role of music in children's socialization, but her emphasis is upon women's memories of their childhood musical activities. She notes that, while Blacking's transformative vision of music has been embraced by South African ethno-musicology, an aspect of his work that has been neglected pertains to his contention that music cannot generate anything new. She claims, however, that '[i]t is in the tension between the "endorsing/confirming" and the "trans-forming" positions that Blacking's legacy should really be sought', as both of these forces can operate simultaneously. Through her discussion of the Northern Sotho *kiba* dance style performed by migrant women on the Witwatersrand she shows how *kiba* draws on girls' experiences in youth and adolescence – when music served to ascribe them specific roles – and how, later in life, these same musical experiences came to be used to frame, and create, a new inclusive version of a 'home'-based identity for migrant women.

Fumiko Fujita's contribution, 'Musicality in Early Childhood: A Case from Japan', also draws its inspiration from Blacking's work on children's music acquisition, linking it to the orientation he pioneered through his investigations of the biological foundations of music as an innate human capability. Fujita conducted ethnographic research in a Japanese nursery school, observing children from the ages of three months to two years, documenting their spontaneous musical behaviour. She notes that the musical activities of young children are deeply connected to their speech patterns and, indeed, she claims that children move fluently between speech and song because both modes of communication are rooted in a common form of musical expression – an intermediate form of vocalization that stands between speech and song, which all small children explore from birth.

John Baily's contribution, 'John Blacking and the "Human/Musical Instrument Interface": Two Plucked Lutes from Afghanistan', presents findings from research that combined his own background in experimental psychology with Blacking's seminal ideas regarding the ways in which some music structures derive from an interaction between the physical properties of the human body and the morphology of musical instruments. Through an analysis of two plucked lutes from Afghanistan, the long-necked Herati *dutar* and the short-necked *rubab*, Baily identifies a number of factors operating at the 'human/musical instrument interface' and shows how, in some cases, the interaction between body and instrument is connected with the structure of the music produced.

The next two contributions by Helena Wulff and Rebecca Sager, respectively, draw attention to Blacking's work on the power of aesthetic experience. Even in his early publications there are hints of a shift away from a preoccupation with the referential content of expressive forms towards an emphasis on experience as the source of meaning for performers and spectators alike, with the latter becoming progressively more marked. One could say, therefore, that Blacking pre-empted, by several decades, the phenomenological orientations that have become almost mainstream within ethnomusicology and ethnochoreology today.

In her piece, 'Experiencing the Ballet Body: Pleasure, Pain, Power', Wulff addresses the dance experience, thereby, like Baily, she highlights Blacking's interest in the anthropology of the body, but she shows its relevance to dance research. She uses Blacking's ethnography on the Venda girls' initiation cycle as a backdrop to her own material on classical and contemporary ballet dancers in much the same way as he drew upon Western music. In this way she shows how dance has a 'dual potential': it can be a means of achieving empowering, transcendental experiences or a powerful means of disciplining and controlling bodies. Ultimately, she claims, people – be they Venda or ballet dancers – dance to experience transcendence, however rare such experiences may be; but when they occur, they are similar – and equally pleasurable – for everyone because of our shared humanity.

Rebecca Sager's contribution, 'Creating a Musical Space for Experiencing the Other Self Within', explores Blacking's concept of the 'other self' – that is, 'the memory or prospect of self in the experience of transcendence'. Blacking contended that one encounters the 'other self' in experiences of 'virtual time' as well as through spirit possession, both of which are commonly promoted through music. In a vivid portrayal of Haitian Vodou ritual Sager shows how a space for the transcendent experience of the 'other self' is created, during which devotees come to embody their highest moral values. As such an encounter has such deep religious significance, Sager refers to it as a 'total musical experience'. She then explores recent research in music psychology, indicating how such non-referential qualities of musical experience as time perception, sound localization and motor-gesture perception not only contribute to music's potential to induce the universally achievable transcendent experiences, but also enhance their persuasiveness, particularly in a religious context.

In the final contribution, 'Bach in a Venda Mirror: John Blacking and Historical Musicology', Britta Sweers explores Blacking's contention that 'Venda music can be a means of understanding *all* music cultures, including western art music' (emphasis in original) to interrogate ethnomusicology's potential contributions to Western historical musicology. She provides an extensive survey of ethnomusicology's links to historical musicology and suggests possible routes for furthering Blacking's lead through a case study of Early Music, an arena that has been shaped by discussions about how to deal with the 'historical other'. Sweers draws attention to the way in which, once again, Blacking pre-empted the calls for ethnomusicologists to turn their attention to Western art music and also notes that the impact of ethnomusicology is becoming ever more present within historical musicology, particularly in so-called 'new musicology'.

Taken together, the chapters in this volume pay rightful tribute to John Blacking, acknowledging both the scholar and the man. They attest to his role as a major intellectual leader of his generation, whose work has remained an inspiration a decade later precisely because of its daring boldness. Unquestionably Blacking, the man of ideas, has set us the challenge of pushing the boundaries of ethnomusicology into new territories where the means of properly investigating daring propositions might become possible. And, in the process, may we not forget his message to the twenty-first century: music contributes to making us human, and therein lies its power to make a difference.

Notes

[1] Since Blacking's death in 1990, numerous discussions of the man and his work have emerged, including Baily (1990a, 1994, 1995), Baily and Grau (2001), Byron (1995), de Carvalho *et. al.* (1991), Fairley (1991), Howard (1991), Kippen (1990) and several others.

[2] For bibliographies of Blacking's academic output see: Byron (1995: 247–52), Kippen (1990: 266–70), and Blacking (1998).

[3] As we know from Jaco Kruger's (1999) research, once conditions allowed for it, both the use of force and the threat of such use became widespead in Venda, unleashing a period of terror that lasted until 1994, when the region was reintegrated into South Africa.

[4] *Vhusha* was the name of the first phase of the Venda girls' initiation cycle.

[5] The *milayo* were two-part phrases that the initiates were required to memorize during initiation.

[6] *Domba* was the name of the third and final phase of the Venda girls' initiation cycle, which was punctuated by the performance of the *domba* (python) dance.

⁷ *Tshigombela* was a Venda recreational dance for unmarried girls; it was usually danced when the weeding was finished and the first maize cobs were available.

⁸ Blacking frequently referred to this drum as the tenor drum.

⁹ Blacking frequently referred to these drums as the alto drums.

CHAPTER TWO

Memories of Fieldwork: Understanding 'Humanly Organized Sound' through the Venda

Keith Howard

John Blacking conducted fieldwork amongst the Venda of the Sibasa District, Northern Transvaal, for 22 months between May 1956 and late 1958.[1] He continued to refer to the Venda throughout his academic life, using his memories of fieldwork as the foundation for grand statements about music in ways that a number of critics now find problematic. David Josephson, in his review of John Blacking's *A Commonsense View of all Music*, writes that:

> Worst of all in a book purporting to examine musical foundations and universals, the supporting material is unacceptably Vendacentric. The evidence cited to support the central contention that music can generate social action comes from the Venda. The journey to identify fundamental structures of music begins by reference to their music. Discussions of music and political freedom are limited to them. The ideal of music-making is posited in them. A quarter of a million people inhabiting a tiny corner of this earth cannot shoulder such evidentiary burdens. (Josephson, 1991: 268)

Joseph Kerman says much the same in *Musicology* (1985a).[2] Many, though, hold the memory of John dear (for example, Baily, 1990a, 1991a, 1995; Fairley, 1991; de Carvalho, 1991; Grau, 1991; Byron, 1995); many more still find Blacking's writings inspirational.

Here, I examine Blacking's reliance on his field experience and explore how he effectively used this to anchor his writings on 'humanly organized sound' – his pithy definition of music as a global phenomenon – in a way that I will argue was not 'Vendacentric' but 'Vendagrounded'. Fieldwork became the basis for his grand statements, the fundamental material with which he attempted to offer illuminating insights into other music that he knew or encountered. His approach inverted earlier diffusionist writing, but came well before its time. Blacking used Venda music to challenge concepts of otherness, an approach that is only now becoming acceptable as academics argue against creating exoticism in their studies of other music cultures. However, the pre-eminence given fieldwork in ethnomusicology throughout the world tends to retain distinction, emphasizing a set of rules within a methodology that compresses together ethnographies about music and musicians written from the early twentieth century to the present. Fieldwork becomes a scientific experiment, resulting in detailed accounts of limited provenance. Blacking, while providing an exemplary model of fieldwork practice, wanted more. As Suzel Reily (in Chapter 1 of this volume) put it, his ultimate aim was to 'dissolve the "other" into a common humanity'.

Placing the Venda

The Venda were not Blacking's first choice for fieldwork study. This is intimated by his early interest in Malaysian *orang asli* music, an interest sparked by military service, helped as he learnt Malay and thwarted when his first job after graduation, as assistant adviser on aborigines in Penang, ended after just six days (for which, see Byron 1995: 2–4). A crisis followed. Blacking stayed on, teaching in an Anglican school in Singapore, writing letters against the army's policy on aboriginal resettlement, composing, performing and preparing his first significant article, an account of aboriginal musical instruments based on collections in museums in Kuala Lumpur and Perak (Blacking, 1954–55). Now convinced that he wanted to apply anthropological fieldwork to music in the region, he sought funding, but without success. His Cambridge mentor, the William Wyse Professor of Anthropology, Meyer Fortes, suggested that he write to Hugh Tracey, with a view to working in Africa. Byron notes that, shortly before, Tracey had mentioned to Fortes that he had secured a large grant to make recordings of African music and was short of skilled assistance (Byron, 1995: 5); Blacking's earlier experience, while still a Cambridge student, of transcribing recordings under André Schaeffner at the Musée de l'Homme would have seemed particularly relevant. Indeed, once in South Africa, Tracey set Blacking to transcribe, analyse and comment on recordings.

Blacking accompanied Tracey on recording expeditions, and this soon led to frustration because of the lack of documentation that Tracey required and expected. Blacking's training in social anthropology and his knowledge of Malinowskian field technique, meant that he wanted more. Fortes helped secure a Nuffield grant, and in 1956 Tracey gave Blacking permission to carry out long-term fieldwork.[3] The grant stipulated that he should work within the boundaries of the then South African Union (Blacking in Howard, 1991: 59), and the Venda were chosen. In his fieldwork, Byron notes how Blacking paid close attention to typical anthropological concerns – to kinship, ritual and economic and political organization (Byron, 1995: 6), observing all he could, taking copious notes, keeping a diary and so on. Baily recalls the note in a contemporary edition of *African Music*: 'Mr John Blacking … is learning to sing Venda songs and play their instruments, since this is one of the most satisfactory ways of gaining knowledge and understanding their music' (Baily, 1990a: xiii). The two disciplines of anthropology and music had met. In this we can see not just the frequently cited introduction of extended fieldwork to ethnomusicology (noted in, for example, Baily, 1990a: xiii; Fairley, 1991: 116), but also a resolution to Blacking's long vacillation between his desire to develop a career as a pianist and his training in social science. Retrospection also allows us to speculate: had he already worked his dilemma through and seen in fieldwork on another music culture a possible way of coming to terms with his own musical background and training?

A certain amount of frustration must have characterized the period following fieldwork. Blacking published a short paper on Venda ocarina music in 1959 (Blacking, 1959c), but his appointment the same year as lecturer in Social Anthropology and African Government at the University of Witwatersrand, Johannesburg, slowed down the writing up of his notes.[4] Fortes once more helped, engineering a Ling Roth scholarship from Cambridge that led to the award of Blacking's PhD in 1965; two years later, *Venda Children's Songs* appeared – a volume that, to his death, he felt was unjustly underrated (Blacking, in Howard, 1991: 63–64).[5] His expulsion from South Africa in 1969, and the authorities' refusal to allow him to return until the mid-1980s, removed the possibility of further fieldwork. Blacking, then, was aware that his primary ethnographic materials had to be framed in historical time. To his data he would add 'headnotes' – memories (Cohen, 1992, cited in Reily, 1998: 47) – and information gleaned from materials collected by others – by Nkhumeleni (Victor) Ralushai, Andrée Grau in 1977 (for which see Grau, 1991: 223–24), and Cora Burnett and Jaco Kruger in the 1980s. He carefully added the appropriate historical frame. Hence, in his posthumous 'The Biology of Music-Making', the Venda make their first appearance three pages in: 'In the *traditional* musical system of the Venda ... outstanding ability in music *was* generally considered to depend partly on the assistance of a spirit of a deceased ancestor...' (Blacking, 1992: 303–04, emphasis added). In *How Musical is Man?* the Venda are carefully positioned as a group of 300 000 living in the undeveloped rural Transvaal; Blacking gives the dates of his research and the main district, Sibasa, in which he worked (1973: 35–36). In *A Commonsense View of all Music* (1987), the Venda first appear on page 19, where the dates of his fieldwork are once more given. Inspection reveals that his Venda data are used to support discussions of broader ethnomusicological issues in a manner that shows the development and unfolding of his knowledge. Ethnography becomes fused with theoretical analysis, so that, while *Venda Children's Songs* is closely argued and assesses the usefulness of analytical techniques, *A Commonsense View* marshals a much greater pool of ideas that, before any mention of the Venda, takes in the music of ancient Greece, Bosnia Herzegovina, the !Kung 'Bushmen', English folksong, Hindemith's compositions and Gregorian chant (Blacking, 1987: 1–19).

Blacking never wrote any definitive account of the Venda. It is commonly assumed that such an account would have secured his permanent place amongst ethnomusicology's Hall of Fame, although this chimes poorly with the realization that he remains inspirational more than a decade after his death less for his Venda knowledge than for his grand statements. He claimed to have three volumes underway by 1989, two commissioned by Cambridge University Press, but all were left unfinished and unfinishable at his death. Nonetheless, exhaustive considerations of aspects of his data do exist, as *Venda Children's Songs* indicates. Again, initiation schools became the basis for articles in 1969 (a series of four articles, plus one more), in 1970 and 1985.[6]

Blacking's field experience was a veritable model of twentieth-century practice. His fieldwork documentation is hard to fault, despite the fact that he himself later said that he 'spent too much time collecting the wrong kind of data' (1985a: 89). His system of diary entries, note-taking, audio and visual recording and so on was taught to generations of his students. His records were careful and extensive, and in a recent reassessment of his work on Venda girls' initiation schools, Suzel Ana Reily notes that she can find no instance where she can question the accuracy of his ethnographic observations (1998: 65). Again, *Venda Children's Songs* (1967) carefully describes the methods used to assemble his impressive collection. He recorded versions of all songs on a portable reel tape recorder at 7.5 inches per second; he transcribed some songs as he learnt them; he learnt songs from both children and adults; he made deliberate mistakes as he sang, noting those that were accepted and those that were rejected by his teachers; he organized tests to learn rhythmic principles; he determined popularity, consistency and difference, pitch and relative pitch when songs were sung in sequence; he asked about the meaning of texts (Blacking, 1967: 33–34). Ample evidence is offered of his extended exposure to Venda music (particularly in Chapter 1). In his transcriptions he synthesizes over 400 recordings recorded in 21 named districts, comparing the same and different songs by the same performer and the same song by different performers (1967: 27). The preface (1967: 5) sets out his reasons: following from Merriam's *The Anthropology of Music* (1964) – although Blacking's fieldwork of course pre-dates it – he notes that, 'if music [is] regarded as human action, music sound can no longer be analysed independently, but must be studied in culture'. So far so good, but he questions the then-standard techniques of analysis (Merriam practised the principal example cited by Blacking – statistical interval counts), since he felt that they would not reveal what he and the Venda knew, namely that children's songs were an integral part of the musical tradition but in many cases sounded unlike other Venda music.

Field technique has been the subject of myriad articles, by Karpeles (recited in Post *et al.* 1994), Merriam (1964), Nettl (1964), Hood (1982), McLeod and Herndon (1983), Myers (1992a, 1992b) and many more. Fieldwork itself is about the only thing ethnomusicologists agree on as characteristic of their discipline, uniting catholic concerns and diverse disciplinary approaches. Some of Blacking's methods – the plural, 'methods', as Rice has pointed out (1997: 102), is surely telling – were, admittedly, idiosyncratic, but most were based on models imported from anthropology. To Blacking, fieldwork remained the primary act that allowed his students, as ethnomusicologists, entry into academy. This, of course, was exactly as Blacking had experienced it after he had shifted his geographical interests to Africa and thereby anchored his dual disciplinary focus. It was, as to many of us, his rite of passage, supported and (hopefully) funded, after which he was qualified for a university post. Writing about his fieldwork – Merriam's 'sciencing about music' (1964: 25) – allowed him to create an ethnographic narrative as he reperformed and interpreted his experiences. He did so, at least to start with, by cementing his anthropological credentials. Hence, during his period at Witwatersrand, he published articles on kinship, riddles and migrant labour, as well as a book that retold the childhood of an African girl (Blacking, 1959a, 1961, 1964b, 1964a). He was aware of potential problems in relating fieldwork to ethnography (as discussed much later by the contributors to, for example, Clifford and Marcus 1986), but resisted the temptation to use strings of anecdotes to prove his ideas, preferring the empiricism of his social anthropological mentors. This approach is most evident in *Venda Children's Songs* where the first chapter begins by positioning the Venda within their region, then describes concepts and definitions of Venda music, instruments and occasions for communal performance.

The way in which Blacking returns to his Venda materials throughout his career resonates with many of us who continue to work primarily on single music cultures. Helen Myers states that fieldwork constitutes the 'most critical stage of ethnomusicological research' (Myers, 1992b: 21) and, for many, like Blacking, fieldwork conducted as part of doctoral research represents the longest period they are ever able to spend outside their home/work environment. Fieldwork has been defined by Jeff Todd Titon (1997: 15) as 'knowing people making music'. Timothy Cooley asserts that it 'distinguishes ethnomusicology and ethnographically-based disciplines from other social sciences' (and from musicology?) to the extent that 'ethnographers derive from fieldwork their most significant contributions to the humanities' (Cooley, 1997: 4). Barz and Cooley's volume on fieldwork (1997) addresses the crisis of representation in postmodernist discourse, an idea that Blacking deftly sidestepped, even in later life, through retaining functionalist and structuralist perspectives. He considered himself to be writing musical ethnography on the basis of anthropology. To this extent, Blacking was a child of his time. But, even as he reflected on his fieldwork in early writings, many of the issues that were to characterize his later career were already present. *Venda Children's Songs* delineates patterns of sound that lie deep below the surface and sets out a 'cultural analysis of music'; it starts to explore music as language and finds parallels between Venda and European art music.[7]

Fieldwork, though, needs to be separated from the paradox of Blacking; our memories of the man, and the continuing role he plays in our thinking about music, tend not to be based on his ethnography. We are more intrigued by his grand statements, his comparisons and the potential application of his ideas to the different musics that we study. Reginald Byron, recognizing this paradox,[8] defends Blacking's first book to make an impact in the international arena, *How Musical is Man?* (1973) as being:

> ... very much in the character of his exhilarating and provocative lecturing style, [with] bold and sweeping assertions [made] on sometimes rather slender evidence, and occasionally none at all, about the innate capacities of humankind. ... (Byron, 1995: 17–18)

Reviews of *How Musical is Man?* were almost universally positive, recognizing the vision and, to a greater or lesser extent, sharing Blacking's identification with fundamental issues. I suggest that the book appealed because it neatly established a role for ethnomusicology and ethno-musicologists, both within the academy and amongst arts promotion agencies, in a way that would not have been possible in a regionally-focused account. It did so by discussing a comprehensive vision for music as a vital part of social life, by moving with apparent ease between Africa and the Western art tradition, and through discussions of musical grammars that questioned existing musicological and ethnomusicological analytical techniques. Most reviews of *How Musical is Man?* sidelined, if not ignored, the fact that Blacking left many questions unanswered – or, more precisely, the fact that he posed more questions than he answered (see, for example, Merriam, 1974; Gilbert, 1975; Rouget, 1977a). Marcia Herndon was more critical, using Blacking's own words to emphasize that this was '"not a scholarly study of human musicality"; rather it is an intensely personal statement' (Herndon, 1975: 143). The same criticism reappears, but in a more damning way, in Josephson's review of Blacking's later book, *A Commonsense View of all Music*:

> ... None of this is enough, however, to support a thesis whose grand speculations and claims require solid foundations, clear organization and impeccable reasoning ... [the] disorganization masks the absence of sustained reasoning and cool evidence, and we are left instead with a patchwork of assertions ... and side-shows.... Much of the musical scholarship is odd and unreliable. (Josephson, 1991: 266–68)

Ethnography can offer a safe refuge for scholarship – a way of avoiding such criticism – but Blacking needed more. And why not? It is surely implicit in most academic careers that one appeals to as wide an audience as possible, or at least to an audience sufficiently wide to enable one to retain a job. Personal research is just one aspect of a university career that, when narrowly focused on the musical ethnography of one geographically bounded group, requires supplementation. I admit that this is a blunt and biased description, but it is clear that Blacking saw himself not just as a researcher but also as a teacher and publicist. Many of his obituaries make much of these latter aspects of his career. John Baily and Jan Fairley, for example, talk of the more than 50 MA and PhD students he trained at Queen's University Belfast from all over the world;[9] this is all the more remarkable because of where Belfast is situated, far from London, and in the 1970s and 1980s identified with considerable unrest. Both discuss his activities for the Society for Ethnomusicology, the Council for National Academic Awards[10] and the European Seminar for Ethnomusicology; both note his role as founder and editor of the *Cambridge Studies in Ethnomusicology* series (Baily, 1990a: xiv–xv; Fairley, 1991: 115, 118). And Blacking's activities were not confined to ethnomusicology; he is also widely remembered as both charismatic and provocative for his writings, conference presentations and broadcast programmes on dance and education.

The defence

In interview with me in 1989, Blacking offered four defences for his continuing references to Venda fieldwork (Howard, 1991: 70). The first recognized a political fact: the South African government had declared him unwelcome, so he was unable to return to personally update his data.

Second, Blacking said: 'I am proud to be, via Meyer Fortes, an intellectual grandson of Bronislaw Malinowski. I have been profoundly influenced by Malinowski's emphasis on deep fine-grain ethnography, and his experiences of the difficulty involved in portraying one society.' Now, to link this to ethnomusicology requires a quick rehearsal of the authorized history of our discipline. According to this history – or at least, this is the way I interpret it – the roots of ethnomusicology are in comparative musicology, a practice steeped in romantic notions of the 'other' and an analytical rational discourse that mirrored late nineteenth-century laboratory-based explorations of science. By the beginning of the twentieth century, scholarship was coupled to nationalistic and bounded folklore studies that isolated the component parts of musical sound. From here, our authorized history relates that a shift from theory to ethnography occurred as Western hegemony was questioned. This allowed Merriam and others, as American members of the nascent Society for Ethnomusicology and followers of Boas, Herzog *et al.*, to graft anthropology on to musicological structural and analytical theories. It also allowed Blacking, in a way that he quickly came to regard as distinct from that of Merriam, to adopt a fieldwork style modelled on Malinowski's *Argonauts of the Western Pacific*.[11] The emphasis given by this cultural immersion through fieldwork reduced the scope for generalized or comparative surveys and increased the output of monographs confined to specific music cultures. This was encouraged by the colonial legacy and then supported after the Second World War by the perception that *we* should know *them*. It allowed for the emergence of related paradigms, chief amongst them Mantle Hood's bi-musicality and reflections such as Hugo Zemp's (1971, and subsequent articles) or Stephen Feld's (1982) on native points of view.[12] And, following from Hood, ethnomusicology adds to social science fieldwork methods what Shelemay has called 'bracketed performativeness' (1997: 200) – the ability to join the music cultures studied by learning to perform, so that 'observation is inseparable from representation and interpretation' (Cooley, 1997: 4; see also Slobin and Titon, 1992: 1). Remember, here, how *African Music* remarked that Blacking was learning to sing Venda songs and play their instruments.

The paradigm that this authorized history presents belongs primarily to mid-twentieth-century discourse. It tends to sideline older ethnographies of music, such as those by Jean de Léry and others collected in Frank Harrison's *Time, Place and Music* (1973) or texts such as Johann Gottfried Herder's *Volkslieder* (1778–79). Indeed, older ethnographies may be more commonplace in ethnomusicology than those following Malinowski would allow for. Consider, for example, the recent collection of early commentaries on Thai music collated by Terry Miller and Jarernchai Chonpairot (1994), projects such as Lawrence Picken's *Music from the Tang Court* (Picken *et al.*, vol. 1, 1991, to vol. 7, 1997), or the common appeals to search for authentic forms in historically-based music reconstructions. Should such works be excluded from the canon? At the same time, the paradigm tends to impose a rosy, if not romantic, gloss on Malinowski, ignoring the revelations of his diary – first published in 1967 – and the forced nature of his incarceration on the Trobriand Islands. It is likely to ignore methodological inadequacies among major scholars such as Margaret Mead or Radcliffe-Brown. It imposes boundaries, so that the field is typically conceived as a geographical or linguistic area – this is how Helen Myers (1992b: 23) considers it. What of, say, international concert tours, or African musicians working and recording in Europe? In anthropology, this paradigm allowed Evans-Pritchard, Meyer Fortes and Raymond Firth, respectively, to continually refine their work on the Nuer, Tallensi and Tikopia. But fieldwork itself, within this paradigm and because of the requirement for long-term immersion, increasingly runs foul both of the local agencies responsible for granting research permission and of an ever-decreasing number of funders.

Blacking, however, moved away from this paradigm in his writings, even though he continued to teach it virtually intact to anthropology undergraduates at Queen's University. The regional boundaries that the Venda inhabit, for example, were collapsed as he broadened his discussion. He saw this in terms of personal maturity: as a scholar matures, so he or she can make better sense of fieldwork data. This was the basis of his third defence. We might see a retrospective defence of fieldwork methods – specifically, the need to keep comprehensive documentation – or a justification for perpetual returns to data that has not been fully analysed. The defence permits reassessment; hence Blacking claimed to have come to understand Venda comments about the relationships between material and spiritual life late in his own life, particularly after he had been diagnosed with cancer[13] and, again, he claimed to understand Venda comments about children as angelic beings only with the arrival of his second family.

Fourth, Blacking stated that '… nobody who still writes about Bach, Schubert or Schumann has to defend themselves' (Blacking, personal communication). Such a comment downplays the notion of musical autonomy and the associated view of music analysts that compositions can be studied as aural phenomenon irrespective of time or place. In this, the grammar of European art music is held to have developed sequentially along a path that can be likened to a jagged continuum, allowing a direct comparison of Bach with Schumann and postulations of musical meaning.[14] (Similarly, Western musical history is typically taught in a sequence that is both chronological and developmental.) As Carl Dahlhaus noted, this does not deny that musical autonomy may be relative (1987: 238) and indicates potentials for degrees of relativity. To Dahlhaus, an aesthetic understanding of Bach or Schumann's music can be bound up in the idea of 'art [music] for its own sake', rather than as a reflection of cultural and political factors. The discipline(s) of musicology/*Musikwissenschaft* has taken this for granted, even if autonomy is largely a nineteenth-century construct, leaving an analytical legacy that converges with premodern ethnomusicology, for example, in Hornbostel's 'pure melody', Merriam's interval counts and Kolinski's trait analysis.

In *Venda Children's Songs*, Blacking's alternative perception received its first extended outing, albeit with little reference to European art music. Blacking writes that he found the analytical tools inherited from musicology inadequate. Rather than see the sequential development of children's singing ability from songs with two tones to songs with three, four or more,[15] he argued that song choice reflected popularity, context and musical style. In keeping with this, he placed his Venda materials in the specific time when they were collected; to him, the reporting of ethnomusicological and anthropological fieldwork was essentially historical. This, too, removes his methodology from musicology, but it mirrors a then-current debate in British anthropology about history. Distrust of an unobserved and potentially distorted history had stemmed from diffusionist discourse and had eventually led to Evans-Pritchard's seminal account, 'Anthropology and history' (1962: ch. 3). Blacking, though, was not prepared to be bound by the resultant strictures characteristic of many anthropological accounts of his time. He was not comfortable with limiting his writing to the observed historical reporting. He sought to escape the chronological parameters of his fieldwork data, believing that they could be held to represent an ongoing tradition. Although this was necessary if his visionary statements were to stand up to scrutiny, I suspect the underlying reason was his need to compare Venda materials with European art music created in the past but still performed in the present: he wanted to write about both with the same brush. Later, to satisfy his acceptance of the anthropological debate, but at the same time to escape the constraints that his 1950s-based fieldwork imposed, he would substantiate his views through both the more recent fieldwork of others[16] and his own increasing first-hand or text-based knowledge of other sub-Saharan musics. In his 1980 film, *Domba: A Personal Record of Venda Initiation Rites*, some shots are clearly recent, including a road sign that post-dates the 1978 'independence' of the Republic of Venda, but he makes no distinction between recent and earlier footage.

To reiterate, then, Blacking's four defences rely on a mix of personal situation, circumstance and experience. He was trained in, and aware of, anthropology and its debates and was keen to apply anthropological fieldwork to ethnomusicological research. But, because his only period of extended fieldwork was in the 1950s, and because he continued to rely on data from that fieldwork, his attitudes to fieldwork in some ways became outdated in later life. Indeed, those of us who studied with him were taught a set of fieldwork techniques that had variable practical utility; his ideas about 'suitable' presents that should be taken into the field, for example, had little chance of endearing me to my East Asian informants. Again, I can find no evidence that he considered potential links between ethnographic representation and colonialism in relation to his own fieldwork data (as discussed, for example, by the contributors to Asad, 1973 and Manganaro, 1990), despite living and teaching in Ulster where such issues were part of local debate. At the same time, he placed anthropological discourse at the service of his own musical interests and passions; his background as a child chorister and then his activities as a composer and pianist cast an enduring shadow over his life and career. It is to this that I now turn, exploring how the Venda are juxtaposed with other musics. This paragraph, though, must end with a brief note on his personal politics. Inspired by Marx, but by nature a humanist and interpreting music from this perspective, I suspect that he would not have been unduly upset by Joseph Kerman's characterization of him: 'Blacking is of the generation of the angry young men of the late 1950s, and he shows it' (Kerman, 1985b: 159).

Juxtapositions

Blacking allowed knowledge about the Venda to illuminate his understanding of European art music. The narrative of fieldwork underpinned his provocative statements because his Venda ethnography was the result of a rigorous scrutiny of data. The same scrutiny is missing from his discussions of Western art music, and this, I submit, explains the critiques of Josephson and Kerman.

A few hints of Blacking's perspectives on the musicology of art music appear in the opening pages of *How Musical is Man?*, but much that he must have known is missing. For instance, in his youth he had composed, and he would surely have been aware of, and concerned with, the post-Second World War promotion of serialism as a method of allowing creative freedom.[17] Again, we know that he had followed the early music movement, notably as it connected with the Dolmetsch family, and he would surely have recognized the contrast between anthropology's distrust of history and the systematic recovery of lost music and instruments that this movement espoused. Once he had discovered Malaysian and African music, what would he have made of Constant Lambert's immensely popular and populist *Music Ho!* (1934) in which the author charts musical decline caused by 'ephemeral and petty ideas' and by 'appalling' popular music and the 'exotic'? Coupled to what is lacking, there is something of the dilettante in Blacking's references to this musicology. This is evident in the general nature of the texts he quotes in *How Musical is Man?*, the bibliography of which includes Edward Hanslick's *The Beautiful in Music* (1891), Alec Harman's *Medieval and Early Renaissance Music* (1958), Frank Howes' *Man, Mind and Music* (1948), Paul Henry Lang's *Music in Western Civilization* (1941), Hugo Leichtentritt's *Music, History, and Ideas* (1946), Wilfrid Mellors' *Man and His Music: The Sonata Principle* (1957) and *Music and Society* (1950), Rudolph Réti's *The Thematic Process in Music* (1961), Arnold Schoenberg's *Style and Idea* (1951), and Alan Walker's *A Study in Music Analysis* (1962). Excluding the last three of these, this is a far more pedestrian list than that which Blacking offers for ethnomusicology or music psychology. And, although these all vanish from *A Commonsense View* with the exception of Schoenberg's *Style and Idea*, in the latter book Blacking cites Jack Westrup's general Western art music history, Hubert Parry's 1896 volume, *The Evolution of the Art of Music* and Lambert's *Music Ho!* The last, incidentally is granted no significant – but surely warranted – critique.

How Musical is Man? presents a critique of Deryck Cooke's attempt, in *The Language of Music* (1959), to provide a linguistic typology for melodic patterning. Cooke's argument is collapsed by the observation that 'changes in musical style have generally been reflections of changes in society'. The context for this observation, of course, is the Venda, and the comment is consistent with *Venda Children's Songs*.[18] Yet, as Blacking expands his theme, and as is characteristic of his writing, he juxtaposes generalized information on European music with specific information on the Venda. We hear about the secularization of music around 1200 in Europe (the monolithic picture of European musical development is simplified, but chimes with so many general histories). This is linked to specific styles of Venda music, and Blacking comments on the degree of assimilation into the body politic amongst the users of each (1973: 58–76).

In fact, a more personal motive lies behind this critique of Cooke. While we can trace in Blacking's writings explorations of links between music and language, and the gradual discovery and selective appropriation of Chomskian ideas, Cooke, whose theory Blacking initially respected, surely stands for much European musicology which Blacking felt he could now, on the basis of his understanding of Venda music, selectively reject. Within this section of *How Musical is Man?* we can see the primacy given the Venda in Blacking's consideration of their national dance, *tshikona*. The Venda say that this is 'the time when people rush to the scene of the dance and leave their pots to boil over' and that the performance of this dance 'brings peace to the countryside'. These comments are matched to Mahler's claim that music performance may take participants to 'the other world'. This, in turn, is transformed by Blacking through a reference to Bali, where music is claimed to stimulate alternative states of consciousness, before he returns to the Venda (Blacking, 1973: 51–53). Mahler is next mentioned ten pages on, as part of a direct critique of Cooke (Blacking, 1973: 60–62). Blacking says that he wants to find out 'what the music says to me' and, because of this, he has 'deliberately never read any analyses'. He asks whether he has 'received the attitudes that prompted Mahler to compose these notes' or whether he merely imposes his personal interpretation. Hidden here is a further broadside at Cooke whose reputation is as much as a Mahler scholar as for his *Language of Music* volume; Blacking rejects the need to refer to Cooke's commentary on Mahler's music.[19] Although there is much in the discussion to recommend it, since a fundamental part of the Venda ethnography is Venda statements about music, where is a parallel consideration of Mahler's own writings beyond just a brief and pithy quote in the tradition of Bruce Chatwin's *Songlines* or of writings about him published during his lifetime?

In *A Commonsense View*, Blacking juxtaposes Edward Elgar with African ensembles. He offers an image of Elgar, 'disgusted by the vulgarity and noise of pomp and circumstance at the British Empire Exhibition of 1924' but still believing resolutely in the transformative power of music – a belief imbibed during five years spent working as an asylum bandmaster. In African ensembles, each 'performer provides only a small part of the total musical pattern' but knows that 'the power of well-performed music can be related to the power that is generated by the extension of individuality in community' (Blacking, 1987: 28–29). This juxtaposition simply does not stand up to scrutiny. Elgar's disgust, for example, surely needs to be seen in its context – in terms of the First World War and its aftermath, nationalism and the setting of words to his most famous march. Again, although Elgar was indeed an asylum bandmaster at the Worcester City and County Lunatic Asylum near Powick between 1879 and 1884, this was well before his career as a composer took off. There is little in our knowledge of that experience to suggest any formative influence imported to his later life, not least since his compositions for patients – largely polkas and quadrilles – were popular dances in contrast to the Edwardian grandeur of his mature works. And Elgar's job was not unusual since, throughout late nineteenth-century Europe, music was commonly used both as recreation and stimulation in asylums – not so much in an aim to be transformative but as something to keep patients occupied.[20]

Blacking returns to Elgar a few pages later and, to defend his essentialist and humanist view, calls on evidence: programme notes written by Geoffrey Crankshaw for a 1971 recording of the *Enigma Variations* that talk of Elgar's alchemy and humanity; an interpretive ballet of the piece choreographed by Macmillan; an impressionistic early 1970s film of the composer's life by Ken Russell (Blacking, 1987: 40–41). These sources, though, explore transform-ation in terms of musical structures – thematic variations and timbral, rhythmic and melodic depictions of character traits – rather than in Blacking's normal social and cultural contextualization. And none dates from Elgar's time, although one small piece of evidence is gleaned from Elgar himself – comments he made about geographical places associated with specific compositions (Blacking cites Moore (1984) for this). At face value, this suggests that the ethnomusicologist in Blacking is at work, but there is more to be considered. Just as Cooke stands for British musicology, associations of place with sound need to be seen as part of the musicological discourse that Blacking grew up with. These associations were expressed in texts such as Cyril Scott's *Music: Its Secret Influence Through the Ages* (1976 [1933])[21] and explored in the spiritual concerns of composers whose works Blacking was familiar with – Scriabin, Debussy, Delius, Holst, Warlock and others. Such ideas have little resonance for Elgar whose one piece titled to invoke a land beyond Britain – the piano miniature *In Smyrna* – has nothing in it that could be identified as Turkish.[22]

Sparked by Percy Grainger's quotation from the Confucian *Record of Rites* (*Book of Rites*; *Ijing*),[23] Blacking, in *A Commonsense View*, moves from Richard Strauss's opera *Capriccio* to a paragraph echoing George List's discussion on speech and song in *Ethnomusicology* (List, 1963: 1–16) although List is not mentioned by Blacking. Grainger is embedded in the text because *A Commonsense View* was originally written while Blacking was resident at the University of Western Australia in Perth where Grainger's music education materials are archived. Quickly, though, Blacking brings more data to his defence, with a reference to Joshua Uzoigwe's doctoral dissertation on Igbo *ukom* drum-row music (Blacking, 1987: 83–89) – a dissertation that Blacking had supervised. The conflict between music and words, he tells us, is his concern here. The Chinese text, however, discusses song as an extension of poetry to express emotion (technically, there is no mention of 'music').

Blacking draws a conclusion in stark contrast to the texts of ancient China, but one which is nonetheless attractive on a first reading: in 'some musical systems, there is no distinction between poetry and music' (1987: 84).[24] In reaching this conclusion he is precise in his references to the Venda – 'rhythmically recited verse was classed as "song"', and six elements define the relationship between speech and song – but attempts no precision when referring to Chinese literature or when differentiating, in the same section, the composer of *Capriccio* (Richard Strauss) from the librettist (Clemens Krauss). Nor does Blacking offer any reference for differentiating Strauss the philosopher from Strauss the musician: the latter, he says, '*seems* to take a *more personal* view ... appropriate for a patriarchal society' (1987: 86, emphasis added). Mahler, Elgar and Strauss – it might prove illuminating to explore Blacking's own compositions to discover what they tell us about the formative influences in his personal style.

In 'The Biology of Music-making' (1992), Blacking contrasts the dexterity of jazz pianists with the hand movements that give flow to the music of Chopin, Debussy and Ravel which, in terms of physical structure, he considers to be different from that of keyboard players from the time of C.P.E. Bach or Mozart (1992: 308–09). For this, he offers no substantiation and no referencing, as this is personal experience from Blacking the pianist. He then refers back to his earlier published analyses of Venda and Nsenga music (Blacking, 1959b, 1973), where, he says, 'symmetrical and physically "easy" movements of the body' were favoured, and to John Baily's movement patterning analysis of Afghan music. One block of material is missing from the text – *The Anthropology of the Body* (1977c), a collection of articles edited by Blacking that allowed him to reassess his understanding. The experience here is less personal and had evolved over time, as he reflected on musical knowledge and understanding acquired during his post-fieldwork career. Again, though, the juxtaposition is of two unequal halves.

Undeniably, however, Blacking encouraged the application of ethno-musicological method to European art music, thereby influencing the development of what some have labelled 'critical musicology'. Hence, while the detail of his arguments may be thin, the thrust remains truly impressive. The discussion that starts from the consideration of Elgar in *A Commonsense View* (1987: 29–34) is particularly noteworthy. First, Blacking notes that the *Enigma Variations* reflected personal memories of people and events, but that Elgar knew that others' responses to his music would be determined by other influences within and beyond the concert hall.[25] This allows him to argue that music association tests will always be inconclusive and that the power of music comes from social, cultural and physical associations.[26] This being so, Blacking asserts that music is a commodity that can be used for an unlimited number of purposes – much, if we are permitted to read beyond what is written in the text, as had happened during and after the First World War with Elgar's

Pomp and Circumstance. From here a set of ideas flow: if a composer's individuality is stressed but a listener's individuality is denied, the popularity of a composition cannot be explained in terms of musical structures; a composer's identity is socially constructed as much as biologically determined; composition, following from Schoenberg's *Style and Idea*, emerges from 'unconscious cerebration' based on 'universal mental processes'; composers such as Mozart transcend the extraordinary to communicate in ordinary ways. These ideas challenge musicology's practices: the first discards the descriptive analysis beloved of Dent's *Master Musicians* series, the second questions how musical analysis can ever reveal meaningful differences between Elgar, Mahler and Strauss, and the third and fourth challenge the notion that composers possess unique and rare musical brilliance. An excursion to the Venda provides justification, then Blacking returns, again challenging the notion of a composer's genius (but now mentioning Franz Liszt) and then illustrating his ideas from personal experience (Blacking, 1987: 40–43).

The parallel discussion in *How Musical is Man?* kicks off with Cooke: 'A composer who hopes to communicate anything more than pretty sounds must be aware of the associations … in the minds of different social groups' (Blacking, 1973: 73). The material now is Britten's *War Requiem*, minuets and the French Revolution, Rameau and harmonic theory, a critique of Max Weber's consideration of the European tone system, Christian polyphony, fourth intervals in the music of Flemish composers, Lutheran chorales used by Bach and the importation of folk music into nineteenth- and twentieth-century art music. The ideas, though, are much the same, and the argument is sandwiched between two segments of Venda ethnography, the first demonstrating how speech tone affects melody and how performance context influences the expressive power of music and the second exploring the relationships between musical structures and social and political groups.

Views of the horizon

The juxtapositions presented by Blacking are implicit, if not expected, within the fieldwork paradigm as it is now practised. As Titon argues, fieldwork is 'an experience of myself in relation to other people … a reflexive opportunity and an ongoing dialogue which … reworks my "work" as "our" work' (Titon, 1997: 94). Hence, the interpretation of fieldwork, at both the documenting/ classifying stages and in narrative retellings, allows the incorporation of past and present experience. The self, according to Heidegger, is understood by placing it in front of cultural works (Heidegger, 1962: 114). To Paul Ricoeur, 'It is cultural works, with the universal power of unveiling, which give a self to the ego' (1981: 192–93). Blacking makes the implicit explicit, and it becomes reasonable, within this, for him to state that he wants to experience what

Mahler's music says on a personal level *to him*, rather than considering another scholar's analysis. Many of his statements about European art music suddenly make sense, as a reflection of his own internalized understanding: Mahler expressed himself in music only when 'indefinable emotions made themselves felt' (Blacking, 1973: 60–61); Britten is an example of how 'composers acquire characteristics of style by listening to the music of the past and present' (1973: 67); performances of Beethoven's *Hammerklavier* sonata by renowned pianists are 'transformative' (Blacking, 1987: 19).

The relationship between experience and understanding in Blacking's writings works on two different levels – one grounded in personal musicianship and one constrained by anthropological fieldwork methodology. The balance between the two is where Blacking the theoretician meets Blacking the visionary; it is precisely because of the fusion between the familiar and the novel that Blacking continues to speak. Blacking, then, was ahead of his time. His writings slip comfortably into post-modernist discourse, or reflexivity – modern-day givens that were less a part of mainstream scholarship during the four decades in which he was active. Similarly, what Arjun Appadurai has called 'deterritorialization' (1991: 192) – shifting the field from the exotic to the familiar, from a detailed consideration of a limited geographical area to a broader canvas and a part of our post-colonial world – held little fear for Blacking.

Blacking's work asks us to question whether ethnomusicological careers can and should be based solely on an understanding of the 'other' – a narrowly defined single geographical or linguistic field – and whether we are not, as Kingsbury has argued, moving towards 'post-ethnographic musicology'.[27] Blacking, though, would surely argue that he could only explore 'humanly organized sound' because his arguments were grounded by his Venda ethnography. He was, then, a product of his time. He had a solid grasp of anthropology, imbued at Cambridge. He undertook exemplary fieldwork amongst the Venda, adding to participant observation the systematic collection of kinship, ritual, social, political and economic data, and thereby challenging the less rigorous music collection practices that, up until that time, had characterized ethnomusicology. He also had personal experience, training and very considerable aptitude as a musician, and brought this to his analysis and discussion.

Hans-Georg Gadamer's notion of horizons provides a tool to fuse these elements of Blacking's persona[28] together. As our experience grows, and if we can view our life as a series of tableaux, so our understanding – our horizons – shift. Tim Rice (1994) has already been here in his exploration of phenomenological hermeneutics. With Blacking, though, a paradox remains: he never allowed the horizon of his 1950s fieldwork to change. There were a number of reasons for this. His fieldwork constituted a bounded period at the beginning of his career, a period frozen in time that was never physically revisited because of his expulsion from South Africa, a period the knowledge of which appeared to be reinforced by those who returned to the Venda in subsequent decades on his behalf, and a period that his ever-increasing commitments elsewhere – as teacher, publicist, board member and so on – effectively prohibited him from ever repeating.

An illustration from gliding, also known as soaring, illustrates the paradox. To the pilot of a glider, the horizon is a visible reference point used to keep the plane at the right altitude to control speed and to restrict yaw in banking. In reality, the view of the horizon shifts as the glider moves through the air. The glider behaves in relation to the invisible column of air that holds it aloft, not in relation to the ground and horizon. Blacking, by focusing on the fieldwork narrative (the horizon), was apt to allow his grand statements to stand with little or no visible substantiation (like the invisible column of air). As he was buffeted by the air supporting the glider – by his formative, internalized understandings and by the acquisition of new knowledge – he kept the horizon as a constant. A glider, though, constantly sinks, descending as it passes through the air, unless the pilot can find lift. The pilot looks for signs of updrafts, hot air signalled in rising smoke or particular cloud formations. Blacking's supporters recognize the hidden substantiation behind what Byron calls the 'bold and sweeping assertions' – the indications of updrafts – and find them most readily in matches between their own formative experiences and understandings and those of Blacking. Blacking not only assumes that his readers will find the matches, but gives substantiation by calling on them from across on the horizon, from his Venda narrative. 'Not good enough,' say his detractors, missing the signs and rejecting the notion that the Venda can underpin this global vision of music. So far, however, his supporters are winning.

Notes

[1] Breaks in the fieldwork period came in 1956 when his first child died, in 1957 when his second child was born, and for a month when he worked with the Gwembe Tonga of the Zambezi valley.

[2] Published in America as *Contemplating Music: Challenges to Musicology* (Cambridge MA: Harvard University Press).

[3] In 1958 Blacking also received a Horniman scholarship from the Royal Anthropological Institute in London to enable him to continue work in the field.

[4] His third child also suffered from leukaemia during this period. Blacking reminisces about this in Howard (1991: 61–62).

[5] The acknowledgements section in *Venda Children's Songs* states that the Ling Roth scholarship allowed Blacking to work on the draft manuscript (Blacking, 1967: 3).

[6] Reily lists the field data he refers to: 106 songs, 322 *mulayo*, 20 rituals, 33 shows, 460 lines of *domba* song texts … (Reily, 1998: 49).

[7] '… ambitious commoners are able to attract a following and further their interests by means of the music that is performed under their auspices. This is similar to the way

in which influential men used the music of Haydn, Mozart, and many others' (Blacking, 1967: 23).

[8] Thus, Byron's criteria for selecting the eight papers by Blacking included in *Music, Culture, and Experience* were that they should be about ethnomusicological understanding, should make characteristic theoretical and methodological points, but that they should bring in Venda ethnography 'only to the extent that the point is given effective illustration' (Byron, 1995: 21).

[9] Many of the PhD students are listed in Howard (1991: 66–67, and fns 12 and 13). As university education moves increasingly towards greater provision of postgraduate courses, the total number of students Blacking taught at Belfast may seem less remarkable, but Blacking's PhD students have gone on to hold senior academic posts in many countries, amongst them Brazil, Britain, Chile, Germany, Greece, Ireland, Japan, Kenya, Nigeria, Poland, Romania, South Africa, the United States, (the former) Yugoslavia and Zambia.

[10] Both identify this as the 'National Council for Academic Awards'. The CNAA was responsible for approving and moderating degree courses in British non-university institutions until the early 1990s.

[11] The link to Malinowski is indicated in *A Commonsense View of all Music* (1987: 24–25).

[12] Kingsbury's *Poisoned Ivy*, a 'story' posted on the Internet (http://www.cybertours.com/~h_kingsbury/pi, last accessed August 2003), discusses Feld, lightly disguised as 'Stephanie Fielding'. What Fielding calls in one article a 'literal translation' of a phrase turns out, according to Kingsbury, to be a 'multi-layered cultural metaphor'. Clifford Geertz (1988) argued that ethnographic writing requires much rhetorical skill, an understanding which, to Tim Rice, becomes 'phenomenologically weighted representations of people making music' (Rice, 1997: 96). The scholar, in other words, mediates to create his or her narrative.

[13] A useful comparison would be Renato Rosaldo's (1993) account of understanding the Philippino Ilongot juxtaposition of grief and rage only after losing his wife while on fieldwork.

[14] Pieter van den Toorn's *Music, Politics, and the Academy* (1997), a robust rejoinder to Susan McClarey and others who argue for contextualization, reiterates the approach. Note van den Toorn's attack on Blacking's *How Musical is Man?* (1997: 38–39).

[15] A parallel exists with the supposedly sequential development of harmony in European art music discussed, for example, in Perischetti (1978).

[16] Andrée Grau took up an offer from Blacking to spend six months fieldwork in Venda in 1977, using funds Blacking had from the Wenner-Gren Foundation (for which, see Grau, 1991: 222–24). Grau observes that what she collected in 1977 was musically not that different from what Blacking had collected 20 years earlier (personal communication, 20 August 2000).

[17] See, for example, the overview in Smith Brindle (1966).

[18] See also his later article on musical change (Blacking, 1977a).

[19] Blacking does, however, admit that he listens to Cooke's performing version of Mahler's unfinished Tenth Symphony (Blacking, 1973: 60).

[20] For a discussion of music in nineteenth-century European asylums, see Kramer (2000a, 2000b).

[21] I have chosen to cite this text because of Blacking's attraction to meditation and the spiritual path of Subud. Blacking stated that his interest began when he and his first wife, Paula Grebers, were struggling to come to terms with the leukaemia of their third child between 1961 and 1963. I do not intend to imply that Blacking would have agreed

with C. Scott's theosophy. Indeed, the thrust of Blacking's *How Musical is Man?* is that all men possess capabilities to appreciate music, whereas Scott saw it rather differently: 'A man is termed "musical" who has a mild liking for claptrap music: (a) by a person who has no liking for music of any kind himself; (b) by a person who also likes claptrap music' (Scott, 1976 [1933]: 16).

[22] *In Smyrna* was written in October 1905. Elgar had taken a Mediterranean cruise, and had disembarked to explore Izmir. An early idea for the piece appears in his sketchbook with the comment: 'In Smyrna (In the Mosque)'.

[23] By 1987, the assigned date given in *A Commonsense View* for when this was written – 2255 BC – was thoroughly refuted.

[24] The Chinese distinction between song and poetry, in contrast, is perhaps best expressed in the Great Preface to the *Book of Odes (Shijing)*.

[25] Although Blacking gives no citation, there is a possible influence here from Christopher Small's consideration of the Western concert hall environment, published as the first chapter in his *Music, Society, Education* (1977).

[26] Blacking cites 1960s scholarship by Donald Ferguson and Alphons Silbermann, plus Rouget's analysis of music and trance. But the reaction here appears to be against the continuing widespread use of musical aptitude tests.

[27] See note 12 above.

[27] In a memorable sequence in Blacking's series for Ulster TV, *Dancing*, Peter Stringfellow is interviewed, saying: 'It's all about *persona*'. To the camera he adds, 'That's a trendy one, you can use that – *persona*.' Blacking did.

CHAPTER THREE

Tracks of the Mouse: Tonal Reinterpretation in Venda Guitar Songs[1]

Jaco Kruger

Twentieth-century South African ethnomusicology reveals a tendency either towards music-making as cultural pattern or the intricacies of musical style. Relatively few researchers have integrated these emphases persistently in support of the axiom that musical style is not only rooted in specific social contexts, but also has socially formative functions (James, 1991). This integrative theoretical approach was one of the inceptive, and most enduring, trademarks of John Blacking's work. His initial field report on Venda music (1957) first related musical style to social function. This relationship was explored consistently in much of his subsequent work, and he eventually formulated its theoretical underpinning as the 'cultural analysis of music'. This theory stated the now-familiar dictum that 'because music is humanly organized sound, there ought to be relationships between patterns of human organization and the patterns of sound produced in the course of organized interaction'. Consequently, it was imperative to describe '*both* the music *and* its cultural background as interrelated parts of a total system' (Blacking, 1971: 93).

Blacking preferred to explore this theory within the boundaries of Venda music of pre-colonial origin. Consequently, he has been criticized for assuming a static stance on culture. However, not only do both his general reports on Venda musical culture (1957, 1965) include references to new musical forms, but his essay on Zionist church music (1980a) is devoted entirely to this theme (also see Blacking, 1986). This important essay is not only one of the first efforts to posit South African musical culture as a form of subaltern expression, but also integrates the role of musical style in this process. Together with early work on urban music by David Coplan (e.g. Coplan, 1980), it marks the beginning of a landmark period in the history of South African ethnomusicology. Musical ethnography of the final two decades of the twentieth century show that subaltern musical cultures have contributed to the reproduction of social health by generating psychological resistance and social solidarity, and providing indispensable strategies against political repression, moral ambiguity and poverty (see, for example, Coplan, 1994; Erlmann, 1999; James, 1999b; Muller, 1999).

These findings contrast with two classical colonial discourses on African musics. The first is traditionalist essentialism which ostensibly identifies and describes intact musical cultures (see De Hen, 2000). The second discourse assumes an evolutionist view of African musical cultures as the acquiescent victims of impinging, commodified musics. Thus a homogenizing colonial epistemology invokes a hyper-real Europe towards which all historical imagination gravitates in the form of a colonial master narrative in which local histories become subaltern variations of European history (Chakrabarty, 1992: 337, 353). Thus, the British weekly magazine, *South Africa*, complained in 1892 of the music of the African Native Choir from South Africa that it was devalued by 'inevitable' European harmonies, while the *Musical Standard* perceived the choir to have 'adopted more or less the European scale, to say nothing of European harmonies' (Erlmann, 1999: 130). These perspectives were echoed by Percival Kirby (1887–1970), an early pioneer of South African ethnomusicology, who suggested that European culture had inescapably 'affected the Bantu in every conceivable way' (Kirby, 1967: 139). African popular dance music was consequently 'always composed after the European manner', and 'based upon European scale systems and their accompanying harmonies' (Kirby, 1968: 276). Similar perceptions of cultural debilitation and replacement continue to underpin interpretations of African musics. Klaus Heimes has suggested that African popular music in South Africa is no longer quite African, because the suprapersonal functions it once had, and which were the source of its transcendental dimensions, have been replaced by other functions. It has become 'a western music because it draws on the western harmonic framework', with the consequent loss of its primordial transcendental dimensions (Heimes, 1990: 69).

These perceptions of structural and philosophical change in African musics correlate with my own initial interpretation of certain styles of Venda acoustic guitar music from Limpopo Province. I encountered these styles first in 1983 as a novice musicologist investigating Venda musical instruments. Like Kirby and Heimes, I too reacted sympathetically and critically to what I perceived as the dilution of local cultural forms. Unwittingly assuming a stance of ethnocentric idealism, I viewed the homemade guitars I encountered with amused disdain. They were rudimentary instruments (see Figure 3.1) of the African 'banjo' type (see Kubik, 1989) which contrasted markedly with the expertly crafted instruments of pre-colonial origin I had learned to make and play (for example, the xylophone and lamellaphone). And so I decided to disregard not only them, but also commercially manufactured guitars because I associated them with cultural imperialism. I lamented the decay of older forms of instrumental music in my field notes, suggesting that the influence of contemporary popular music was not only 'shocking' but also 'smothering' musical creativity.

Figure 3.1   Mbulaheni Netshipise, Tshififi, 27 November 1989

However, my continued exposure to guitar styles (including those associated with homemade guitars) sensitized me to their strategic functions and the structure of their forms. So I met the guitarist, Mashudu Mulaudzi of Tsianda, early in 1986. Mulaudzi treated me to a stunning performance in which I recognized a startling cross-cultural fusion of harmonic sequences. Further investigation revealed that, although these guitar styles may appear to conform rather simplistically to the stylistic norms of certain commodified musics, some of them in fact reinterpret the tonal template of Venda music of pre-colonial origin. And so I came to discover for myself a basic principle of African musics in situations of cultural contact, namely that foreign musical syntax and semantics are reformulated and resignified in dynamic interaction with local cultures (see, for example, Kubik, 1974; Rycroft, 1977).

An important challenge in the interpretation of transculturated musical forms clearly is to resolve 'the almost insuperable contradiction between a political actuality based on force, and a scientific and human desire to understand the Other hermeneutically and sympathetically in modes not influenced by force' (Said, 1993: 66). The making of modern African subjectivities is not determined by the dichotomy of conqueror and conquered, and imperialism and its legacies cannot, in any sense, be described as uncontested and unambiguous historical moments (Erlmann, 1999: 3–4). Instead, we accept as axiomatic that culture is a continually reconstituted 'assemblage of separable parts' (Moore, 1989: 38), and that the capacity of humans to creatively interpret and expressively engage historical circumstances is the essence of culture rather than evidence of its death or decline (Coombe, 1997: 85). Ethnic boundaries are rarely, if ever, overrun in cultural blitzkriegs. Instead, they become 'contact zones' (Pratt, 1991) where cultures converge and wrestle in the exploration of commonalities and differences that are expressed in new cultural forms. Our challenge is to determine what degree of commonality and variation exists in the perception and interpretation of cultural patterns across perceived boundaries (Kubik, 1979: 221). In particular, we must be receptive to when and how newly encountered cultural patterns may be recognized as reformulations of intracultural practices, and resignified in forms appropriate to cultural contact.

Resistance through symbolic inversion

Processes of social reorganization and cultural resistance in subaltern communities are underpinned by a quest for meaningful social identity. This quest is related to what W.E.B. Du Bois has described as a 'double consciousness' (Du Bois, 1969, cited in Erlmann, 1999; 156). This state of awareness is rooted in a 'deep sense of alienation and from the bitter experience of being part of modernity and at the same time excluded from it' (Erlmann, 1999: 200; see also Comaroff, 1996, p. 30). Two contradictory strategic viewpoints often emerge from this state of awareness. The first adopts many of modernity's utopian assurances and narratives, while the second assumes an oppositional, even separatist, stance against modernity's irrationality. Located in the dynamic intersection of these radical positions are many local communities that are swept along by empires and world economies, yet 'remain rooted, in important respects, in their own regimes of production and exchange' (Comaroff, 1996: 34).

Fundamental in these regimes of production is the adaptive reformulation of historical cultural patterns. Deborah James points to our expectation of a uniform effect on local communities of the transforming power of capitalism. We tend to ignore social and cultural specificities, particularly the emotive appeal of 'tradition' which speaks of 'home' and 'origin' to many physically and culturally dislocated people (James, 1999b: 16, 27). James accordingly shows how the cultural bedrock (*wa setso,* of 'traditional' origin) of *kiba* dancing has effected the socioeconomic mobility of Sotho women based in rural areas of Limpopo Province. Eric Makhado, a student at the University of Venda, similarly explained[2] the role of older dances in the contemporary politics of neighbouring Venda communities by quoting the following expression: 'The offspring of the mouse follow ancestral tracks' (*Nwana wa mbevha ha hangwi mukwita*).[3] Makhado's comment relates to a time of change and conflict when the concepts of Venda 'tradition' and 'culture' had become topics for heated communal discussion and resources for social action (see Kruger 1999).

The nature of historical patterns and the extent to which they are invoked in cultural redefinition identifies the position of their practitioners in relation to centres of hegemonic social and cultural production. This process plays powerfully into making and marking new social classes and rupturing existing complexes of signs (Comaroff, 1996: 21). Jean Comaroff appropriately uses the term 'bricoleur' to describe members of a marginalized grouping located in the crucible of British imperial and Tswana cultures. The identity of the bricoleur is visible in the calculated combination of European and local forms of dress which symbolizes an effort to harness imperial power, yet evade its authority, thereby configuring 'an enduring identity at a distance from white markets and morals' (Comaroff, 1996: 34).

And so resistance to domination assumes many forms. Subaltern studies show that marginalized populations do not necessarily vent their defiance in the arenas of combat defined by dominant cultures. Instead they often do so in places diffused in the everyday world, jarring the conventional perceptions of the orthodox observer with 'defiant reformulations of mundane practice' such as writing, speech, bodily gestures, social space, clothing and music-making (Comaroff, 1985: 25, see also Guha, 1992; O'Hanlon, 1988; Pratt, 1996). Blacking (1980a) accordingly suggested that South African Zionists expressed Africanist aspirations in the way they sang church hymns. Although some Zionists were perfectly capable of singing European hymns, they preferred to adopt the 'Zionist style', thus attempting to render the incorporative, universalizing, and totalizing codes of colonialism ineffective and inapplicable (Said, 1993: 60).

Subaltern cultural reconstruction involves efforts to increase power, and even reverse power relations, by means of processes of symbolic inversion (Da Matta, 1984; J. Scott, 1993: 172–82, V. Turner, 1969). Thus, the status elevation in performance of certain lowly Venda musicians legitimizes them as important social critics and induces personal and communal psychological regeneration (Kruger, 1999–2000). However, processes of symbolic inversion also grapple with hegemonic aesthetic forms to test their potential for integration and subordination by means of an array of opposites, negatives and oppositions (Said, 1993: 60; see also J. Scott, 1993: 166–72). This then becomes 'a struggle against ideological evidentness on the terrain of that evidentness, an evidentness with a negative sign, reversed on its own terrain' (Pêcheux, 1982 cited in Parry, 1994: 176–77). Veit Erlmann accordingly detects in the dress of the African Native Choir a pattern of bricolage similar to that identified by Comaroff for the Tswana. This syncretic dress pattern hints at 'the subversive potential of colonial mimicry and the possibility of reversing the received subject–object relationship of the colonial order' (Erlmann, 1999: 106). Similarly, Jean and John Comaroff detect, in a moment in colonial history, the evocative effort of a Tswana convert to subvert Christian religious meaning and power by means of a 'brilliant bricolage of symbolic objects and verbal utterances' that functioned beyond the comprehension and control of missionary authority (Comaroff and Comaroff, 1989: 287–88).

This chapter further explores the kind of musical thought and practice identified by Blacking for Zionists, namely that music, like the codes of dress, religious ritual and language, does not merely involve the appropriation and redefinition of imperial cultural codes but often also resistance to them by means of the construction of explicitly, as well as implicitly oppositional representations of the 'conqueror's own speech' (see Pratt, 1996: 29). Like the calculated domestication of imperial sartorial codes in Tswana bricolage dress patterns, Venda guitar songs reveal certain obvious streams of syncretic awareness. I have shown how Venda guitarist Solomon Mathase uses the antiphonal structure and verbal messages of his songs in a deliberate endeavour to resist moral ambiguity accompanying rapid change (Kruger, 2001). Mathase selectively merges pre-colonial moral ethics with Christian principles, thus revealing consciousness of the strategic potential of imperial codes (see Comaroff and Comaroff, 1989).

But this strategy of resistance may not be expressed in the obvious practices and formal structures of Mathase's music only. Blacking's work on Zionist church music shows that music also may express implicit codes of resistance. Although Zionist hymns were based on European models, they had been reformulated to conform to certain local musical practices. So Blacking identified in them the presence of African features such as call and response form, drum accompaniment, thick harmonic texture, parallelism, and contrapuntal and harmonic addition (Blacking, 1980a: 53–55). He suggested that melodic and harmonic elaboration in particular affirmed the philosophy of maximum human individuality within the largest possible community – a social maxim he often cited in regard to *tshikona*, the ancient bamboo-pipe dance (see Blacking 1973).

This discussion accordingly proposes that the cross-cultural fusion of harmonic sequences in certain Venda guitar songs expresses a resistant, Africanist ideology. Although the tonal progressions of the music may appear to reflect the inexorable impact of globalization and commodification, they could be regarded as a structural substratum on which asymmetrical power relations are reversed. In particular, I will emphasize the role of enculturated patterns of aural perception, suggesting that they unconsciously induce a process of defiance. Because this process takes place on the terrain of apparent westernized popular music, its actual oppositional tactics may elude cultural outsiders. Implicit codes of opposition are often shielded from centres of power because of their localized articulation. However, their often culture-specific nature also may conceal patterns of resistance. As such, they not so much involve the deliberate concealment of some political agenda as a process in which resistance goes unnoticed behind a veil of apparently familiar sound.

The methodological challenge that emerges from this theoretical position relates to the fact that Venda guitarists express little or no awareness of patterns of resistance in the structural minutiae of their music. This problem also was identified by Blacking (1980a: 37) who noted that musical meaning invokes the problem of relating intentional social interaction to non-verbal modes of expression. Blacking addressed this problem by merging his cultural analysis of music with the Zionist 'folk model'. Consequently, he not only analysed musical thought, behaviour and structure in *emic* terms, but also related them to religious tenets and political consciousness.

My investigation into structural meaning in Venda guitar songs accordingly first locates musicians in the economic and political vortex of the second half of the twentieth century. Like Zionist musical culture, Venda guitar music is posited as an adaptive response by a largely subaltern grouping attempting to modernize certain time-honoured social values. The musical roots of this response are shown to be embedded in musical styles of pre-colonial origin whose theoretical principles are summarized in the second part of this chapter. Finally, I analyse the retention and reinterpretation of certain of these principles in guitar music.

The ideologies of *muzika wa sialala* guitar styles

The strategic use of historical symbolic resources to counteract anomie and achieve modernist aspirations is articulated strongly in South African musics. The Venda guitar styles discussed here accordingly belong to a cultural category known as *muzika wa sialala* ('modern old music'). *Muzika* obviously derives from 'music' and contrasts with *nyimbo* ('songs'), music of pre-colonial origin. *Sialala* is an archaic term for pre-colonial culture that has enjoyed increasing popularity since the 1980s. It derives from -*lala*, ('to sleep') which is used as a euphemism for death and thus refers to persons or objects from the distant past. Some younger, school-educated musicians describe the term *muzika wa sialala* in English as 'cultural music', reflecting revitalized local awareness of the strategic function of cultural continuity.[4]

According to guitarist and poet Phineas Mavhaga,[5] *muzika wa sialala* is any style of contemporary song that articulates social themes conventionally addressed in *nyimbo* or critically evaluates contemporary social experience against the template of pre-colonial forms of morality. As in other African musical cultures, the presence in *muzika wa sialala* of Western instruments and stylistic patterns (and sometimes also English song texts) is therefore not regarded as undermining attempts to revitalize social relationships of pre-colonial origin (see Kaufman, 1972). The articulation of pre-colonial values in *muzika wa sialala* should not be dismissed as some dysfunctional historical legacy. Venda acoustic guitar styles are generally markers of a marginalized grouping still engaged in certain older forms of economic and social production. This grouping includes a large contingent of poor migrants with strong links to rural bases in the mountainous, north-eastern part of Limpopo Province. It also incorporates a subaltern population eking out a living on small pockets of arable land on the periphery of emerging local towns, often in combination with intermittent phases of migrant labour and low-level activity in the informal economic sector. Colonized at the turn of the nineteenth century, this area comprises the former Venda 'homeland' which was created during the apartheid era and reincorporated into South Africa in 1994. Catapulted from a horticultural subsistence economy into capitalist production in the twentieth century, *muzika wa sialala* communities struggle with chronic unemployment[6] and poverty, as well as a rising rate of violent crime:

Mukukulume wo lila	**The cock crowed**[7]
Mukukulume wo lila, wee.	Alas, the cock crowed.
Wa ri: Konkokolikoko!	He said: Konkokolikoko!
Wo lila nga tshifhinga-de naa?	When did he crow?
Wo lila nga madautsha.	He crowed very early one morning.
Nga kotaphasi fo	At quarter past four to wake up
u tshi vusa vhashumi.	those who have to go to work.
Ri ye mushumoni, wee.	Oh dear, we have to go to work.
Naa a thi ri no ri kharali nda	Did you not say that when
nga pfa mukhuwa a tshi ri ndi	a white man is looking
khou toda muthu wa u shuma	for a garden boy that I
gadeni boy, ndi ni vhudze ni do	must inform you so that
ya na shuma naa, muthannga?	you can go and work, young man?
Mukukulume wo zwifhela phambo, wee.	Alas, the cock lied to the hen.
Wa ri: Mukegulu o tevhula vhuse, wee.	He said: Old woman, spread the ground maize kernels.
Ndi dziedzi, mmawe!	Oh mother! There is misery![8]
A thi funi u shuma, wee.	Oh dear, I do not like to work.
Ni do tshila ngani nwananga Nnditsheni?	How will you survive, Nnditsheni, my child?
Ndi do la matari sa mbudzi: Meee!	You will eat leaves like a goat: Meee!
Ndi do la damba sa nguluvhe: Hotshi-hu!	You will eat herbs like a pig: Hotshi-hu!
Ndi do la hatsi sa kholomo: Mooo!	You will eat grass like an ox: Mooo!

Muzika wa sialala styles crystallize experiences of cultural disorientation. Many musicians express feelings of estrangement from both the pre-colonial order and an often elusive modern world. The early colonial era in which older musicians grew up did not adequately prepare them for the demands of a changing environment, while persistent patterns of inadequate schooling, poverty and unemployment have also entrapped many younger musicians. Both generations often experience their social environment as a 'battle site' and a 'wasteland' where people fail to observe even some of the most fundamental historical conventions of ordered interaction: women and young people transgress the boundaries of their pre-colonial social statuses,[9] sexual immorality abounds, and political corruption and crime is rife:

Heli shango	**This country**[10]
Heli shango, heli shango lo naka.	This country, this country is beautiful.
Vha ri, li dinwa nga vhathu.	They say, it is troubled by people.
Nne ndi humbula vhusiwana.	I remember misery.
Nne tho ngo funzwa.	I am not educated.
Nne tho ngo ya tshikoloni.	I did not go to school.
Nne thi divhi na u vhala.	I do not know how to read.
Vhatali a vha fheli.	There are many clever people.
Nne ndi khwine ngauri ndi dabadaba.	I am better because I am ignorant.
Nne thi vhoni ndi tshi ndinaho.	Nothing troubles me.
Ndi khou amba nga u sa funzwa.	I say this because I am not educated.
Ndi khomphethisheni.	There is competition.
Ndi mupfufhi u sa mphire.	Everyone wants to be at the top.
Vho tou thanyesa.	They are too clever for their own good.

The structural position of *muzika wa sialala* musicians is reflected in the articulation in guitar songs of a religiously legitimated cosmological model that invokes ancestral and Christian moral principles (see Kruger, 2001). *Muzika wa sialala* is similar in this respect to electrified *mbaqanga* jive that emerged from the turbulent apartheid conditions of the 1960s. Both performance cultures have been responses to a central dilemma in urbanizing Africa, namely the creation of a model 'at once authentic and modern, indigenous but not isolated or provincial, African but not ethnically exclusive' (Geertz, 1973; cited in Coplan, 1982: 125). *Mbaqanga* jive projected images of a once autonomous rural African past when people habitually honoured cohesive moral and political values in contrast to the supposed individualism and immorality of modernity. The presentation of images of a self-sufficient African idyll thus not only contributed to a sense of resistant nationalism and self-regard, but also mobilized extant psychocultural resources (Coplan, 1998: 775–77). Similarly, many *muzika wa sialala* guitarists live in peri-urban areas that used to be rural villages as recently as 15 years ago. Their performances not only articulate processes of urbanization and new relations of production, but also selected patterns of pre-colonial economic and social production. *Muzika wa sialala* guitar songs thus express strong historical, spiritual and economic ties to the soil, celebrate nature as a moral prototype, advocate historical forms of authority and kinship, and promote time-honoured values that are aimed at supporting the poor, insecure and lonely. These values centre on friendship, compassion, interdependence and equality:

Lupfumo lwa kale	**Riches of old**[11]
Vhathu vha kale nazwino	People of old were rich indeed.
vho vha vho dzula.	
Mara vha tshi hola zukwa, wee.	But they only earned five cents.
Zwino, ri nga ita mini? Wee.	Alas, now what must we do?
Zwino, ri nga lidza mini? Wee.	Alas, now what must we sing?
Musalauno nazwino ngoho	Nowadays we are truly ashamed.
wo shona ngoho.	
Musalauno nazwino ngoho wo	Nowadays we are truly overcome.
kundiwa ngoho.	
Zwino, vha tshi hola tshelede.	Now, even if we get money,
Vho vha vho kundiwa.	we are overcome.
Vha fhirwa nga vhathu vha kale.	People of old were better off.
Na kholomo dzo vha dzi hone.	They had cattle.
Vho vha vho dzula.	They were rich.
Vhuswa nahone vho vha vha tshi la.	They also used to eat porridge.[12]
Zwino, ndi nga ita mini? Wee.	Alas, now what must I do?
Tsha khwine ndi u ya u lima ngoho.	Indeed, the best thing is to go and hoe.
Thamusi ndi do pfuma ngoho	Perhaps we will become truly rich.
ro vha ro dzula.	

Pfananani	**Mutual understanding**[13]
Vha ri muzila kha u vhuye	They say tradition[14] must be reinstituted
shango li lale.	so that there can be peace.
Vha ri tshikale kha tshi	They say the past must return
vhuye shango li lale.	so that there can be order.
Na nne ndo zwi vhona	And I realized how
zwa ri nndwa i bva ngafhi.	conflict[15] started.
Vha ri, vhatshena na	They say, white people
vhone a vha fani vhothe.	do not all behave the same.[16]
Tshikale kha tshi vhuye.	The past must return.
Ri tshile rothe.	We must all live.

Rothe ri a fanana	**We are all the same**[17]
Vho pfuma hani?	How rich are you?

Vho naka hani?	How beautiful are you?
Vho vhifha hani?	How ugly are you?
Vhanwe ndi mpengo.	Some are mad.
Kana ndi dabadaba?	Or are they just fools?

Ri khou vaya samu.	We are leaving together.[18]
Rothe ri a fanana!	We are all the same!
Ro begwa rothe nga Mudzimu washu.	We all were brought into this world by God.

Ndi khwine vha mmbenge.	It is better to hate me for saying this.
Humbula vhakale vha nthuseni.	Honour the ancestors so that they can help us.

Hu na vhutshilo dzinani la Yeso

There is life in the name of Jesus[19]

Vhathu vha hashu, idani ha Yeso.	Our people, follow Jesus.
Ngovhani u sa vha na Yeso,	To be without Jesus
vhutshilo ndi mutshinyalo.	is to struggle in life.

Vha tshi vhona vhakalaha vha	See the old men who try to be young.
sa kalahi. Thoho ndi mmbvi.	Their heads are grey with age.
Minwaha ndi mahumi	They count their age in multiples of ten
a vha litshi u dzhola.	but they still engage in illicit love affairs.

Zwi itwa nga vhana.	Children do the same.
Ndi mulandu wa zwivhi.	It is sinful.

Vha tshi vhona vhathannga vha	See the young men
hone, vha tama vhasidzana.	who befriend girls.
Vha milela na maduda.	They swallow their own mucus from lust.

Marukhu vho khatha a guma nga	Their trousers are cut off at the knee.
magonani. Vha edza phatholushaka.	They act like studbulls: builders of a nation.

Vha tshi vhona vhasidzana vha hone.	See the girls from here.
Vho tshipa badi, u ngari ndi	They are very cheap, as cheap
banana dza ngei Tshakuma.	as bananas at Tshakuma market.
Dzirokho vho tsheya dza guma	Their dresses have a slit
nga zwitikoni.	down the back.
Vha tshi ri: Ndi dzifesheni.	They say: It is fashionable.
Vha vho tou di rengisa sa nama	They sell themselves like canned
ya tshikotini a hu na bikani.	meat which needs no cooking.

Ndi vula ule.	You just open it and eat.
Gwanda, mufana!	Eat, boy!

The basic values of *muzika wa sialala* are enacted in the setting of many guitar performances, namely local bars (*tshipoto*, *sosa*). These bars are private homes from which homemade and bottled beer is sold. Beer drinking is a social institution of pre-colonial origin associated with cohesive family and communal rituals (see Blacking, 1965: 31–33). David Coplan has shown in his writings on the twentieth-century musical culture of Johannesburg that the function of urban shebeens as hubs of the local economy was rooted in their articulation of the historical functions of beer drinking (see, for example, Coplan, 1985). Accordingly, bars are not so much places where beer is available, as places where people can go to socialize.[20] These places sometimes are referred to as bars of 'old people'; although they host gatherings of poor people who share time-honoured world-views, rather than gatherings of elderly people. Bar culture therefore not only plays an important role in the local economy, but it also functions in a therapeutic manner to entertain, relieve tension and mediate conflict, while its actions, aesthetic expressions and ritual objects formulate social values.

But bars of 'old people' do not shun the often adverse present. They are dynamic settings for the formulation of adaptive cultural patterns. Musicians know that change is irreversible, and many consequently attempt to participate as fully as possible in a new world. One of the commodified influences in *muzika wa sialala* acoustic guitar styles is jive (*dzhaiva*), the well-known dance from the repertoire of kwela bands that flourished in urban areas during the 1950s. Gerhard Kubik notes that kwela belonged to a conceptual framework associated with social emancipation and increasing power, social status and intensity of life (Kubik 1974, p. 13). The texts of *muzika wa sialala* songs similarly reveal buoyant, yet ambiguous, optimism and excitement about the very concepts and institutions that are criticized for bringing about confusing change:

Ri dzula Mukumbani.	We live in the district of chief Tshivhase.[21]
Ri dzula dzithavhani.	We live in the mountains.
Ri dzula miedzini.	We live in the valleys.
Ri ri a la. Ri a fura.	We have enough to eat.
Mme anga vha tamba tshimodeni!	My mother dances in a modern style!
Khotsi anga vha thula mavhotana ...	My father dances by shaking his buttocks ...
Ngoho, Venda lo shanduka.	Venda has changed indeed.
Ho fhatiwa zwikolo, na	Schools, flats and roads
fuletse na dzibada ...	have been constructed ...

Kushango huku kwa	The small village[22] of
Ngulumbi kwo nakesa.	Ngulumbi is beautiful.
Na tshikolo, na madi, na mavhone ...	There is a school, piped water and electricity ...
Ngulumbi, shango lavhudi.	Ngulumi is a good place.
Civic association fhano Ngulumbi.	There is a civic association here at Ngulumbi.
Li nyaga vhashumi i vha na biko.	It needs dedicated workers.
Hayani ha havho ndi ha vhudi.	Their homes are well cared for.

Many *muzika wa sialala* guitarists are migrant labourers, and their songs express a shift towards urban-based cultural forms influenced by the mass media. *Muzika wa sialala*, correspondingly, is an aesthetic category related to detribalization, urbanization and wider social integration. Thus the well-known wedding song *Tshitiriri tsho lila* ('The whistle is blowing')[23] invokes a pan-ethnic urban–rural continuum, while songs like *Vhana doroba thina* ('Children of our place')[24] and *Mmbwa yo fhedza thulwana ya marambo* ('A dog finished a heap of bones')[25] reveal the influence of the radio and the recording industry.

Muzika wa sialala guitar performances articulate a set of powerful symbols by means of which performers construe themselves as social beings living in a changing world. Studies of African popular culture show that emerging African cosmopolitan images are negotiated through participation in interactive sartorial, culinary and musical styles (Coplan, 1985; Waterman, 1990). The symbols of *muzika wa sialala* include fashionable clothing and cosmetics, bottled beer and modern instruments such as guitars and keyboards. The dance steps of *muzika wa sialala* also differ from older styles associated with beer drinking, such as *malende* dance songs. The basic *malende* dance step is vigorous. The torso is the fulcrum for flailing arms and legs that stamp the ground aggressively in continual cross-rhythmic opposition to clapping and singing. The dance steps of *muzika wa sialala* are not as rhythmically complex as *malende* dancing. The basic movement comprises a simple sideways movement of the body. The feet are lifted only slightly, and they are usually brought down on the beat. Unlike *malende* dancing, the hips often are gyrated and the buttocks pushed backwards. This is referred to as *thula mavhota* ('shake the buttocks'). These pelvic dance movements are regarded as sexually immoral by older people, and their occasional use by *malende* dancers is regarded as daring. In contrast, they are common at *muzika wa sialala* performances where male and female dancers also often hold hands or embrace (see Kruger, 2000). Although men and women may perform *malende* together, they do not usually make bodily contact.

Some younger guitarists in particular express vitality and creative thought in their musical engagement with a changing society. They recognize the seed of vibrant new life in the apparent disorder. Often, poverty and suffering cannot suppress youthful optimism and the exuberant celebration of life. So when he was 20 years old, Mmbangiseni Madzivhandila (b. 1968), a vegetable vendor, sang 'Even if you enjoy life here on earth, you will not enjoy it like me'.[26] The subject of Madzivhandila's vast narrative world is that of a young man living in a changing society. His is a wonderful, sad world, filled with many new things and experiences: the local casino with its glittering lights and fashionably dressed people; beautiful 'Chinese'[27] and Tswana girls; planes, trains and cars that can also transport you in the dream world of musical narrative; dancing to powerful high-fidelity sound; pantyhose, permed hair, high-heeled shoes, deodorant, beauty cream and wedding outfit of a beautiful girl – all tempered by the harsh reality of HIV/AIDS, violence, police, jail and mortuaries (Kruger 1993: 348–403).

The *nyimbo* legacy in *muzika wa sialala*

This discussion explores the predominating structural legacy of *nyimbo* music in *muzika wa sialala* guitar songs, namely ostinato harmonic patterns. These patterns are defined by Kubik as 'a distinct sequence of harmonic progressions, by a specific motional structure, by a specific length expressed in elementary pulses, and by certain melodic implications' (Kubik, 1974: 23). John Blacking (1959c) identified this fundamental principle of older forms of African music as shifting tonality,[28] and he subsequently analysed it in detail (Blacking, 1967, 1970b). My intention therefore is to summarize only those of its aspects that have been retained in *muzika wa sialala* guitar songs.

Although there exists no term in Tshivenda for 'scale', a general conception of a scale as a fixed store of tones is implicit in the term *mutavha*, which denotes the set of heptatonic bamboo pipes used in *tshikona*, one of the most important *nyimbo* dance songs (see Blacking 1965, 1973 and Figure 3.2 below). Other *nyimbo* categories comprise pentatonic and hexatonic songs, but all songs follow the same structural conventions, and *tshikona* may therefore be used to illustrate the principle of shifting tonality.

Tshikona has achieved fame as a bamboo-pipe dance. It therefore is not always apparent that performers sometimes sing when not blowing their pipes and dancing as a team. When this happens, they usually gather near the drums for individual dancing and to praise important persons. Although the music of *tshikona* comprises a sequence of seven chords, the progression between the first and last chords of the pattern is most important. Blacking defines the first chord as *phala* (chord A–D in Figure 3.2) and identifies it as one of the tonal centres in *nyimbo* music.[29] The chord on which the pattern ends is referred to as *thakhula* (from *takula*, 'to lift'; chord B–E in Figure 3.2). It is located approximately a whole tone above *phala* and 'lifts' the pattern back on to it (*phala* and *thakhula* are indicated by [P] and [T] respectively in all figures).

Figure 3.2   The upper tones of *tshikona*, transposed down a semitone
Source: Blacking, 1970: 15.

Blacking accordingly suggests that Venda 'melodies may be called bitonal, in the sense that they shift from the influence of one implicit or explicit tone-centre to another' (Blacking 1970b: 18).

Figure 3.2 also explains patterns of harmonization, without which the tonality shift in *nyimbo* music cannot be fully understood. The chords of *nyimbo* music are generated by the principle of harmonic equivalence. Harmonically equivalent tones belong to the same mode in which a melody is set, and they are placed an octave, fourth, or fifth above or below a tone.[30] Viewed vertically, the *tshikona* pattern demonstrates that Venda melodies may be conceptualized as a stream of chords and that they must be explained in terms of an implicit harmonic framework.

The *phala–thakhula* tonality shift assumes two basic forms, referred to by Blacking as instrumental and vocal models (Blacking, 1970b: 20–21). In the instrumental model, exemplified by *tshikona*, the tonality shifts from *phala* to *thakhula*. In contrast, the vocal model (derived from the tonal structure of songs from *domba*, the girls' initiation school) features a tonality shift from *thakhula* to *phala*. Thus in Figure 3.3, performed by Vele Mulaudzi of Khubvi,[31] the tonality of the song shifts from *thakhula* D to *phala* C. In addition, some *nyimbo* music features a retrograde form of the tonality shift. In such cases, melodic phrases (usually corresponding with call and response patterns) begin with 'passing' tones, and move towards *phala* and *thakhula* respectively. In Figure 3.4, produced on the *lugube* mouth-resonated bow (see

Pitch = D; original = G; mode = hepta-based pentatonic;
2 pulses = 138

Figure 3.3   The vocal model of the tonality shift

Pitch = D; original = E♭; mode = hepta-based hexatonic; 2 pulses = 160
Interval distance between fundamentals: D – E = 200 cents; E – F = 100 cents

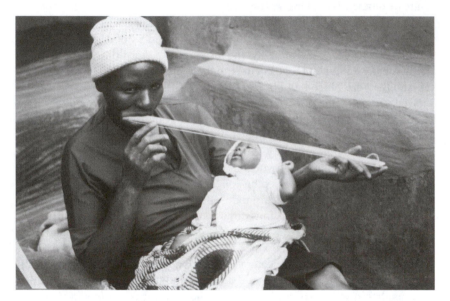

Figure 3.4   The retrograde version of the instrumental model of the tonality

Figure 3.5   *Lugube* mouth-resonated bow played by Flora Shonisani, Khubvi, 1984

Figure 3.5) by Flora Shonisani of Khubvi,[32] the first melodic phrase moves towards *phala* A and the second towards *thakhula* B.

The melodic phrasing in Figure 3.4 also points to another fundamental structural principle of *nyimbo* music, namely the balancing of metrical and tonal phrases (see Blacking, 1970b: 7). Thus, each melodic phrase in Figure 3.4 comprises eight pulses and centres around one of the main tonalities. The melodic phrases also follow the typical descending contour of *nyimbo* melodies (see Figure 3.2), which is another familiar characteristic of many older forms of African music. As shown below, the presence of this melodic shape is often an indication of some form of bitonal shift in *muzika wa sialala* guitar songs whose tonal structure appears ambiguous.

The above-mentioned features of the tonality shift of *nyimbo* music enjoy a
clear, if transformed, legacy in *muzika wa sialala* guitar songs. However,
mention must also be made of another possible unconscious link between the
tonal structure of *nyimbo* and *muzika wa sialala*. This link is related to the root-
progressions of certain instrumental songs, such as those produced on mouth-
resonated bows. Certain of these bows were an integral part of courting,
marriage and divorce rituals in pre-colonial times. Although these bows have
now virtually disappeared, an investigation during the early 1980s revealed a
few remaining active players, as well as an extant ability among many rural
people to perform on them (Kruger, 1986).

The root-progressions of bow songs are articulated in sequences of
fundamentals over which mouth or gourd-resonated harmonics are generated
to produce melodies. Bow fundamentals are created by plucking the string of
the *lugube* and *tshihwana* bows with the fingers or a plectrum, scraping the
notched surface of the *tshizambi* mouth-bow to cause vibrations in its palm leaf
cord, or beating the string of the *dende* gourd-bow (see Figures 3.6–3.8).

Figure 3.6   *Tshihwana* **mouth-resonated bow played by Nngwedzeni
Tshamano, Phiphidi, 1984**

Figure 3.7   *Tshizambi* **scraped mouth-resonated bow played by Lukas**
Ramabanda, Tshivhilwi, 1984

Venda bow music corresponds to Xhosa bow music from the Eastern Cape
in the sense that it provides an ideal model for an in-depth analysis of the tonal
and harmonic progressions underlying melodies because, in them, these
progressions are 'literally pared down to their bare essentials' (Hansen, 1981:
672). Certain Venda bow songs thus reduce the relatively extensive and
densely structured harmonic sequence of *nyimbo* categories like *tshikona* to a
clear, sparsely harmonized bitonal shift.

This is evident in Figure 3.9a, the musical score of a song performed on the
tshihwana braced mouth-bow by John Mphaphuli of Tshianzwane.[33] The vocal
melody (Figure 3.9b) comprises a hepta-based hexatonic mode that is reduced
to a tetratonic mode in its representation on the bow (Figure 3.10). The bow
song features two chords only, generated by the segments of the braced string

Figure 3.8 *Dende* **played by Elias Ndou, Mangaya, 1984**

that are tuned approximately 300 cents apart (roughly equivalent to the interval of a 'minor third'). These chords represent *phala* tonality (chord C–G) and *thakhula* tonality (chord A–E), with the whole tone shift evident between melody notes G and A.

An additional relevant feature of mouth-bow music is evident in Figure 3.10, a song produced on the *tshihwana* bow by George Phophi of Malavuwe.[34] The string segments of Phophi's bow are tuned to an interval distance of approximately 700 cents or a 'fifth'. The lower fundamental (note D) represents *phala* and the upper fundamental (note A) *thakhula*. The *phala–thakhula* whole tone shift occurs between the first and last melody tones (notes D and E), which occur at the distance of an octave and fifth over their respective fundamentals.

Pitch = G; original = B; mode = hepta-based hexatonic;
4 pulses = 84

Figure 3.9a   *Vho-Lutanga*: vocal version

Pitch = G; original = B; mode = hepta-based tetratonic;
interval distance between fundamentals = 300 cents; 4 pulses = 88

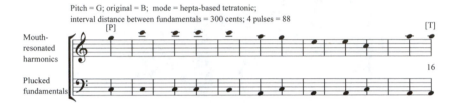

Figure 3.9b   *Vho-Lutanga*: instrumental version

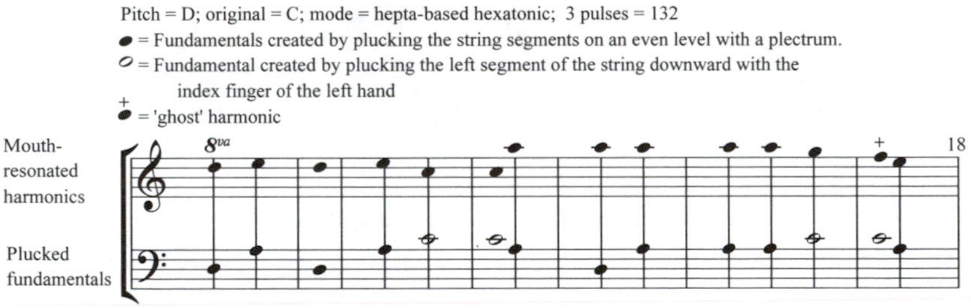

Pitch = D; original = C; mode = hepta-based hexatonic; 3 pulses = 132
● = Fundamentals created by plucking the string segments on an even level with a plectrum.
○ = Fundamental created by plucking the left segment of the string downward with the
           index finger of the left hand
● = 'ghost' harmonic

Mouth-
resonated
harmonics

Plucked
fundamentals

**Figure 3.10   Song performed on the *tshihwana* mouth-resonated bow
featuring root-movement of a fifth**

The two basic fundamentals are obtained by striking the string segments on an even level with a plectrum.[35] A third fundamental (note C in Figure 3.10) is produced by striking the left segment of the string from above with the index finger of the left hand (which holds the bow), thus exciting both segments of the string.[36] Many bow songs feature a third root which increases the number of available melody tones and hence also the potential of rendering acceptable instrumentalized versions of vocal songs. However, performances of *tshihwana* songs in which only two roots occur seem to suggest that the third root may be regarded as of secondary tonal importance.

While certain *tshihwana* songs are the only ones in the Venda bow repertory to feature root-progressions which include an interval of approximately a 'fifth', the interval of roughly 500 cents (a 'fourth') features in songs produced on the *tshizambi* mouth-bow and *dende* braced gourd-bow. Thus, Figure 3.11, performed by Piet Musisinyani of Mangaya,[37] is based on the vocal model of the tonality shift. The harmonic sequence moves from *thakhula* tonality D–A at the beginning of the pattern a 'fourth' up to tonality G, and finally to *phala* tonality F–C. Although the movement from the end of the melody to its beginning is from C to A, a whole tone progression from D (the harmonic equivalent of A) to C is implied.

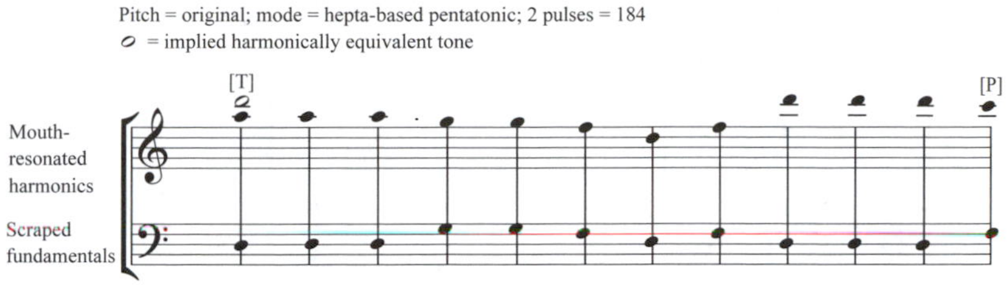

Pitch = original; mode = hepta-based pentatonic; 2 pulses = 184
○ = implied harmonically equivalent tone

Figure 3.11   Song performed on the *tshizambi* scraped mouth-resonated bow, featuring root-movement of a fourth

Synthesizing *nyimbo* and kwela

The foreign roots of *muzika wa sialala* are embedded in processes of musical diffusion from the United States, especially after the Second World War. Kubik notes that 'traces of all the successive waves of African-American music transmitted by the mass media can be found even in local traditions remote from the cities, in reinterpreted but still recognisable forms' (Kubik, 1999: 155). One of the dominant tonal schemes of these musics derives from the 12-bar blues and its use in jazz and rock styles. American big jazz band music of the 1950s inspired pennywhistlers who initiated a new swing-based dance music, initially referred to as 'jive', until the recording industry, seeking an appropriate label, coined the term 'kwela' (Kubik, 1999: 165–66). Kwela was shaped by the refusal of the recording industry to market any music not structured according to commercially successful formulae, particularly simple 'four-bar cyclical sequences of primary chords topped with two or three melodies which repeated and alternated with each other' (Allen 1995, p. 3). This three-chord pattern has featured in various forms in subsequent styles of South African popular music such as *simanje-manje* (isiZulu: 'things of today'), its urban form *mbaqanga*, and its Venda off-shoot *dzhaiva*.

Two fundamental characteristics of the three-chord pattern are relevant here. First, many contemporary musical styles in South Africa feature a reduced form of the 12-bar blues. Kubik notes that musicians tend to think in terms of African short, cyclic forms, and that they regularly omit the passage from C7 to the two F measures of the second line by one measure in either direction (Kubik, 1999: 175–77; Figure 3.12). Secondly, this chord pattern features rigid bass lines that reveal hidden, non-European harmonic sequences that should not be misinterpreted as the conventional three-chord progression (Kubik, 1999: 173).

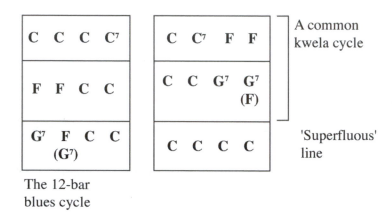

Figure 3.12   Reduction of a 12-bar blues to an eight-measure cycle
Source: Kubik (1999: 177)

Richard Waterman noted in 1952 that slaves and their descendants in the Americas subjected African harmonic forms to a remodelling process that resulted in 'European-inspired African music' (Waterman, 1952: 209), while Bruno Nettl subsequently noted that 'the presence of western harmony in non-western music is in many instances limited and symbolic' (Nettl, 1985: 38). Blacking first referred to the fusion of *nyimbo* root-progressions and three-chord sequences in Venda music during the late 1950s. He noted that the regular movement of the root-progression a whole-tone above or below a tone which may be called the 'tonal centre' was a feature of much Venda music. 'Unambiguous shifts of tonality' thus not only characterized Zionist hymns (Blacking, 1980a: 54), but also the 'tonic-subdominant-dominant' strumming often heard on guitars (Blacking, 1959c,: 23).

This type of tonal reinterpretation also has been identified in other African musical cultures. Thus, in his essay on the celebrated Congolese guitarist Mwenda Jean Bosco, David Rycroft shows the application of older forms of modality and root-progression within what mistakenly appears to be a conventional Western chord pattern (1961: p. 85). An extract of Zulu urban music performed on an *igqongwe* homemade guitar similarly suggests that what seems to be a straightforward imitation of the three-chord sequence is in fact perceived by the musician as an ostinato pattern derived from older styles of bow-playing (see Rycroft, 1977: 242–43). This type of phenomenon has been described most extensively by Kubik who notes that:

> In new African music played with western instruments the old concept of root progressions is projected into tone and chord material of western provenance. Guitar chord progressions such as F-C-G7-C and other cadential patterns may thus have a meaning in the context of musical practice in Africa different from that in European music. They are not necessarily explained in terms of tonic, subdominant and dominant functions. The western chords are also unconsciously approximated to the traditional root progressions by a selection process emphasising certain layouts, certain inversions and so on. In this way the voice combination, both local and instrumental, assume a particular flavour within the framework of these ostinato patterns, which are often experienced rather as linear multi-part structures. Tonality and multi-part techniques re-approach traditional practice. (Kubik 1975: 24).

Herskovits's seminal work on transculturation (1958 [1938], 1952) first pointed to the resilience of enculturated processes of perception and cognition. New cultural codes encountered in situations of contact are projected against entrenched behavioural and cognitive patterns. The power of enculturation is so compelling that auditory perception is difficult to modify and is probably even irreversible (Kubik, 1985). The stereotypical Western perception of the imitative character of modern forms of African music, as well as the African reinterpretation of American popular styles, point to the habitual interpretation of unfamiliar tonal models in terms of enculturated patterns whose immense power virtually 'coerces' new material into recognizable shape (Kubik, 1979: 242). This process involves the application of existing elementary patterns that 'scan' new sound complexes to release certain of their structural elements and bring them into congruence with their own (Kubik, 1979: 234).

Accordingly, when Venda musicians who grew up in *nyimbo* performance cultures encounter three-chord sequences, they tend to isolate in them what sounds like the bitonal shift. This bitonal shift is reinforced with certain melodic and metric features of *nyimbo* music that subordinate and resignify the three-chord progression. This pattern of restructuring is effected by means of two basic strategies. The first undermines the primacy of the 'tonic' chord (for example, C) while resignifying its relationship with the other chords. The second assigns pivotal status to the 'subdominant' F and links it inseparably to the 'dominant' G. These strategies are illustrated in Figures 3.13–3.16.

Figure 3.13 is an extract from a song[38] by guitarist Piti Ravhura (b. 1961) of Gondeni. Ravhura is a blind musician who busks in the towns of Thohoyandou, Makhado and Giyani. In performance he sits on the ground, pulls his legs up,

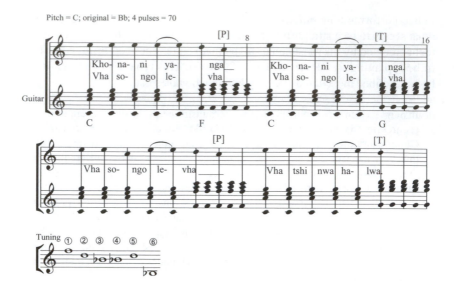

Figure 3.13   *Khonani yanga,* **by Piti Ravhura**

and, like most local guitarists, places the guitar on his right thigh. He sits hunched over the instrument, with his face very near to the soundbox. The neck of the guitar is horizontal to the ground, and Piti uses the second and third fingers of his left hand to depress the strings over the top of the neck. Perhaps because of his blindness, he vamps a basic harmonic pattern only, with little rhythmic variation.[39]

Figure 3.13 seems to comprise a straightforward, even unimaginative, primary chord sequence (C-F-C-G).[40] However, Kubik has shown that Western structural categorizations of world musics with African roots tend to obscure the actual nature of pitch resources and patterns, and that vocal and instrumental melodies regularly pursue their own strategies. As such, it is necessary to abstract vocal lines from their instrumental accompaniment and to consider them, and their tonal systems, in isolation (Kubik, 1999: 86, 126). Using this approach, it becomes clear that Figure 3.13 in fact is structurally identical to Figure 3.4 in several respects. Both songs feature a 16-pulse cycle that is divided into two metrically and tonally balanced phrases. Figure 3.13 also follows the retrograde version of the instrumental model of the bitonal shift. The first eight-pulse vocal melodic phrase follows a familiar descending contour towards *phala* C in chord F, and the second phrase towards *thakhula* D in chord G. The whole-tone shift in Figure 3.13 between *phala* F-A-C and *thakhula* G-B-D has clearly motivated the tonal ascendancy of these chords in *muzika wa sialala* songs.

In contrast, chord C is clearly not perceived as 'tonic' harmony in a Western sense. Instead, it functions as a secondary tonality and corresponds structurally to the third bichord found in mouth-bow music (see Figures 3.4 (p. 52) and 3.10 (p. 56)). This third chord generates root-movement of a fourth and fifth, shown to be features of certain mouth-bow songs (see Figures 3.10 and 3.11). In addition, there is no sense of melodic flow from chord G to chord C to support a dominant-tonic relationship. This undermining of the conventional Western relationship between these two chords is a common feature of *muzika wa sialala* songs that is shared by many blues songs in which vocal lines have a similar tendency to circumvent the 'dominant' (Kubik, 1999: 126).

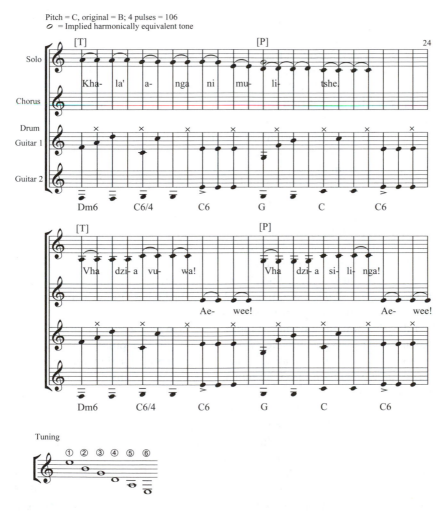

Figure 3.14   *Khaladzi anga,* by Mmbangiseni Mphaga

Figure 3.13 thus seems to take the form of a conventional eight-bar kwela pattern that is truncated to a bitonal shift with a third chord derived from bow music. Clearly, this reformulation falls within the 'tolerance limits' of the tonality shift in *nyimbo* music (see Kubik, 1979). When the Venda bitonal memory is projected on to the three-chord sequence, the two systems are brought into alignment at a point where they are congruent. As a result, the chords that a Western musician may understand as 'subdominant' and 'dominant' are interpreted by Venda guitarists as *phala* and *thakhula*. This type of fragmentation of patterns into 'subpatterns' that, once again, can be structured into complex units gives rise to 'inherent' auditory patterns which emerge from a musical totality featuring characteristics such as fast tempo and discernible pitch layers (Kubik, 1979: 223–24, 232–38). The bitonal progression of *nyimbo* music similarly appears to be perceived by Venda musicians as an inherent pattern. This is suggested not only in the reduction of the harmonic sequences of vocal songs to a straight *phala–thakhula* alternation in mouth-bow songs, but also by the fact that *muzika wa sialala* musicians are able to detach a bitonal shift from three-chord progressions, and reconfigure it in terms of *nyimbo* structural conventions.

Figure 3.14 shows a related way in which Western harmonic flow is subverted. This song was performed by Mmbangiseni Mphaga (b. 1965) of Mukula, a clerk in the Department of Public Works in Thohoyandou. He is leader of an 11-member band called Current Stars, but Figure 3.14 dates from the 1980s when there were only two friends with him in the band. When I recorded the small group in 1986, Mphaga played lead guitar, Nkhangweleni Ramaswiela (b. 1959) bass guitar and Norman Rantsana (b. 1971) played drum on the resonant body of an old, broken guitar. Plectrum-plucked[41] arpeggio and single-line patterns gave their songs an open and at times, even delicate texture. The musicians also distinguished between their guitars in terms of timbre. The lead attack was delicate and light, and the acoustic bass guitar was thumped heavily to achieve an electric bass guitar effect.

Like Piti Ravhura's song, Figure 3.14 also is metrically and tonally balanced. The 24-pulse cycle is divided into two 12-pulse phrases, each centring around a main tonality. Although the opening vocal melody includes an apparent progression from 'dominant' G to 'tonic' C, any sense of Western harmonic flow is weakened by a preponderance of chords in inverted form that creates a harmonic ostinato effect. In contrast, the descending melodic curve in the first vocal line hints at an underlying bitonal framework. Closer scrutiny reveals that this song in fact follows the vocal model of the bitonal shift. Thus, in the vocal melody, *thakhula* A in chord F-A-D leads to D in *phala* chord G-B-D. Although the vocal melody does not move from *thakhula* A to *phala* G to produce an explicit whole-tone shift, note G not only is present in the guitar parts, but the whole-tone shift in fact emerges clearly from the melodic phrases A-C-E and G-C-E in the subsequent melody line (see second system). Viewed from the perspective of the three-chord convention, this tonal movement also occurs between the 4th and 5th degrees of a C-scale (see Figure 3.13), although Mphaga employs a D minor or 'supertonic' chord in first inversion to obtain the 4th degree.

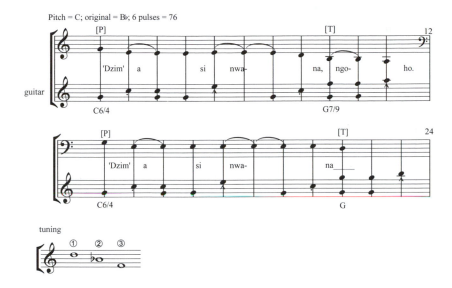

Figure 3.15 *Mudzimu a si nwana*, **by Mbulaheni Netshipise**

Figures 3.15 and 3.16 illustrate a second way in which the harmonic interrelations in the Western three-chord progression are resignified to fit a bitonal shift. Figure 3.15 is a song performed in 1989 on a home-made guitar (*gomboza* – 'an empty container') by Mbulaheni Netshipise of Tshififi (see Figure 3.1 (p. 39)), who was 16 years old at the time. Mbulaheni was a member of a group of boys I found wandering along a rural road over a weekend. Such groups are quite common. They often not only include a person carrying a guitar, but also a person carrying a radio or a soccer ball. These objects are popular symbols of the social identity and aspirations of poor rural teenagers.[42] Home-made guitars also provide a cheap, yet valuable way of exploring and consolidating musical technique and practising performance. Performances on these guitars involve the basic principles of guitar-playing, and they establish the foundation for subsequent performance on commercially manufactured guitars.

Figure 3.16 is a song performed by Mashudu Mulaudzi (b. 1963) of Tsianda.[43] Mulaudzi comes from a broken family and grew up in utter poverty. He abandoned his schooling in grade seven when he was 17 and, since then, has worked as farm labourer, gardener, fruit vendor, photographer and busker.

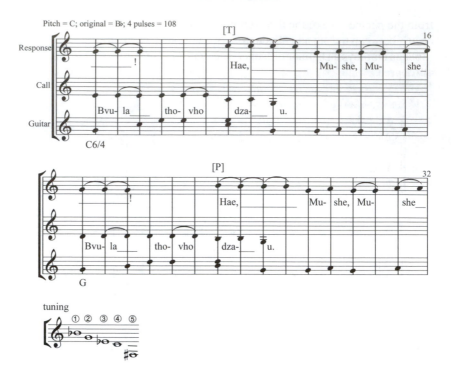

Figure 3.16   *Mushe*, by Mashudu Mulaudzi

Mulaudzi is a brilliant musician who never seems to exploit his professional potential. He habitually busks for a few days until he has earned enough to cover just his most basic living expenses and then lives off this amount until he is required to perform again. He appears to produce far below his ability, projecting the image of a carefree rough diamond who allows every day to unfold of its own accord. However, this is a front that conceals a fervent desire for social acceptance. Figure 3.16 dates from a period during 1988 when he searched for social identity in several local Christian churches. However, abandoned these churches when he discovered that they could not support him as a full-time musician.

From a western perspective, the harmonic sequence in the guitar part of Figures 3.15 and 3.16 shows an alternation between C6/4 and G(7/9). The appearance of the C chord in inverted form not only subverts a possible 'tonic' function, but also provides a strong ostinato effect (see Figure 3.14). Ostinato patterns in Venda gourd-bow performances (see Figure 3.8 (p. 55)) function as supportive sound vehicles for extensive spoken narratives (see Kruger, 1986). Mulaudzi not only performs on a modern version of this bow[44] but, as the text of Figure 3.16 shows (note 42), his guitar performances involve narratives of similar dimension (also see the text of 'There is life in the name of Jesus' (p. 47)).

Nyimbo tonal structuring in Figure 3.15 is confirmed by the descending contour of the melody that starts on *phala* G, and ends on *thakhula* A (the ninth in the G chord), and its harmonic equivalent D in the second system. Figure 3.16 in turn also features a metrically and tonally balanced structure. The 32-pulse cycle is divided into two 16-pulse phrases of which the first centres around *thakhula* harmony G-C-E and the second around *phala* harmony G-B-D. The *thakhula–phala* whole-tone shift occurs in the vocal melody between tones C and B.

Unlike Figures 3.13 and 3.14, Figure 3.15 features two chords only. There is a hint at a third harmony (unison A, pulses 15 and 31) in Figure 3.16, but this presence is so weak that the song, like Figure 3.15, essentially seems to take the form of a straight bitonal shift derived from certain mouth-bow songs (see Figure 3.9 (p. 56)). The presence in Figure 3.15 of the seventh (F) in the G chord reflects the ubiquitous use of the 'upper blues note' in South African popular music. This note is perceived by local musicians as the seventh partial of the natural harmonic series (Kubik, 1999, pp. 182–3), and it appears in songs performed on the *tshihwana* mouth-bow (Kruger, 1986).

Conclusion

Tonal–melodic structuring in *muzika wa sialala* reminds us that the often sensible and lucid appearance of cultural codes may in fact conceal alternative structural and value systems. A diminishing world apparently conditioned by overwhelming homogenizing forces easily fools us into technical explanations of globalization which may misinterpret the meaning of local musics. Thus, in Africa, we often hear imitations of Western music instead of recognizing creative processes in which a concern for characteristically local themes and sounds has given birth to adaptive musical codes (Blacking, 1980c: 196). *Muzika wa sialala* accordingly emerges as a narrative of continuity that opposes the failure of modernity to generate meaningful local identities by invoking the transcendental dimensions of pre-colonial culture: while sounds and styles may change, and eras may pass, African musics continue to be animated by the philosophy that people and their relationships are what make music (Tracey, 1989: 2).

The case of cultural continuity in Venda guitar songs, as conditioned by unconsciously embedded aesthetic patterns, affirms our understanding of two important cultural patterns. First, the lodging of African tonal designs below the conscious level is evident in many contemporary African and Afro-American styles. Tonal resilience in *muzika wa sialala* gives credence to Kubik's final shattering of the myth of rhythm as the only enduring African legacy in the world of contemporary music (Kubik, 1999). In fact, *muzika wa sialala* has retained very little of the wide array of rhythmic patterns of *nyimbo* music (see Blacking, 1970b, 1969c–f). Second, there is an apparent surface acquiescence in musical styles in situations of contact that often conceals deeper structures of resistance. The appropriation and syntagmatic rupturing in *muzika wa sialala* of the three-chord sequence not only undermines the very coherence of a system of dominance, but turns a symbol of coercion into a dynamic force of transcendence (Comaroff, 1985: 198, 225). *Muzika wa sialala* musicians have managed to retain the power of indigenous discourse in a metaphoric recasting of the social order.

However, cultural continuity does not imply a naïve return to some mythical harmonious past, since resistance often necessitates deployment of elements of the very codes it opposes. *Muzika wa sialala* emerges as a symbolic system that reproduces enculturated patterns by way of resistance, while also resignifying them as cultural codes appropriate to social change. The ancestral mousetrack has not changed course; rather, it has been encroached upon by other expanding cultures and become a border zone whose song structures do not articulate straightforward symbolic inversion, but a tonal dialectic expressive of permanent, dynamic change.

Finally, despite our vast store of knowledge of human nature, the non-European 'other' continues to be represented as mysterious and bizarrely diverse, a virtually different human species whose members and cultures can be objectified and displayed like botanical specimens.[45] It is worth recalling the divisive apartheid conditions of the 1950s and 1960s that were experienced not only by Zionists and jive musicians, but also by Blacking, who argued that technological progress and the visible contrast between cultures do not provide convincing evidence of essentially different kinds of humans (Blacking, 1969b). The conjunction of the Venda bitonal shift and the three-chord sequence affirms that some important perceptual and cognitive processes underlie the use of all symbolic systems (Harwood, 1976). This is neither to deny cultural specificity, nor to advocate some kind of sociobiological determinism. But it does underscore the potential, in any situation of musical contact, of the ongoing reconfiguration of the innate human capacity for musical expression, rather than an accidental commonality between essentially different cultures. This recognition has important consequences for how we view the human species, organize ourselves culturally and politically, and formulate the ethics and philosophies of science.

Notes

[1]   I am indebted to Deirdre Hansen for her evaluation of a draft of this essay.
[2]   Thohoyandou, 1994.

[3] Lit. 'The child of the mouse does not forget the mouse track'.

[4] Venda historical cultural symbols enjoyed a revival during the period of separate development (1948–1994). Although these symbols were often discredited because of their oppressive hegemonic use, some of them have been retained in the post-apartheid era to shape local identities (see Kruger, 1999). Strong contemporary awareness of Venda ethnic identity is concomitant with the invoking of familiar symbols in processes of re-empowerment and social reordering. One of the most enduring forms of continuity is a form of boldly coloured female dress (*nwenda*) that, despite its colonial origins, has come to symbolize cultural continuity and identity. As recently as 2001 a local shop refused to sell *nwenda* cloth to a white entrepreneur on the grounds of its ethnic exclusivity (*Beeld*, 3 August 2002).

[5] Tshikambe, 23 March 1992.

[6] The current official unemployment rate in Limpopo Province is 36 per cent, but unofficial estimates range as high as 50 per cent.

[7] Nnditsheni Ramukhuvhathi, Madamalala, 11 July 1990.

[8] Referring to chronic hunger in a poor family, exacerbated by a lazy husband.

[9] The negative evaluation of the changing status of women in *muzika wa sialala* guitar songs can be related to the fact that guitarists are almost exclusively male.

[10] Solomon Mathase, Ngulumbi, 23 May 1992.

[11] Nndanganeni Luambo, Muhuyu, 9 July 1987.

[12] *Vhuswa*, a porridge-like staple food made from ground maize.

[13] Solomon Mathase, Ngulumbi, 23 May 1992.

[14] Lit. 'tribal tax'.

[15] Lit. 'war'.

[16] A simultaneous acknowledgement of the destructive effect of colonization and the need to avoid racial stereotypes.

[17] Solomon Mathase, Ngulumbi, 6 June 1992.

[18] A reference to joint travelling (usually on foot or by minibus taxi) by people living in a close-knit community.

[19] Mashudu Mulaudzi, Thohoyandou, 13 July 1990.

[20] It is not unusual to see people (especially women) drinking soft drinks only at beer houses.

[21] Song extracts, Solomon Mathase, Ngulumbi, 3 December 1989 and 25 May 1991. The Tshivhase district incorporates the town of Thohoyandou.

[22] Now an eastern suburb of Thohoyandou.

[23] Solomon Mathase, Murangoni, 5 May 1990. This song describes an interethnic marriage formalized with a wedding contract (not required with older, intratribal marriages). The train takes the married couple from an urban area back to Venda where the woman presumably is to join her in-laws:

Tshitiriri tsho lila.	The whistle is blowing.
Tsho lilela Selinah.	It is blowing for Selinah.
Ho saina mama/papa.	It is a sign mama/papa.
Saina, saina, saina.	A sign, a sign, a sign.
Mukusule ndi mini?	What are dried vegetables?
Ndi nama ya Vhavenda.	They are the favourite Venda food.
Tshidimela ndi mini?	What is a train?
Ndi tsimbi dza makhuwa.	It is the iron machine of white people.

[24] Solomon Mathase, Murangoni, 5 May 1990. This song denounces anti-social behaviour, and urges cooperation, represented by the dance metaphor.

Vhana doroba thina.	The children of our place.
Vhana doroba thina,	The children of our place are
vha na pemberera.	dancing excitedly.
Tambani zwakanaka.	Dance well.
Tambani zwakanaka masimbana, iwe!	Dance well, witch!
Nguwe, nguwe!	It is you, it is you!
Muthakhati ka loya.	One who bewitches.
Vhana vha Vhanyai.	Children of Zimbabwe.

[25] Solomon and Robert Mathase, Murangoni, 5 May 1990. This song apparently originated with famous kwela pennywhistler Albert Ralulimi.

Mmbwa yo fhedza thulwana ya marambo!	A dog finished a heap of bones!
Hu pfi!	So they say!
Vho i vhona yo dzula nga u tumba!	They saw it squatting!
Hae, vho i vhona.	Hey, they saw it.
Tshinetise na Nndanduleni,	[The singers are,]
hu pfi,	so they say,
ndi vhana vha Hamathase.	children of Mathase's place.

[26] '*Kana ni nga diphina hafha shangoni, ni nga si diphine u fana na nne.*' Tshakuma, 03/07/88.

[27] The Venda government of 'traditional' leaders (the Venda National Party) offered tax incentives to foreign companies during the period of nominal independence (1979–1989), attracting entrepreneurs from East Asia.

[28] See Hansen (1981: 665–701) and Rycroft (1971) for the application of this principle in Xhosa and Zulu music.

[29] The anchor role of *phala* is reflected in its description by musicians as 'the caller'. This explanation refers to the function of the *phala* horn, namely to summon people to the homestead of a leader for meetings and musical performances.

[30] They are appropriately called *zwifanaho* ('things which are similar'; from *–fana*, 'resemble').

[31] 30 April 1984.

Vho-mma-vhasali wa wela.	Young boys are attending their first initiation school.
Zwezwi ni swike ni tshi amba.	Do not reveal the laws of the school.

[32] 6 June 1984.

Ha-Manwadu, Tshitandani.	Botswana, Louis Trichardt.
Ha-Manwadu vho lovhelwa.	There has been a death in Botswana.

[33] 26 April 1984.

Rine ri funa Vho-Lutanga.	We like Mr Lutanga.
Na Vho-Gole vha tamba ngavho.	And chief Mphaphuli plays political games with him.

(Lutanga was a popular leader of the *domba* puberty school.)

[34] 14 May 1984.

Idani, ri tambe rothe musidzana.	Come girl, let us play.
Idani, ri tambe rothe na Dafita.	Come, let us play with David.

[35] Plectrums usually take the form of a sturdy thorn or a safety pin.

[36] Fundamentals produced by exciting both string segments of the *tshihwana* bow sometimes elicit 'ghost' harmonics which do not belong to the harmonic series of the fundamental over which they seem to appear (note F in Figure 3.11). This aspect of *tshihwana* music requires further investigation.

[37] 7 June 1984.

I ya vhuya mulobilo, golongonya.	Here the rain comes pouring down,
I ya vhuya tshikwarani, golongonya.	pouring down over the ridge.
Nndu khulu dzi na biko.	Big houses are warm.

[38] 22 October 1987.

Khonani yanga, vha tshi	My friend, when you drink
nwa halwa, vha song levha.	beer, do not be vicious.
Vha tshi levha, vho do rwiwa.	When you are vicious you will be beaten.
U gai Ndini? Ndini o tuwa	Where is Ndini? Ndini has left because
nga tshone tshibonda.	she was beaten with a walking stick.
Kholidringi.	Drink cooldrink only.
Mello Yello.	Drink Mellow Yellow.

[39] It is unlikely that Ravhura's limited technique and lack of musical variation is related to his blindness only. The noisy streets where his acoustic performances take place are not conducive to delicate finger-plucking or performing complicated harmonic and rhythmic patterns. What is required is powerful strumming, a loud voice and entertaining narratives that lure pedestrians.

[40] Chord symbols are used in Figures 3.13–3.16 to facilitate explanation. Their use does not suggest any Western tonal conception by musicians.

[41] Plucking by means of a plectrum or the fingers is described as 'lifting' (*tota*, 'to lift') the strings in contrast with vamping or 'scratching' (from *kweta*, 'to scratch').

[42] Kubik notes that the popularity of homemade banjos among Zambian male adolescents is partly due to the gap created by the breakdown of educational systems 'and the consequential loss of ideals with which the younger generation can identify' (Kubik 1989, p. 5).

[43] With Judith and Florence Mamarigela, 04/07/88.

(Sung)	
Hae Mushe, bvula thovho dzau.	Hey Moses, remove your sandal.
(Spoken)	
U mmbulahela mini iwe Mushe?	Why are you killing me, Moses?
Ndi a u vhulaha ngauri u Muegipita.	I am killing you because you are an Egyptian.
Ndi do u vhulaha nda u fukedza nga	I am going to kill you and bury you in
mutavha.	the sand.
Khoulaa Mushe! A tangana na	There is Moses! He meets the bush

tshitaka tshi	which is
tshi khou duga tshone tshi sa swi.	aflame but not burning.
Ha bva ipfi lihulu la Yehova la ri:	There came the loud voice of Jehova, saying:
Mushe, bvula thovho dzau u gwadame phanda hanga.	Moses, remove your sandal and kneel before me.
U dibule vhuvhi hau hothe.	Confess all your sins.
Mushe a ri: Ndo vhulaha Muegipita.	Moses says: I have killed an Egyptian.
Yehova a ri: Ndo zwi divha.	Jehova says: I knew that.
Zwino ndi a u ruma ha ngei Kanana.	Now I am sending you over there to Canaan.
Nga itsho tshifhinga ndi musi Vhaisraele	At that time the Israelites were
vha tshi khou pandamedziwa nga Vhaegipita.	being pursued by the Egyptians.
Vhaegipita vho namela dzibere.	The Egyptians were on horseback.
Hu tshi pfala vhukikiriki!	One could hear the galloping of horses!
Hu tshi khou duba buse.	One could see billowing dust.
Vhaisraele vha swika Mulamboni wa Yorodane.	The Israelites arrived at the Jordan River.
Ha bva ipfi lihulu, la Yehova la ri: Mushe,	There came the loud voice of Jehova, saying: Moses, raise your staff and hit
imisa thonga yau u rwe aya madi.	the water.
Hu do bva ndila khulwane vhukati ha madi	A big road will appear in the water.
A rwa ala madi.	He hit that water,
Ha mbo bva bada khulwane vhukati ha madi.	and a big road appeared.
Ha vha tshimangadzo tshihulwane ngamaanda	It was a wonderful surprise.
Vhaegipita vha tshi da vho namela dzibere.	The Egyptians followed them on horseback.
Vha tshi ri vha a dzhena fhala lwanzheni,	When they were about to enter the sea,
madi a kuvhangana a mbo di vha kumba vhothe!	the water converged on them and swept them all away
Ngauri vho vha vha sa na lutendo.	because they did not have faith!

<hr>

[44] This instrument is referred to as *dende* or *tshikotikoti* (lit. an 'empty tin'). It comprises a dented five-litre oil can over which three rubber bands of different thickness and width are tied. As with the original gourd-bow, sound is elicited by striking the rubber bands (tuned to the same interval as the braced string on the gourd-bow) with a length of thatch grass.

[45] The National Geographic Society circulated a promotional brochure in 2001 for a publication dealing with 'exotic cultures' by offering a photographic sample of a 'dazzling' variety of the 'customs, traditions, religions, languages and lifestyles' of the world. The sample shows colourful folk costumes, facial and bodily decorations and social practices of various non-European groupings.

CHAPTER FOUR

Black Background: Life History and Migrant Women's Music in South Africa

Deborah James

As an undergraduate in Witwatersrand University's Anthropology Department, which Blacking had left some years previously, I read his Venda material eagerly. My excitement on unearthing his articles, and on finding the great tome of his dissertation in the library, was the greater for what I'd felt was the department's – and the university's – relative lack of interest in the anthropology of music at the time. This lack of interest was surprising given the intensity with which, his former students assured me, his charisma as a teacher had been experienced. Finding Blacking's writings was a great source of encouragement to me. Consciously or unconsciously, it pointed me in the direction of my own future research interest, which echoed his in some respects. Like him, I became fascinated by the role played by music in socializing children, and young women in particular. My perspective on this, however, was to investigate how adult women saw the music of their childhood in retrospect, and to try to understand how it had shaped, or been shaped to form, their later musical experiences.

Blacking's own interest in these matters can be seen from several articles he published during the 1960s, covering the music and symbolism of the three stages of Venda girls' initiation – *vhusha*, *tshikanda* and *domba* with its famous 'python dance' (1969a, 1969c–f) – as well as in the more comprehensive material on Venda music and on Venda children's songs (1964c; 1967) and in an earlier report (1957). But it can also be seen in a very different piece of work. In this, Blacking used the autobiographical writings of a Venda adolescent girl of Lutheran faith, Dora Thizwilondi Magidi, for the text of his book *Black Background: The Childhood of a Young South African Girl* (1964a). The Christian childhood it portrays seems to have only a tenuous connection to the experience of the female initiates in the academic articles – a tenuousness highlighted by the fact that many of the photographs with which the book is illustrated are of the female initiation rituals which Dora, as a Christian, was destined never to undergo. That the two kinds of girl saw themselves as distinct from each other is indicated by Dora's use of the term 'salempore girl' to describe her traditionalist counterparts (Blacking, 1964a: 158).

Blacking's interest in the part played by music in a young woman's upbringing, seen against the backdrop of broader Venda society with its patriarchal and hierarchical structure, and of South African society shortly after the decade of apartheid's most comprehensive implementation reveals a central tension in his attitude towards music more generally. It also contains a clue as to why his detailed studies of the Venda have had relatively little influence on subsequent studies of music and performance culture in a South African context, although his more general works (Blacking, 1973, 1977a, 1980a) have been acknowledged in this canon (see, for example, Erlmann, 1991; James, 1999b).

The tension is that between music as a designator of a fixed and unquestioned place in the social order, established through age, generation, gender and degree of royal connection, and music as an expression of alternative visions of social order, perhaps able to be used strategically in pursuit of such visions. His writing on girls' initiation, for example, shows how each stage is marked by highly formulaic learning of musical and speech patterns. These are memorized not so much for the knowledge they can impart as for the fact that they are automatic affirmations of status, denoting unalterably the phase a girl has reached in the life cycle. Affirming this idea that music marks a ranking within the context of pre-existing social statuses, Blacking remarked in his dissertation that music is incapable of expressing anything new; that it 'can only confirm sentiments that exist but cannot create new ones' (1964c: 108, 334). This remark is perhaps in keeping with his view, expressed nearly a decade later, that of all systems of symbols musical ones are the most resistant to change (1977a, cited in Erlmann, 1991: 11). Even when people embraced new, Christian types of worship and the new musical forms accompanying them, he saw these as conforming, fundamentally, to the original patterns. Christian adolescents, for example, might learn hymns and biblical phrases rather than the traditional initiate's music and *milayo* (laws), but these had the same function of designating status rather than being transmitters of knowledge or the means of enabling a fundamentally new and different outlook on the world. From one point of view, then, the Lutheran culture of Dora Magidi's childhood was every bit as ascriptive as the traditional Venda culture of the 'salempore girls'.

But bearing an apparently different message are remarks to be found elsewhere in Blacking's Venda work, and indeed it is these which could be said to have had most impact on subsequent studies – mainly focused on migrant and/or popular forms – in southern Africa. Music, he says, involves a symbolic removal from the everyday scheme of things; hence, those performing it are able to achieve states of mind or sociability which would be unattainable under non-musical circumstances. On one level, this can be seen to occur in the musical expedition (*bepha*). In this, chiefs or headmen – mostly from the ruling Singo clan – sent commoner boys and girls on competitive musical visits to neighbouring rulers' villages in an expression either of political fealty or dominance, depending on the relative status of the other chief concerned (Blacking, 1962). From the perspective of the commoner youths involved, such expeditions provided opportunities for enjoyment by engendering a 'spirit of fellowship' (1962) and, in particular, for anarchic cross-dressing and transvestite behaviour, which were afforded during the days of musical performance and competition involved (1965: 78–79). Here, certainly, was a case of symbolic distancing from normal patterns of behaviour. At the same time, from the point of view of the royals who harnessed the energies of these commoner youths, the *bepha* was of primarily political significance. It was 'an agreeable means by which a ruler [could] cultivate indirectly the continued loyalty of his people and remind them of his position' (1962: 62), and also by which he could assert, or affirm, his status in relation to that of those positioned at other points in the hierarchy of chiefs and headmen. For these royals, then, the sense of symbolic distancing from normal life which communal music involves was something to be used strategically, in the construction or affirmation of alliances.

While the enjoyable cross-dressing of *bepha* might be viewed as nothing more than a sort of Venda 'ritual of rebellion', Blacking makes the point about symbolic distancing, and transformation, more strongly elsewhere. In a discussion of the national reed-pipe dance *tshikona*, he demonstrates the transformative and transcendent power that music may have in certain settings, in part through its establishing of 'virtual time' (Blacking, 1973: 27, 51) and hence of special kinds of social relationship between participants. Where social integration may not have existed between participants before the dance, it would certainly have come into being in the course of its performance: in such a setting the themes of 'humanly organized sound' and 'soundly organized humanity' interlock (1973: 95–97). In such situations, music becomes 'an instrument indispensable to the transformation of man and his world' (1973: 49), as it was in the hands of such geniuses as Bach or Beethoven.

It is interesting, however, that Blacking's Venda material lays little stress on musical innovation or syncretism as a means of achieving this transcendence. He was interested in the 'political freedom' (inextricably linked to 'musical freedom') which independent African churches seemed to have (Blacking, 1980a). But it was a freedom which lay more in the Africanness of their music, and hence in their escape from mission structures and strictures, than in a creative merging of African with Christian elements. If one looks at the Lutheran childhood described in *Black Background*, it appears every bit as circumscribed and hedged in by institutionalized musical routines – school choir practices, Eisteddfods, weddings, singing competitions – as the childhood of one of Dora's more traditionalist counterparts described in

Blacking's scholarly articles about girls' initiation (1969a, 1969c–f). Reading between the lines of this book, it does not seem that the key to music's role as a transformative force was to lie in a merging of Venda with Christian forms. And yet it is precisely in this kind of syncretic, 'popular' music that subsequent generations of ethnomusicologists in southern Africa have sought, and found, a transformative role.

Leaving aside the question of syncretic forms, it is Blacking's view of music as having an almost heroic capacity to alter the world, or at least to reconstruct it satisfactorily in settings of extreme harshness and intractability (Blacking, 1980b, cited in Erlmann, 1991: 11), that has subsequently become something like the conventional wisdom among scholars of especially migrant, popular and other modernizing or neo-traditional styles of music in southern Africa (Coplan, 1985; Erlmann, 1991; James, 1999; Muller, 1999). This perspective, in its most extreme form, could be called 'methodological idealism'. The methodological idealist tends to mine all forms of musical activity, no matter how apparently quiescent, for their expression or embodiment of resilience in the face of oppression and hardship in South Africa. It is in this – the second of the two aspects in Blacking's work – that the imprint of his work can be discerned on ethnomusicological studies in the region. But my claim here is that the first aspect – in which music demonstrates or confirms apparently unchanging social/structural relationships, rather than transcending these – is a neglected aspect of Blacking's legacy. It is in the tension between the 'endorsing/confirming' and the 'transforming' positions that Blacking's legacy should really be sought, and it is in understanding their interrelations that scholars would do well to deploy their energies in further research on popular and/or migrant styles.

Blacking's resolution of this inherent tension in his own work was to differentiate between the varying functions of different kinds of musical activity: put simply, to claim that certain kinds of music achieve one end while different kinds achieve the other (Blacking, 1973: 44). But my own work on the musical culture of adolescents and of female socialization in the Northern Province (formerly northern Transvaal) suggests that the two functions can be intrinsically linked. I have found that the musical culture of girlhood and initiation, while used by adolescent girls and their parents as endorsements of specific fixed points in the life course and to denote apparently immovable gender orientations, membership of religious groupings and attitudes toward customary as against modern behaviours, can serve – in the context of migrant society – as a basis for later-established identities in which music plays a transformative role.

This relates, in turn, to the question of syncretism: my study suggests that the worlds and musical cultures of church/school on the one hand and tradition on the other are not as separate as they were alleged to be in Blacking's Venda material or as they have been insisted to be in some anthropological studies

(Mayer and Mayer, 1971). Rather than conceptualizing them as distinct social spheres, a more accurate representation would be yielded – in Venda terms – by thinking of a complex interweaving of the Lutheran Dora Magidi's experiences with those of the salempore girls. As I will demonstrate below, the life course of a young woman from the Northern Province typically incorporated a range of experiences – both school and *sotho*,[1] Christian and traditionalist – which might have been thought incompatible because of their ownership by incompatible social/religious communities. But this intersection of mission/school culture with traditional or neo-traditional influences, in the course of the adolescences I investigated, was not merely a matter of bricolage, in which parts of separate cultures were randomly or indiscriminately blended to form a new mixture. Rather, women leaving home to become migrants identified a voice with which to express a very precise combination of elements: they aspire to live in an autonomous fashion, benefiting from that which a modern or church-oriented route might provide, but they express this in terms which will enjoy a hearing within the male-dominated and traditionalist-oriented world of Northern Province migrancy.

Music of initiation: school and *sotho* culture

My examples are drawn from two studies. One was conducted in the early 1990s, among Northern Province migrant women working on the Witwatersrand who met regularly to sing and dance in a style called *kiba*, only recently acknowledged as the female equivalent of the formerly exclusively male genre known by the same name. The other, which dovetails with the first in some respects, was conducted in the later 1990s among men and women growing up in a Lutheran community, on a farm about two hours' drive north-east of Johannesburg.

To look first at the performers of *kiba*: the fact that men and women were in the 1990s recognized as partners in this musical enterprise obscures some major discontinuities. One can see the contrast if one looks at a single performance group, such as Maaparankwe (those of the royal leopard-skin clothing). Its male performers are mostly traditionalists (*baditshaba* – lit. 'those of the nation') from the Pedi heartland of Sekhukhune, who have been dancing *kiba* and playing its end-blown metal pipes since their childhood in the reserve. Their patterns of work and residence as migrants, and those for their forebears of several generations, were largely determined by the ethnically-based monopolies within particular mines and service sectors, formed on the basis of male initiation regiments (*mephato*) (Delius, 1989: 582–83; Molepo, 1984: 28). As they moved from compounded mine labour through a series of less restrictive forms of employment and residence, such as domestic service and later industrial employment, they took *kiba* with them. For male players, then, this music was a constant and ongoing feature of life.

For future female *kiba* players, in contrast, musical experience was discontinuous and shifting. They came from the northern area known as Leboa (the north),[2] and had grown up while their families were rent or labour tenants on white- or black-owned farms outside of the reserves, living largely off the proceeds of agriculture or of farm labour. For these families, the belated move from the farms to one of the small northern reserves drew both male and female family members into their first-ever exposure to labour migration. The women who were to become singers of *kiba* departed for town in search of a job without ready-made ethnic support groups.

It was only on arriving on the Witwatersrand that *kiba* women began to construct or become involved in broader social networks. While these were initially church-based and linked to associations of men from specific reserve areas in Leboa, women were later to form their own *kiba* groupings on the basis of the friendships they had made with other women from a more broadly-defined home area. Sometimes, as in the case of Maaparankwe, they went into partnership with male partner-groups that were selected for their professionalism in dancing. Performing their sung and danced version of *kiba*, which they saw as part of *sotho* music/traditional music (*mmino wa sesotho/wa setöo*), provided an opportunity to escape from the restrictive male controls of the more conventional migrant associations.

I mentioned the church as a basis of social networks: most of these women had grown up in communities of Christians (*bakriste*), so the fact that they performed *kiba* did not signify a straightforward continuity with past practice. Starting some time after they arrived to work on the Witwatersrand, for most it represented a revival of a pre-adolescent involvement in *sotho* culture which had culminated in initiation. In the ethnically diverse Northern Province, many of them had grown up speaking languages such as siNdebele – or, like Dora, TshiVenda – and performing styles of music more commonly associated with those languages.[3]

Since my broader discussion of how these women, during the phase of life when they became mature mothers, built up an identity based on selective application of *sotho* ideals, morals and musical principle, has been published elsewhere (James, 1999a, 1999b, 1994), I will touch on it here only in passing. The ostensible reason for their use of *kiba* is expressed thus: 'Home is where this music is sung. We don't want to forget the tradition of our home people'. This statement sums up the enterprise, but conceals the true nature of this 'home'. They had not met before they came to the Witwatersrand. They started with few contacts except an uncle or brother, eventually started watching male dancers on Sundays, and decided to start their own club. The few who knew this dancing taught the others, more joined, more learned: the sense of what 'home' was gradually expanded to include more and more dancers. Women's involvement in this unusual form of ethnic organization provided a range of benefits. Some of these – financial aid and support and help with securing jobs in cleaning and domestic service – were more easily measured. Others – a sense of identity in the city, deriving some impact and audience respect from its connection to the male genre, but having its own coherence – were less material but perhaps more important.

Women's performance, then, while apparently harking back to a shared origin (*setöo*), spoke more of a commonality developed among friends in town than of a culture they had personally transported, intact, from the countryside. But its origins were, in complex ways, to be found in these performers' upbringing. In order to find out how, and to establish in what ways this mature identity drew selectively on, and yet transformed, the musical and social experience of youth, I needed to adopt an approach which foregrounded individual singers' accounts of their own musical life histories.

These histories, it turned out, diverged considerably from each other. Part of the difference lay in the complex set of landholding arrangements in the northern Transvaal of the 1960s and 1970s. In a country notorious for its patchwork of different forms of tenure, this seemed to present an extreme example. There were three basic types of landholding, which varied concomitantly with forms of livelihood, culture and music.

Some future singers' families were living in quasi-feudal conditions, as labour tenants on white farms. A second category of people lived, as owners or tenants, on African freehold farms. These were mostly Christians who had bought land away from the reserves in an attempt to live as independent peasant producers, remote from burden to some obligations to the chiefs in the reserves. A third had been born and reared in reserves, where their families were dependent on chiefs for their access to land. The patchwork-like quality yielded by these different types of landholding was one which the apartheid government attempted to rationalize, with its plans in the 1960s and 1970s to remove all Africans in the first two categories – those living in so-called 'white' areas – and resettle all of them in the 'black areas' or reserves. But, for the girls and adolescents who were later to become *kiba* singers, whose families, removed from their original homes, began to converge on these reserve areas, the result was one of considerable dislocation.

It was not only, however, the government's infamous plans which lay behind these removals. While writers on South Africa have tended to highlight resettlements which were involuntary, and attributable to the depredations of apartheid – especially the infamous 'black spot' removals, and the evictions of labour tenants off white farms (Desmond, 1971, Surplus People Project, 1983), the move to the reserves was also occasioned, at least in the case of many farm labour tenants, by the desire of family members to have a more modern life. They wanted to live in conditions of greater civilization (*tlhabologo*) and to have easier access to schools, shops and churches than was possible on the farms. Although not all were Christians or church members, their favouring of church-oriented culture resulted from a modernizing course adopted by them and their families – an orientation which in part resulted from, but also contributed to, the rapid resettling of their families, as of other Africans, in the reserves during this period. In this flux of social and property arrangements, the adolescent musical culture in which these future female migrants participated was one in which choir, concert and church songs were favoured, but with a selective use of customary *sotho* elements.

In the context of this social and cultural flux, one childhood experience which all future urban singers of *kiba* from these areas were to share was *koma* (initiation), although their disparate social backgrounds meant that their attendance at this ritual was prompted by widely differing, even contradictory, impulses. Former labour tenants who had moved off white farms were still sufficiently steeped in the customary ways – despite the desire to live in a more modern manner – to send their children to initiation without much question. In contrast, those families who moved to the reserves from independently-owned freehold farms ('black spots'), where Christian belief had predominated, often found themselves in new situations where a Christian ethic was not as entrenched as it had been in their former homes. The peasant daughters who had moved from these farms were initiated because of pressure from peer groups encountered in their new homes, sometimes against the wishes of their parents. For the Lutheran Machaba sisters to be initiated was to rebel against the authority of their father, but to conform – albeit more out of a desire to 'fit in' than out of an espousing of traditional values – with the social mores of their age-group in the reserve. In the reserve village of GaKgare to which they moved, where most children were dressed in skins in contrast to their own dresses, they had felt isolated and conspicuous. After attending *koma*, they found that their status as initiates and their membership – shared with their peers – of initiation regiments (*mephato*) served to lessen the gap which had divided them from these age-mates.[4] But the experience was not to carry the same sense of unification and bonding as it would have done for the Venda initiates of Blacking's account, if only because they were later to become migrants who would rely on very different kinds of musical solidarity for their sense of belonging.

The Machabas were girls very much like Dora, the heroine of Blacking's *Black Background*. Although her family, like theirs, was strongly Lutheran in orientation, she nevertheless longed to dance the girls' *tshigombela* (Blacking, 1964a: 82–86) when she saw her friends and neighbours – the 'salempore girls' – doing so. Her parents were opposed to this, but they eventually relented and allowed her to join the team. But their tolerance was not limitless: they stopped short of letting her go with her team on a *bepha* expedition. One can only speculate about whether her longing to imitate her peers might, as with the Machabas, have extended to initiation had her childhood, like theirs, been disrupted by a move from a predominantly Christian community to one where initiation was the norm.

Even where future *kiba* singers attended initiation, the Leboa villages where they spent their adolescence espoused a culture oriented to school and to modernity. One might imagine that the differences between uninitiated and initiated children would be de-emphasized in such a context. Studies of 'traditional' rural music-making in southern Africa have stressed how musical performance differentiates gender and age roles from each other (Blacking, 1967, 1969b; Johnston, 1971, 1975; Huskisson, 1958), with smaller categories, each specific to a particular occasion and social status and never sung outside of this, eclipsing any broader totality of music or song (Merriam, 1964: 262–70). Adopting a mission-influenced musical culture has been assumed, in contrast, to engulf all generations and sexes in its grip. But this was not the case in Leboa communities, where musical markers of status were important despite the apparently homogenizing effects of Christianity.

Although the pre-initiatory phase *bothumasha* (uninitiated girlhood) was thought not really to exist in such communities, since 'there was now *tlhabologo*' (civilization), it was still marked off by age-specific musical practices and thus distinguished from the subsequent phase *bokgarebe* (initiated girlhood). *Bokgarebe*, like its male equivalent, was characterized by an abandoning of children's songs such as *dikoöa töa go bapala* or *dikoöa töa go aloka* (playing songs, for skipping and the like). Initiated girls, like initiated boys, began to sing in the music of a school or mission culture which had become general to all social classes and categories in these northern reserve areas. They were learned at school, through a mixture of oral and literate transmission, and performed by school choirs: a performance context which gave this genre its name – *kosa töa dikhwaere* (more commonly known in the literature as *makwaya*).

In a similar vein, Dora's brief foray into singing *tshigombela* had ended abruptly when she started school. This was the defining moment which not only separated her from the performance practices of childhood, but also which detached her definitively from the 'salempore girls' with whom she had had a brief musical partnership. In the strongly school-oriented reserves of Leboa, in contrast, what distinguished an initiate from a child was her leaving behind the *sotho* songs of childhood and becoming immersed in the performance of this genre of choir music – a genre embracing both Christians and non-Christians in its grasp.

Makwaya first came into being as a result of the impact on local sung traditions in southern Africa of Christian hymnody, whose successful implanting in this context was probably due to the fact that 'traditional music in the south is predominantly vocal, characterized by choral singing in complex, overlapping responsorial patterns' (Manuel, 1988: 28–29). The impact of hymn-singing was profound: the imprint of its three-chord harmonic structure can be detected in a wide range of popular South African music including not only *makwaya* but also stretching from *marabi*, through kwela and *mbube*, to the mainly media-disseminated *mbaqanga* (Manuel, 86, 108).

Most of what has been written about *makwaya* stresses its initial association with the nascent African middle class in both rural and urban contexts (Coplan, 1985: 72, 118; Manuel, 1988: 107). It was transmitted mainly through a medium available only to literate people – the tonic sol-fa system of notation – although the development of the genre in an urban context saw some choirmasters switch over to a way of teaching songs more oral in its focus, in which their choirs sang 'by heart' or 'out of their heads' (Coplan, 1985: 117). The aspect of *makwaya* that has not been examined is the gradual increase in its popularity in the rural districts of South Africa. Here, although in its strictly religious form as African hymnody it was sung only by churchgoers, its most frequent performance occurred in schools by scholars on both sides of the Christian/traditionalist divide.[5] Although identified at its inception with the African middle class, its later developments took it across boundaries of income, occupation and status into the ranks of those who derived their income from unskilled migrant labour. In the areas of Leboa where urban *kiba* singers grew up, as in many other labour-sending areas of rural South Africa, this music became a major form of cultural expression for school-going children and adolescents.

In the reserves of Leboa where these girls lived, initiation did, then, mark off children from post-initiates, but it did so largely by endorsing their inculcation with a mission-style musical culture. Although the formal attributes of *makwaya* or *kosa töa dikhwaere* may have had little overlap with that of the indigenous songs it replaced, the competitive social contexts within which it was sung show striking similarities with indigenous ones. Here one can see evidence of the accuracy of Blacking's perception – that musical activities confirm existing structures and sentiments and that music symbols are resistant to change. It is interesting, for example, that the *mothetha* (choir for girls and girls under the leadership of a senior boy) to which the Machaba sisters belonged, although singing *dikoöa töa dikolo* (school songs) did so within a setting remarkably similar to that of the Venda *bepha*:

> We'd go with our school choir to visit other schools, and spend the night. We'd hear their songs, and learn them, and take them as our own.[6]

This practice of musical competition and learning leads me to mention, in parentheses, the adolescent musical culture of a much more overtly and unreservedly Christian community, living a few hour's drive to the south-east of these Leboa communities. This was a community similar in ethos, perhaps, to Dora's, and to the one living on the freehold farm where the Machabas had lived before moving to the reserves. These were the Lutherans of the farm Doornkop who formed the nucleus of that farm's inhabitants until the 'black spot' removal of 1974. In the course of investigating their 1994 reclaiming of the farm, some 20 years later, I asked about their early – and, in particular, their early musical – experiences there.

In some ways their musical activities were very similar to those of the Lutheran Dora. Wearing special uniforms, they joined the strongly Christian-oriented Wayfarer movement which, in South Africa, was an African equivalent of the Boy Scout movement (see Blacking, 1964a: 101–07). Within the context of this movement, and of school and church, they spent a large proportion of their time learning and singing choir songs. But they also had much in common with the reserve-dwelling traditionalists from whom their forebears had been so keen to distinguish themselves. One of these was the prevalence of confirmation groupings (*dithaka*) which undertook activities strikingly similar to those of the initiation regiments (*mephato*) to which traditionalists' children belonged in the reserves. Another was the favouring of a musical competition/expedition format, much like the *bepha*. A great deal of time and energy was spent in practising for, and in carrying out, competitive events in which the chief rivals were children from other Christian communities in the neighbourhood or members of other branches of the Wayfarers. Even here, before the removals that caused such flux and disruption in rural districts of the Transvaal, there were interchanges and striking continuities between school and traditionalist culture, despite people's attempts to distinguish strongly between these. Music on the farm Doornkop, as elsewhere in that province, was giving adolescents a specific point in the life course at which to fix themselves.

To return to the singers of *kiba*: the significance of initiation in the rural areas where these people grew up was a complex one. It was not a mark of group identity that excluded non-traditionalists, since it incorporated Christians of long standing and of recent conversion alongside those who had never been churchgoers. Neither did it mark a commitment to a traditionalist or custom-bound social order: indeed, while *koma* itself represented perhaps the most intense experience of *sesotho* and its ways yet undergone, especially for those of long-standing Christian affiliation, it also heralded a phase in most girls' lives when the things of *sesotho* would be put behind them almost completely, at least for a while. But it did lay the basis for proficient practice of *sotho* cultural forms when these girls, as women, began to sing *kiba* in town. The songs and music of *koma* were secret and, strictly speaking, should not have been repeated outside of this context. But their basic structure and style was characteristic of Northern Sotho traditional music (Huskisson, 1958) – polyrhythmic, hexatonic and with descending cadences – and similar to those of present-day women's *kiba* (see James, 1994). It was at *koma* that most informants, but especially those whose parents were Christian and so taught them no *sotho* music, learned, through oral transmission, to sing in a *sotho* style.

Black background: the case of Julia Lelahana

Among those who were later to sing *kiba* in town, there was then a general
orientation towards modernity, to be followed much later by a selective revival
of *sotho* culture. But this general trend needs qualification, if one bears in mind
that children of different sexes – even those within one family – are socialized
in very different ways. While it is true that the school culture that took root in
these northern communities was not strongly differentiated by gender, as can
be seen from the case of the mixed choirs, there were some important cultural
and musical differences between boys and girls. Girls were required to perform
more duties in the domestic domain, were less free to move beyond it for long
periods of time, and were less likely than boys to be given anything further than
a primary school education. In some cases, this meant that girls were thought of
as 'more *sotho*' than their brothers. Their orientation to the domestic sphere
often led to their acquisition of forms of musical or oral culture from mothers
and grandmothers where boys, at school, were not in a position to acquire
these. And it was these girls in particular, more *sotho* than boys and more *sotho*
than some of the other women with whom they would later club together to
sing in town, who would later assume key roles in teaching and developing
kiba in the urban context.

The case of Julia Lelahana, later to become the leader of Maaparankwe's
women's section, is one which demonstrates a complex interweaving of
gendered experience with the effects of the social disruptions mentioned
earlier. She grew up on the farm Bijlsteel, about 30 kilometres north-east of
Pietersburg, 'ran away' to work on a nearby farm and eventually moved with
her parents to a village in the Moletöi reserve in Lebowa. But this major move
had not been the only one in Julia's life: her parents had moved to this farm,
where her paternal grandparents were living as labour tenants, after being
evicted from the soon-to-be-demolished African location adjoining Pietersburg
where Julia had been born. It was because of this move away from town that
Julia, the youngest of five children, had no education at all, while her older
siblings, brothers and sisters alike, had been schooled in the location up until
the time the family left for the farm.

Growing up in this context, she was remote not only from the school culture
described above, but also from the culture of people initiated in the reserves.
The songs she sang as a child were not the mixed choir songs of boys and girls
but those of the herdboys with whom she worked and played. As a young girl
she was sent to herd cattle together with boys of her own age on the farm, and
they had taught her to make and play a string instrument called *botsorwane* or
setseketseke. Perhaps with the hindsight of a migrant career, she observed:

> I was not shy and I had no problem in playing things that are *senna* [of men/meant
> for men]. I did this because I was a herdgirl.[7]

It was her lack of schooling that set this girl apart from all her older siblings. But the contrast she noted between herself as *motho wa sesotho* (a *sotho* person) and her brothers as *batho ba dikolo* ('school people') was due not only to this educational disparity but also to her acquisition of an interest in *sotho* ways from her parents and older relatives. She learned *go reta* (praising) from her mother and grandparents, with whom she spent much time around the house. Another means by which she acquired a love of the ways of *sesotho* was through a kind of cultural inheritance from her father, who was a diviner, a maker of drums for spirit-possession drumming, and a player of men's *kiba*.

Julia, with her exposure to and interest in *sotho* things beyond the boundaries of initiation and despite her background in a generally mission-oriented area, was later to become a key figure in the development of urban *kiba*. In 1993–94 she was the *malokwane* (leader) of the Maaparankwe group, heading the singing, teaching songs learned at home to her fellow-singers, embellishing existing songs with new words or actions and providing extensive interpretation of these words and actions if called upon to do so. Her relationship to the music was in contrast to that of some of her fellow singers, who had learned all the songs from others, who mostly sang the chorus rather than the lead part, and who were hard-pressed to explain the significance of particular songs. Leading figures like Julia tended to be those who were exposed to some *sotho* ways in their own and in relatives' homes. Conversely, the musical followers were often those whose early exposure to this music was restricted to what they learned at *koma*.

The cultural background of the girls who spent their youth and adolescence on the farms and later in the reserve villages of Leboa was a complex one. A variety of inputs contributed to the overall culture of modernity to which they and their families aspired, but these inputs were refracted, and in certain respects deflected by their refraction, through the lens of gender. Although most desired to live in a modern way, their role within the household gave some, like Julia, a leaning towards *sesotho*.

Diversity merged in music

In the process of gathering life and music histories from *kiba* singers, it became clear to me that their differing experiences in adolescence nevertheless converged in particular ways. In addition to the shared experience of *koma* there were some other things they had in common. Many had been forced into labour migrancy, as domestic servants, when a father's death or desertion left their families penniless; and it was the position of oldest child which – despite being women – made them feel responsible for their families in this way. Some had been briefly married, but all ended up as single mothers exclusively responsible for the upkeep of their own children and other kin.

But it was not only in their objective socioeconomic circumstances that there were commonalities in these women's disrupted lives. If, on the basis of these regional diversities, they eventually came to have a single homogenous experience of 'home', it was through music that this was achieved. When they first decided to sing together, they discovered that their sense of *sotho* music (*mmino wa sesotho*), although its basic aspects had been learned through initiation, was regionally varied and hence far from uniform. But this changed as they practised together under the tutelage of influential musical figures such as Julia Lelahana and as, with the passing of time, they engaged in a process of reciprocal teaching and learning. Competitive performance formats created ever-increasing pressure to make of women's *kiba* a highly polished and unified style. It was thus that multiple and initially somewhat mismatched styles of performance were adjusted to create a standardized and homogenous music and dance style (James, 1999a).

Conclusion

Lived in the midst of turbulent and disruptive experiences in the northern area of Leboa, the childhood and adolescence of future female migrants was one in which musical experiences definitively demarcated particular positions in the life course. They gave those who had faced the insecurity of relocation a way of affirming customary connections, and those aspiring to a modern life a way of entrenching and fortifying their commitment to civilization (*tlhabologo*). They also allowed those whose circumstances denied them any easy social or cultural connections to draw nurture from the almost forgotten musical backgrounds of their parents. Although initiation played an important part in this, its role was not the well-established one of providing a solidary peer group in which all future activities could be undertaken, or of affirming adherents' membership of a well-defined ethnic community in contrast to other ethnicities in the neighbourhood. Nor did it incontrovertibly divide boys from girls. Rather, it was a watershed between a childhood marked by traditionalist children's music and culture and an adolescence marked by school- or church-oriented music and culture. At the same time it served, in its teaching of *sotho* music, to lay a foundation of musical principles to which many initiates would return only in adulthood, in the process of constituting of a very different kind of ethnic identity and group of peers.

For these young women, as for those Blacking described (1964c: 108, 334; 1969a, 1969c–f), the musical experiences of childhood and youth were ones which circumscribed identities and statuses. But the fixity and secure social positioning they achieved was a fleeting one. By seizing at moments of stability within the flux and mobility of changing identities and social arrangements in the northern Transvaal of the 1960s and 1970s, it may be that girls like Salome and Andronica Machaba were doing more than simply trying to 'fit in' with those around them. As well as yielding to the temptation of attempting to belong in communities from which they felt somewhat estranged, they were, albeit unknowingly, acquiring the groundwork for the musical culture which would characterize their adulthood. It was on these musical foundations that their future life as autonomous wage-earning mothers, within the largely male-dominated world of urban migration, was to be built.

To understand the relationship between the ascriptive nature of these youthful musical experiences and their future imaginative transformation by migrant women, one needs to recognize the complex meanings attached to terms of religious affiliation. In the changing world of rural/urban connections in twentieth-century South Africa, terms such as 'Christian' (*mokristi*) and 'traditionalist' (*heitene*) were not adjectives describing distinct and separate identities. Although these terms were conceived of as denoting opposite polarities on a continuum of social experience – and often had connotations of class as well (see James 1997) – in the life of a single individual they could be woven together into a new totality. Like the gender polarities which music's strict subdivision had informed in more thoroughgoingly traditionalist Northern Sotho communities (Huskisson, 1958), these polarities of religious belief, sociocultural orientation and class have been intertwined with each other to yield new, heretofore unknown, combinations. It is as though the experiences of Dora and those of her friends and erstwhile dancing companions, the 'salempore girls', were encompassed in the life of a single individual.

The legacy of Blacking's Venda work for understanding the musical culture of migrants lies, then, in understanding how music, in its ascriptive and transformative aspects, affects and is used within the life histories of individuals. Blacking's legacy can lead us to try to comprehend how innovative individuals, produced by pitting themselves against the powerful social forces that have moulded them as people, assimilate musical influences in the process of maturing, and later use these to create new and transcendent situations.

Notes

[1] Where Sotho denotes a language or a set of musical or other features which have been attributed to a group of people by analysts, it is spelt with a capital and is not italicized. The language officially known as Northern Sotho (SeSotho sa Leboa), also called SePedi, is an example. But where, as the noun *sesotho* or as the adjective *sotho*, it denotes a language, a way of dressing, a state of being, a way of life, or a set of qualities which informants themselves have enunciated or commented on, it is italicized and spelt without a capital. In this commoner form, *sesotho* is rarely qualified by terms such as 'northern' or 'southern' (*sa Leboa/sa Borwa*). See Comaroff and Comaroff (1989: 276–96) for a similar usage.

[2] Local people's classification of the area north of Pietersburg as Leboa (the north) should not be confused with Lebowa, the name of the former bantustan or homeland set aside by the apartheid government for the Northern Sotho or Pedi.

[3] SeTswana, *seSotho sa borwa* (southern Sotho) and *seSotho sa leboa* or *sePedi* (northern Sotho) are all cognate languages with common sociolinguistic roots, belonging to the linguistic family termed Sotho. The speakers of vhaVenda have close relationships to the northern Sotho, although conquest by a Shona-related people from north of the Limpopo makes matters linguistically more complex. The speakers of siNdebele, belonging to the Nguni linguistic family, moved from the east coast to settle in the areas now called Mpumalanga and the Northern Province in the late seventeenth century, well before the era of warfare and migration sometimes called the *difaqane*. For fuller information on the socio-linguistic relationships between the speakers of these various groups, see Krige (1937), van Warmelo (1952, 1974) and Wilson (1982).

[4] Andronica and Salome Machaba, recorded discussion with DJ (Deborah James) and PM (Philip Mnisi) on 19 October 1991. This was in contrast with girls in the Pedi heartland, Sekhukhune, where uninitiated girls of the same age were still singing the songs of *mathumasha* (uninitiated girls), including a rain-making song crucial to the agricultural viability of society.

[5] Even in the mission contexts where it initially took root in the nineteenth century, it provoked not so much the slavish imitation of which some writers have complained (Andersson, 1981: 16) as the inventive and eclectic responses of such genres as *makwaya* (Manuel, 1988: 107). The case of *makwaya* shows that people's use of cultural forms originating in the mission does not necessarily have an 'overwhelmingly imitative character' as is claimed by the accounts that Ranger criticizes (1975: 6), or signify 'the colonization of consciousness' (Comaroff and Comaroff, 1989). Even within the mission context and among converts, people may transform the religion of the colonizers into something significantly different, as Hofmeyr has shown in her excellent study of the oralization of literate Christianity in an area that is part of Leboa (Hofmeyr 1993: 68–83). New and syncretic cultural forms which arise among churchgoers, as *makwaya* did, may spread through a variety of channels to reach – and to be actively sought out by – even those people who do not count themselves among the ranks of the converted.

[6] The format of visiting, competing with and learning from one's hosts, as well as having much in common with *bepha*, also shows similarities to the process of visiting and imitating which characterized the spread of *kiba* (see James 1999b, ch. 3).

[7] Julia Lelahana, recorded discussion with DJ and PM, Johannesburg, 13 October 1991.

CHAPTER FIVE

Musicality in Early Childhood: A Case from Japan

Fumiko Fujita

Introduction

John Blacking's chief concern was to explore the nature of human musicality, and his great interest in this issue can be noted throughout his writings. During his fieldwork amongst the Venda of the northern Transvaal in South Africa, he discovered a society in which all normal human beings were regarded as capable of making music (Blacking, 1973) and in which no one was excluded from participating in musical performance (Blacking, 1967: 191). Drawing on this experience, he highlighted the contrast between the Venda concepts of musicality and those held in the modern industrial society of his background, in which only a few people were regarded as musical. His research, therefore, has drawn attention to the ways in which the cultural interacts with the biological, often stifling innate human capabilities.

In Japan, my native country, notions of musicality have developed through the encounter of Western and Japanese musical systems. There is no original Japanese term equivalent to the English word 'music' to refer collectively to all categories of 'humanly organized sound'. As traditional Japanese music is closely connected with drama, dance and songs, it does not exist separately from other performance genres, and therefore no generic term emerged. What did emerge as a comprehensive term is *geino*, which translates as traditional Japanese performing arts, and it refers to all categories of 'humanly organized sound and movement' (see Kikkawa, 1959: 28). As Western culture became ever more present in Japan, a Japanese translation for 'music' became necessary, and the word *unmake* came to be used for this purpose, while the term *ongaku-sei* could be glossed as 'musicality'. Thus, in Japan, an association has developed between *ongaku* and Western music, which also defines 'musicality' as a characteristic of people who perform Western music. It could be said, therefore, that in Japan, Western music, rather than Japanese music, has become the yardstick against which a person's musical aptitude is measured. The social and historical backdrop against which these associations emerged dates back to the Meiji period, which introduced Western music as the main focus of school music education in Japan. This focus has persisted up to the present, such that Western music has now been taught systematically in Japanese schools throughout the country for over 120 years, clearly establishing the link between musicality and a proficiency in Western musical performance.

It is, of course, absurd to assess the musicality of the Japanese exclusively in terms of their proficiency in the performance of Western music. Indeed, many elderly Japanese are unable to sing Western songs proficiently, while being excellent performers of traditional Japanese folksongs; similarly, there are many children who find it difficult to perform the Western instrumental music that is taught in schools, but engage competently in Japanese folk ensembles (*hayashi*). This, therefore, is a clear indication that, in Japan, there is a discrepancy between people's 'natural' musical tendencies – that is, the musical competencies that develop through daily interaction within the Japanese cultural setting – and the socially-constructed notion of musicality that has become dominant in the country. Given these circumstances, a better understanding of the intrinsic nature of Japanese musicality might be gained through research that examines the early stages of music acquisition among Japanese children, viewing the process in everyday settings.

Processes of music acquisition were central to John Blacking's concerns, and he not only highlighted the link between human musicality and overt, culturally distinct musical activity, but also developed methodologies for investigating it. Through his research on Venda children's music and music-making he was able to focus on the very context in which the natural maturation processes intersect with learned behaviour. Drawing on his elaborate and detailed documentation of the lives and musical activities of Venda children in their cultural setting, he discussed their processes of music-making and pointed to certain relationships between the lives of the Venda and their style of music.

One aspect of Blacking's study of Venda children's songs involved outlining the relationship between Venda speech patterns and their musical structures, and he ultimately concluded that the structure of Venda children's songs was deeply influenced by speech, both in terms of its rhythmic elements and its melodic contours. He described the transformation process of Venda speech into the songs in the following way:

> The rhythmic patterns of the children's songs are not typical of children's music that has been recorded in other parts of the world; they are understood best as elementary *Venda* rhythms. ...
>
> Speech-tone is an important element of Venda speech, and it can sometimes affect the meaning of a word. The Venda do not expect a song to sound like ordinary speech, but nevertheless the melodies of songs are closely related to speech-tone patterns. ... When songs are composed, it appears that words and music interact in the following way: an idea framed in words is set to music that is partly influenced by the speech-tone patterns of the words and their prevailing

rhythm. Once the meter and the melody of the song are established, they influence the composition of further 'lines' of the song. (Blacking, 1967: 192)

Blacking proposed a mode of musical analysis premised on a distinction between two dimensions of the musical product: its deep structures and its surface structures, an idea that sprang from his concern for the relationship between speech and melody which emerged during his analyses of Venda children's songs. Drawing on this work, Blacking claimed that:

> ... the surface structures of Venda music ... can be heard and learned by any human being who can perceive and reproduce pattern of sound.
>
> But there are other aspects of the Venda musical tradition which are forever changing and which cannot be learned except by total participation in Venda society and by unconscious assimilation of the social and cognitive process on which the culture is founded. These are the deep structures of Venda music, which determine what comes next in a melody and how a new idea may be expressed in music, how many times a pattern will be repeated on a given occasion and why. They are structures in a dynamic sense, in that they include the potential for growth and development, and so they might better be described as processes. (Blacking, 1971: 95)

Blacking emphasized the importance of conducting research into the deep structures of human musical behaviour, an endeavour he referred to as the 'cultural analysis of music'. According to Blacking:

> The purpose of the technique is not simply to describe the cultural background of the music as human behaviour, *and then* to analyze peculiarities of style in terms of rhythm, tonality, timbre, instrumentation, frequency of ascending and descending intervals, and other essentially musical terminology, but describe *both* the music *and* its cultural background as interrelated parts of a total system. Because music is humanly organized sound, there ought to be relationships between patterns of human organization and the pattern of sound produced in the course of organized interaction. (Blacking, 1971: 93)

What is notable here is that Blacking consistently discussed the deep and surface structure of music from the viewpoint of the music-maker. In other words, in discussing the structure of music, he proposed a theory regarding the structures of human musical behaviour. As his work matured, his ideas about how the generative processes of human music-making derive from deep structures developed into his notion of 'musical intelligence' (Blacking, 1992). 'Musical intelligence', he claimed, comprises the cognitive and affective equipment with which people make music and musical sense of the world.

The musicologist and forerunner of Japanese ethnomusicology, Daigoro Arima, studied music in Vienna, where he took a PhD at Vienna University for his thesis *Japanische Musikgeschichte auf Grund der Quellenkunde* (*A*

Philological History of Japanese Music) in 1933. His research concerns centred on the investigation of Japanese performers' emotions during performance in an effort to identify the distinctiveness of Japanese musicality. He concluded that Japanese performers assimilate a set of musical principles which allow them to perform properly; there is a close link between spoken Japanese and the traditional repertoire; and good breath control is a central element of aesthetic evaluation. Although, unlike Blacking, Arima did not undertake systematic field research, his approach, research methods and quest for the basis of human musicality suggest parallels with Blacking's concerns. The main points in Arima's characterization of Japanese musicality can be summarized as follows:

1. During performance, Japanese musicians are restrained by the tune or melodic pattern (*fushi*) of the piece they are performing; this structural backbone serves as the basic constitutional element of music performance. [1]

2. Japanese music is closely connected to the spoken language and it is strongly ethical in orientation. *Ongaku* (traditional Japanese music) is mainly made up of vocal music that is based on recitation (Ebisawa, 1987: 35 and Fujita, 2003: 68). There are many song texts that can be performed to a single melodic contour, and it is up to the performer to construct variations in accordance with the ethical meaning of the text being performed (Ebisawa, 1987: 37).

3. For the Japanese proper breath control is a central indicator of musical competence, and this is true of both vocal and instrumental music (Arima, 1951: 15). Breathing is considered to be closely connected to human motivation and human emotions. Moreover, it is through breathing that mutual time agreement is established among co-performers during performance.

4. The principles of Japanese music can be found in a wide range of common, everyday performances, such as daily conversations, hawkers' cries, the lines used by *sumo* yellers or *kabuki* performers' formalized speech; thus, these principles can be learned through practical experience in everyday life (see Ebisawa, 1987: 148–53; see also Fujita, 1989: 13; Fujito, 2003).

As a researcher who was keen to study Japanese children's musical abilities, I was strongly drawn to Blacking's perspectives on human musicality and his view of musical performance as the natural outcome of the human being as music-maker. Furthermore, he approached the study of music in relation to the specific sociocultural context of its performance, in order to assess the impact of culture on the biological and vice versa. I found that many of his observations regarding the procedures employed by Venda children in their music-making also held true for the Japanese children I was observing. All normal Japanese children are musical when their musical activities are approached from Blacking's perspective. Moreover, their musical perform-ances are deeply connected to their speech patterns in a manner similar to that of the Venda children. Japanese children employ numerous intermediate forms of expression that lie between speech and song, such as calling, story-telling and chanting. These forms involve instances in which a word or a phrase is uttered metrically or melodically. Blacking also noted the use of such forms in the Venda children's song repertory (Blacking, 1967: 155).

In 1983, I was fortunate to have been accepted into the postgraduate programme at Queen's University Belfast, where I undertook a project on Japanese children's musicality under Blacking's supervision. In 1987 I completed my PhD thesis titled: *Problems of Language Culture and the Appropriateness of Musical Expression in Japanese Children's Performance* (Fujita, 1989). For the thesis, I observed children's musical performances not only from the perspective of the musical product, but also as a means of understanding the learning processes involved in generating the musical structures. In particular, I was interested in detecting musicality – the innate human musical capabilities – by observing the ways in which children made musical use of their voices and their body movements in everyday settings, and the conditions that stimulated such behaviour. To link the project to Arima's findings on Japanese music, the observation of the children's musical activities also involved grasping the feelings the children expressed through their musical performances, their levels of breath control and the ways in which their melodic and rhythmic phases changed when they shifted from speech to song.

My observations led me to conclude that Japanese children make music by employing a form of musical expression that is deeply connected to their speech patterns. The framework that structures the forms of musical expression among Japanese children is based around a basic unit, namely a single breath, from inhalation to exhalation, that is used to produce phrases, words or syllables in the Japanese language. The musical sound that is produced by children is determined by three parameters:

i)   the intensity of the child's expressive intent;
ii)   the duration of the child's breathing cycle; and
iii)   the sound structure of the Japanese language. (see Fujita, 1989: 217)

Ultimately, therefore, musical activity links the self, a wilful being, to biological (breathing cycle) and cultural (language properties) contingencies. The main finding of the project suggest that the principles of Japanese children's music-making are conducive to musical creativity, substantiating Blacking's notions of 'musical intelligence' (Blacking, 1992: 310). The study also demonstrated that the children gained great pleasure from musical communication:

When the children sang [a] song with others, individual children tried out their own ways of singing, and at the same time listened to the others' ways of singing. They compared their singing with others and evaluated their own performance. Then they modified their own way of singing, always striving for the best results. When children recognised that their breathing cycles were synchronized with others, they felt the communicative pleasure of sharing a common time with others by making music. (Fujita, 1989: 186–87)

Since completing my doctoral research, I have begun a longitudinal research project on the development of musical competence among Japanese children. Observation began in 1997, and it is being conducted within the context of daily life at nursery schools, involving children from the ages of three months to six years. This chapter presents some of the findings of this project that pertain to observations undertaken at the Kohitsuji Nursery School.

The project and the setting

The aim of the research is to obtain information about the way in which Japanese children acquire musical skills in early childhood and about the processes involved in the development of their musical competence within the specificities of their sociocultural environment. To collect the data, two or three researchers visit the nursery school one morning a week for a period of around two hours. During these visits the researchers observe the children's musical activities and their musical experiences. The observation period proceeds for six months each year, amounting to a total of 21 days of observation a year. The long-term project was planned so that the children who were in their first year of life in 1997 would be observed up to the age of six, which is when they leave nursery school. Observation is undertaken in a natural setting, and the observers focus their attention on the voices and movements of the children and their teachers in an effort to detect instances in which these behaviours could be defined as musical. Musical behaviour is distinguished from ordinary behaviour according to one of the following two criteria: it is performed producing a sound which consists of a tone of fixed pitch with intervals, or it is performed with recurrent pulses.[2] The musical activity is recorded on videotape in such a way as to also render evident the broader social environment in which it occurs. The videotapes are transcribed as soon as possible after the recordings, usually within a week, aided by context notes and memory.

Kohitsuji Nursery School is located at the corner of a public housing project built by the Higashi Yamato City Council, in the northwestern part of Tokyo. The nursery is run by a Christian group, and its educational policy has a Christian basis. There are 110 children in the school, and they are divided into six age-groups, ranging from three-month-olds to six-year-olds. The children of each age-group are cared for and educated by four teachers, a scenario that is common throughout Tokyo. The daily schedule of the nursery varies according to the age-group of the children, their physical and mental state, the weather and other factors. The daily schedule for the three-year-olds might look something like this: arrival at the nursery at about 8:40; free activity until 9:20; morning service and group activity from 9:20 to 10:50; lunch and relaxation from 11:00 to 13:00; nap from 13:00 to 15:00; snack at 15:00; free activity until 17:00. The nursery makes a point of having a child-centred educational orientation so that the children can engage in activities freely and spend a relaxed and happy time while they are away from home. The nursery, however, does not have a systematic music education programme, although musical activities are integrated into the general educational programme. It includes hymn-singing during morning service and the singing of songs in the context of story-telling, games or musical exercises. As Table 5.1 shows, most of the songs that the teachers present to the children are in a Western style, as is common in many Japanese nursery schools. However, the children tend to sing the Western repertoire in a monotone that bears a closer resemblance to the fluctuations in the song text than to its melody (Fujita, 1994: 188–89).

At the time of writing, the project had been going on for three years. It began in April 1997, and during 1997 the 12 children in the youngest group were the focus of observation. Their ages ranged from three months to one year and five months. In 1998, there were 19 children in the group under observation, and their ages ranged from one year and two months to two years and two months. In 1999 there were 22 children in the group, ranging in age from two years and one month to three years and two months.

The musicality of Japanese toddlers

The observers documented the musical behaviour of both the children at the nursery and that of their teachers. Each instance was classified into one of two categories: it was either considered to be 'music' or an 'intermediate form'. The instances classed as 'music' included those forms of musical activity that would be regarded as musical performance by the wider Japanese society. The 'intermediate forms' would not normally be classed as music in Japan, although they stand between speech and song; this category includes such forms as calling, rhythmic speech, chanting and other such behaviours. Table 5.1 summarizes the instances of musical events that were documented over the three-year period of observation, and it indicates the number of times each type of event was observed in each age-group.

Table 5.1 shows that the most frequent type of musical activity involving the teachers was that in which there was 'rhythmic movement accompanied by music in a Western style'. However, when the children engaged in musical activity without an adult, the use of western style songs was relatively rare. On

Table 5.1　Children's musical activities at Kohitsuji Nursery School

	Type of musical activity	Children in their first year of life (1997)		Children in their second year of life (1998)		Children in their third year of life (1999)	
		Frequency of musical activities instigated by a teacher	Frequency of musical activities instigated by the children	Frequency of musical activities instigated by a teacher	Frequency of musical activities instigated by the children	Frequency of musical activities instigated by a teacher	Frequency of musical activities instigated by the children
Music	Rhythmic song and movement to western style music	'Omocha no cha cha cha' and other such songs — 91	0	'Te wo tatakimasho' and other such songs — 133	'Happy Birthday' and other such songs — 53	'Kyanpu da hoi' and other such songs — 129	'Omocha no cha cha' and other such songs — 41
	Rhythmic song and movement to Japanese style music	0	0	'Genkotsu-yama no Tanuki-san' and other such songs — 1	'Genkotsu-yama no Tanuki-san' and other such songs — 1	'Genkotsu-yama no Tanuki-san' and other such songs — 1	1
	Onomatopoeic melodies	0	0	0	'Obi pu pu pa pu' and other such songs — 14	0	'Dadda chikko' and other such songs — 15
	Commercial Music or TV songs	0	0	0	'Draemon no uta' and other such songs — 1	'Dango san kyodai' and other such songs — 7	'Dango san kyodai' and other such songs — 18
	Background Music	0	0	'Hataraku kuruma' and other such songs — 40	'Zo san' and other such songs — 6	0	'Dadda chikko' and other such songs — 0
	Subtotal	91	0	174	75	137	75

Intermediate forms between speech and song						
Traditonal game songs	'Inai inai ba' and other such songs — 38	0	'Yoi don' and other such songs — 30	'Inai inai ba' and other such songs — 23	'Mo ii kai' and other such songs — 6	'Akkanbe' and other such songs — 6
Phrases from commercial music uttered rhythmically	0	0	NEC Commercial Music, Okaimono — 1	0	0	0
Rhythmic utterances and movements	'Tsukushi san' and other such phrases — 38	'Basu basu' and other such phrases — 22	'Tanpopo san' and other such phrases — 180	'Janpu' and other such phrases — 90	'Sumire san' and other such phrases — 204	'Oshimai' and other such phrases — 107
Babbling or uttering of onomatopoeic words in rhythmic fashion	'Tan tan tan tan' and other such phrases — 45	'Po pon' and other such phrases — 420	'Wan wan wan' and other such phrases — 16	'Wa chi ton ton' and other such phrases — 133	0	'Buran buran' and other such phrases — 30
With rhythmic movement	Clapping hands to produce a pulse — 41	Clapping hands to music — 339	Clapping hands — 13	Pounding a table with the hands — 158	Pounding a table with the hands — 0	Pounding a table with the hands — 74
Subtotal	162	781	240	404	210	217

Note: A musical performance which occurred within a certain situation was counted as a single event, even though the same performance may have been repeated several times.

their own, the children were most frequently documented employing one of the intermediate musical forms. This suggests that if one is to understand how children acquire musical competence, it is necessary to investigate how children learn to perform the intermediate forms, and also to look at how they make the transition from rhythmic speech to song. In the following section I will outline the developmental trajectory that was observed in the nursery school. This trajectory indicates that the children begin by performing rhythmic movements, then start to engage in the production of rhythmic speech sequences and only then begin to develop the ability to perform more complex musical forms.

Musical performance among children in their first year of life

The musical activities of children between the ages of three months and one year and two months are very different from those of older children. As they are in a stage prior to language acquisition, their musical behaviour is all non-word-based, remaining limited to rhythmic movements and rhythmic babbling. Their playful vocalizations often display a clear rhythmic order of recurrent pulsations but do not contain a melodic order of fixed pitches with intervals.

During this period the children appear to gain considerable pleasure from shaking and beating on things, such as toys, tables, the floor, poles and other objects. When they were observed playing in the paddling pool, for instance, they often paddled the water surface with their hands and they repeatedly scooped up water in a cup, which they then poured back into the pool. Thus, many of their actions were repetitive and cyclical. It was also observed that whenever they explored new ways of moving, they listened carefully to the sounds that resulted from their action. Once a child had taken an interest in a movement or a sound, he or she concentrated his or her attention on it, then moved into action and tried to do it repeatedly. Through these explorations and rehearsals, the child would learn how to organize his or her actions and to render them in progressively more coordinated ways.

The descriptions above indicate that children engage intentionally and performatively in their own processes of music acquisition. They begin by taking an interest in the sounds which they have heard and they then make the actions that will produce them; they then repeat the actions over and over again, striving to achieve a refined sound. Recent studies into the ways in which children learn through interaction with their environment have begun to reveal the precision and refinement in the strategies that children employ in their own learning. Jerome Bruner, for example, has shed light on the intentionality involved in children's language acquisition, indicating that children make a deliberate effort to communicate. His research was undertaken within the playful setting of a child interacting with his mother during a game of 'peek-a-boo'. Bruner noted that there is a sequence to the toddler's language acquisition: the child begins by establishing sustained eye-to-eye contact and then singles out or touches a 'new' object, often accompanying the act with a proto-demonstrative such as 'da'; this is followed by a double consonant-vowel syllable such as 'bi-bi' or 'nana', and then 'ada'; from then on, the child moves step-by-step into conventional utterances (Bruner, 1983: 131). Swedish educator Marita Lindahl's doctoral research, *Experience and Learning* (1995), is one of the few projects on children's learning processes to have been undertaken in the pre-school context. She observed ten children between the ages of 13 and 20 months for a period of three months in their pre-school and demonstrated how they learn from their environment by monitoring their own actions. Her findings indicate that one-year-olds follow a particular learning sequence: first they grasp the purpose of the action, then they attempt to master their environment, focusing their attention on different phenomena in order to discern the world about them, discovering differences (Lindahl, 1995: 181–89). Although neither Bruner nor Lindahl were concerned with issues of cultural specificity in children's learning processes, they have demonstrated that the learning process of young children emerges through their negotiation with the environment. This suggests that the study of music acquisition should also be undertaken in natural settings. In what follows I will demonstrate how Japanese toddlers learn and develop their musical competence in interaction within the cultural setting that surround them, drawing on examples of musical performances that were observed during the research period.

In April, at the beginning of the observation period, none of the children in the group uttered actual words; they only produced babbling sounds. Once babbling had begun, they progressed rapidly into using these sounds as well as onomatopoeic words to produce rhythmic utterances. Their rhythmic babbling during this phase suggested that they were trying to talk or to sing. Shiori, for example, seemed to be trying to call a teacher when he made the sounds: 'wei we, wei we'; and he seemed to be attempting to imitate the singing of another person when he joined in with 'da, da, da'. Almost all the young children's utterances were accompanied by bodily movements. In the early days they generally performed gestures or movements of an impulsive sort in conjunction with their vocal sounds, but in time the movements became more intentional and well coordinated with the vocal sounds they were accompanying.

While processes of maturation are implicated in the stages through which young children progress to achieve musical competence, they also seem to acquire a sense of how to use their musical abilities in social interaction, as the following episode, recorded on 20 September 1998, suggests:

It was a very hot day when the teachers of the youngest age group decided to let the children play in the paddling pool. In the beginning, the toddlers remained silent, simply soaking in the paddling pool, but soon they began to play with the water; they slapped the water, they created showers with watering cans, and they played with the water in other ways. The teacher sprinkled water on each child's head, uttering the onomatopoeic word 'jah', which imitated the sound of the flowing water. Taishi, who was one year and two months at the time, responded to her by repeating the word, 'jah', in rhythmic co-ordination to the teacher's utterance.

On this day Taishi uttered the word 'jah' with considerable clarity. The first time Taishi had been observed uttering the word 'jah' was on 6 August, when he was playing in the paddling pool. On that day he only uttered it once, using a low voice. The episode above recounts the second instance in which he was observed uttering this word. Up until then, Taishi had only reacted to his teacher's use of 'jah' by stretching his hands forward to receive the water; when he had accompanied the hand movement with an utterance, it had been with the syllable 'dah'. Yet on this day, when the teacher poured the water onto his head saying, 'Hai, jah', Taishi responded by clearly saying 'jah' as he raised his right hand in high spirits. Then the teacher reiterated the word 'jah', this time using the same duration and tempo Taishi had used in saying the same word. To do this, both Taishi and the teacher synchronized their breathing cycles. Following this event, Taishi answered the teacher by saying 'jaah', prolonging the 'a' in the word. Once again the teacher responded by imitating the child, using the same duration as Taishi, yet again synchronizing her breathing cycle to his. As the two engaged repeatedly in this game, the more their utterances acquired metrical balance (see Figure 5.1.)

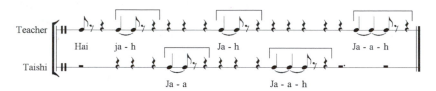

* The bracket indicates a single breathing cycle.

Figure 5.1   Rhythmic speech interaction between Taishi and the teacher

The teacher then gave her watering can to Taishi and said, 'Do it yourself, like this, jah', and she poured water on Taishi's head with another watering can, saying, 'Hai, jaah'. Then Taishi threw his watering can down and raised his hands up and responded 'jaah' in time to her actions.

I found it very moving to see how Taishi learned to say the word 'jah' in an interactive context with his teacher. Taishi uttered the word 'jah' within the comfort of a familiar environment in which he was experiencing the pleasurable sensations of feeling the water on his body and of seeing it being poured affectionately on him. It was within this setting that the teacher interjected with the word, 'jah', suggesting a relationship between the word and feelings of pleasure. Indeed, 'jah' became a means of communicating these feelings, and the vocal inflections the child and the teacher explored with one another allowed them to achieve a high degree of mutual coordination through the metrical synchronization of their breathing cycles. The interaction based around the word 'jah' generated feelings of joy for both child and adult, and the word provided them with a special vehicle through which to communicate these feelings to one another. Furthermore, the very musicality generated by the rhythmic quality of the successive interjections enhanced the pleasurable feelings surrounding the episode. In effect, the way in which Taishi and his carer engaged musically with one another highlights that which Blacking referred to as 'the special kind of social experience' which musical performance affords (Blacking, 1985a: 65). For people to perform together, they must attend closely to one another. Much of the pleasure that derives from musical performance is directly linked to this experience of mutual attendance and synchronization of the body amongst performers. It is, therefore, of particular interest that the social benefits of musical activity are experienced and explored by children from a very early age.

Musical performance among one-year-olds

When children reach the age of one, they begin to acquire a repertoire of words, but frequent babbling still persists. Thus, this new resource can now become a part of their musical behaviour, as in an episode observed amongst the one-year-olds on 20 April 1998:

> On this day the one-year-olds went to the park near the nursery school. The children were merrily playing in the sand or running about here and there as the fancy took them. Naoto (one year and ten months), who had only started walking about six months earlier, was now trying to run. He often fell down when he ran, for it was not easy for him to run because he was still in a nappy, but he did not give up trying. He ran to the bench about six meters ahead calling: 'pai yah, pai yah, pai yah, junbanko yo-h'. This phrase juxtaposes the babbling syllables 'pai yah' with the words '*junbanko yo*' (you must wait for your turn).

In this seemingly mundane act, Naoto produced a metrical sequence when he uttered the babbling syllables 'pai yah' in a single breathing cycle, which he repeated three times: 'pai yah, pai yah, pai yah'. He then proceeded to a lower level of metrical time unit, dividing the time unit of his breathing cycle into three units using the syllables 'pai-ya-h', as shown in Figure 5.2. Then he continued his performance by uttering the words '*junbanko yoh*', a phrase the teacher often said to the children. This phrase was twice as long as the breathing cycle he had employed in the previous phrases; yet it preserved the metrical beat previously established, although now he had divided his breathing cycle into six equal time units by grouping the syllables of the phrase.

In effect, the way in which Naoto produced the meter in his musical performance mirror's Blacking's explanation of the way in which Venda children create metrical order. For the Venda, he claimed that: 'Once the basic metre of [a] song has been established in the first word-pattern, or "line", the remainder of the text generally conforms to this pattern, and the number of syllables per "line" is controlled accordingly' (Blacking, 1967: 156).

Figure 5.2   Movement with rhythmic utterance in Naoto's performance

As shown in this example, when one-year-olds begin to run, they often accompany the movement of their legs with rhythmic babbling or words in their vocabulary. Other movements are also frequently accompanied by verbal sounds. This suggests that such rhythmic utterances are likely to aid the child in performing certain types of deliberate movement, just as the movements may aid in the production of the rhythmic vocal sounds.

As the children enhance their rhythmic skills, both verbally and bodily, they also become better able to use them in their interactions with other children. Thus, at around the age of one and a half, this resource begins to be used more and more frequently in child-to-child encounters. The following episode, which took place on 1 July 1998, documents such an interaction:

> The group of one-year-olds enjoyed playing with sand in the garden, and on this day they were covered with sand. Then the teachers started to wash the children's hands and legs one by one, before they entered their room. While the children were waiting their turn, Hideki (one year and nine months) and Shumpei (one year and five months), who were squatting down and facing each other, jumped up alternately calling 'poi', generating the rhythmic pattern of Figure 5.3.

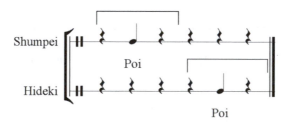

Figure 5.3   The musical interaction between Hideki and Shumpei

This episode shows how Hideki and Shumpei created well-defined rhythmic movements and utterances through their coordinated interaction with one another. They created the rhythmic movement together by imitating one another's utterance of the word '*poi*', synchronizing their breathing cycles. They both clearly enjoyed their performance, and an important source of their pleasure derived from the fact that they recognized that it was the outcome of their ability to produce well-balanced vocalizations and movements, in which each time unit was produced by a single breathing cycle which they had synchronized with one another to generate a shared rhythmic sequence. This example vividly shows how children communicate with one another and express their sense of well-being through musical performance. The activity was so enjoyable to both of them that they repeated it 30 times, stopping only when their teacher called out their names.

Musical performance among two-year-olds

The two-year-olds showed rapid progress in language acquisition. Almost all the children of this age-group were able to count rhythmically from one to ten. They expressed their feelings or opinions with two or more words uttered in a rhythmic fashion, as could be noted when Shiori made his position clear to another child: '*Shiori ga ichiban*' ('I am first'). The children were also observed engaging in communicative interaction with other members of their group using conventional teasing words, as when Nagisa rhythmically called out the teasing phrase, '*akkan be-*', as she pushed her cheeks down with her hands.

Children of this age take great interest in singing action songs. As part of their daily routine, the teacher let the children sing two or three kinds of action song that followed the principles of Western music. The children engaged enthusiastically in singing the songs and, by the age of two, they were usually able to generate a sufficiently convincing rendition of the rhythm of Western-style songs, although the melodic contour of the songs was disregarded; however, when they sang songs in a traditional Japanese style they could perform both the rhythm and the melody correctly. On 3 June 1999 the two-year-olds showed a marvellous ability in achieving a fluent performance of the action song '*Genkotsu yama no tanuki san*' ('The Baby Raccoon').

To introduce the song, the teacher told the story of the raccoon's family along with the song text of '*Genkotsu yama no tanuki san*' to the 18 two-year-olds, showing them paper puppets of father, mother and baby raccoon. Then she sang the song working the puppets rhythmically. The children took a great interest in the story, and they joined together to sing the song with the teacher for a total of six repetitions.

Genkotsu yama no tanuki san

The baby raccoon in the Genkotsu mountain

Genkotsu yama no tanuki san	The baby raccoon in the Genkotsu mountain
Oppai nonde nenne shite	Suckling and sleeping at the mother's breast
Dakko shite onbu shite mata ashita	Carried in the mother's arms then on her back, and saying bye-bye
Jan ken pon	(Call used for the game 'stone, paper, scissors')

The first time the teacher sang the song, the children concentrated on listening to her singing and on watching the gestures of the baby raccoon, and only three of the children joined the singing. The second and third times through, half the children began to sing, accompanying their singing with the gestures of the baby raccoon. The fourth time through, half the children stood up to sing the song, to which they now jumped. The more they sang the song, the more excited they became. They became especially enthusiastic each time the song reached the final phrase for the game of *janken* (stone, paper, scissors). By the fifth and sixth time the song was repeated, most of the children were standing and singing the song to the accompaniment of the gestures of the baby raccoon.

This example exemplifies a number of aspects involved in the way in which two-year-old child performers acquire their musical skills. In this instance they began by placing themselves within the story of the song text and then proceeded to perform the gestures of the baby raccoon in time to the teacher's singing, synchronizing their breathing cycle with hers. Next, they sang only the

* indicates that the pitch performed was lower than notated.

Figure 5.4   Shiori's performance of '*Genkotsu yama no tanuki san*'

last syllable of each phrase together with the teacher, and then they sang the whole song with her. This suggests that the last syllable of each phrase becomes prominent in the children's consciousness, because it marks the moment of their next inhalation.

The way in which the children organized their breathing to perform the song can be noted in Shiori's (three years and one month) perfomance (see Figure 5.4); she began to sing '*Genkotsu yama no tanuki san*' by herself immediately after her enthusiastic participation in the episode I have just described.

Shiori sang each song phrase in one single breathing cycle (bracket 1 in Figure 5.4), but she subdivided the basic time unit provided by the breathing cycle in various ways that assisted her in her performance. For the first line of the song she divided her breathing cycle into two equal time units, using the phrases '*genkotsu yama no*' and '*tanuki san*' (bracket 2). She further divided these phrases into two more equal time units, using the word units '*genkotsu*' and '*yama no*' for the first half of the phrase and '*tanukisa*' and '*n*' for the second half (bracket 3). These word units were also subdivided into equal units: '*gen*', '*kotsu*', '*yama*', '*no*' for the first half and '*tanu*', '*ki sa*', '*n*' for the second (bracket 4). Thus, she sang the song metrically by subdividing the basic time unit given by her breathing cycle into a hierarchical rhythmic order by grouping the words and syllables into ever smaller, but equal, units. The rhythmic order she was able to generate in this way is characteristic of Japanese speech patterns, in which all syllables are generally equal in duration.[3]

The observations conducted for this project suggest that two-year-olds are able to sing this particular song because its melodic contour follows that of the speech tones of its text.[4] Indeed, other traditional children's songs in which the melody is related to the contour of the text are also easier for two-year-olds to sing than those without this characteristic. The texts of traditional children's songs suggest that many of them may have originated from children's rhythmic speech games. It is likely, therefore, that the song melodies were produced through transformations of the speech games, generating a genre of traditional Japanese children's songs with close links to the tonal patterns of children's rhythmic speech commonly found in 'intermediate forms' of musical activity, namely those that lie between speech and song.

A common feature of many traditional Japanese children's songs is that their melodic contours are more directly connected with rhythmic speech than with ordinary speech. This suggests that the transition from speech to song takes place through rhythmic speech. Thus, the 'intermediate forms' provide a key to explaining how the melodies of children's songs are influenced by speech-tone fluctuation. With respect to the relationship between speech tone and Venda children's songs, Blacking claimed that '[t]he melodies of the children's songs [were] never slavish imitation of speech-tone, but both they and their rhythms [tended] to be influenced by its fluctuations' (Blacking, 1967: 167). Based on the observations conducted at the nursery school, it appears that children move fluently between speech, rhythmic speech and song. The children found it easy to switch from speech to song and vice versa because both speech and song employ a form of musical expression that is common to both modes of verbal communication.

Conclusion

In this chapter I have attempted to provide a detailed account both of the ways in which young Japanese children acquire musical proficiency and of the sequence involved in their musical development within the context of their daily life. This sequence could be summarized as follows:

1. Children under one year of age engage in considerable non-word-based musical activity, involving repetitive action and vocalizations, such as rhythmic movements and babbling.
2. One-year-olds often produce rhythmic movements and rhythmic utterances of words and other vocal sounds. Their movements are often accompanied by rhythmic utterances. They show great interest in making rhythmic utterances and movements in response to the actions of other children.
3. Two-year-olds take a great interest in performing action songs, and they have developed techniques to assist them in learning to perform such songs. They begin by mastering the action sequences of the song, which assist them in controlling their breathing; then they sing the endings of each phrase in the song at the appropriate moment, which triggers the next inhalation; and finally they sing all of the phrases of the song.
4. Children between the ages of three months and two years show remarkable development in terms of the acquisition of musical competence that run parallel to their language acquisition and their physical growth. All of the children, even those as young as three months of age, actively engage in forms of behaviour that require the organization of movement and vocalizations in musical ways.
5. Children draw on their repertoire of 'musical forms of expression' – that is, the framework of their music-making – to engage in vocal behaviour and movement patterns that are coherent with their immediate emotions and feelings. To do this, they first synchronize their breathing cycle with others, and then they organize their movements or utterances according to the characteristics of the sound structure of the Japanese language.

This research project was strongly influenced by John Blacking's perspective on the musicality of the human species, and it has demonstrated that the ways in which Japanese toddlers engage in musical activity is deeply connected with the development of speech competence. Through their daily expressive and communicative interactions with others, they assimilate the 'forms of musical expression' that define the culturally-specific principles of music-making, but they also assimilate a sense of the appropriate contexts for musical performance. In time, they become progressively more able to control their movements and vocalizations, both rhythmically and melodically, thereby enhancing their musical competence.

As Blacking noted from his observation of the musical performances of the Venda children, this project also indicates that all normal Japanese children are musical, and their musicality reveals itself in their daily activities. Furthermore, children have developed their own mechanisms to acquire their musical skills, and these techniques challenge many of the pedagogical tenets underlying programmes of music education. Their musical competence is acquired through their spontaneous engagement with forms of musical expression that are deeply connected with the speech patterns of the Japanese language, rather than through processes involving the abstract assimilation of musical elements, such as rhythmic and melodic patterns found in musical works.

Recently increasing attention in the field of music education has been given to the study of the intuitive ways in which children acquire their musical skills, and many of these projects have been inspired by Blacking's perspectives on human musicality (see Fujita, 1990; Young, 1995; Mang, 2000). The findings of these investigations show that the strategies young children deploy in processes of music acquisition are deeply connected with their speech development, and therefore they are marked by both cultural and biological factors. Blacking pioneered research into the intrinsic nature of human musicality and its interaction with the cultural environment. Further research on the music-making of children in a wide range of different cultures may bring us closer to an understanding of the biological foundations of human musicality. Undoubtedly, such understanding is likely to have a significant impact on current thinking in music education.

Acknowledgements

I wish to thank the children and staff of Kohitsuji Nursery School, and the member of my music education seminar in Kunitachi College of Music who assisted me with the observational research. I would also like to thank Dr Suzel Reily for her assistance with the English of this text. Through her kind suggestions and help on an earlier manuscript, I was able to deepen and give shape to the ideas I wished to communicate in this chapter.

Notes

[1] Arima claimed that *fushi* can be understood as a Japanese equivalent to the ancient Greek concept of *nomos* and the European Medieval concepts of *Weise* or *Ton* (see Ebisawa, 1987: 173–74; Fujita, 2003: 65–67), as these terms indicate the use of fixed melodic and rhythmic patterns that function as the basis of performance.

[2] I have defined the distinction between musical performance and ordinary performance following a proposal put forward by S.F. Nadel (1930: 531–46; see also Fujita, 1989: 47–49).

[3] The Japanese language is commonly held to be a tone-language, with lexically significant, contrastive but relative pitches on each syllable (Pike, 1948: 3), and it has a strong tendency for each syllable to be of the same duration. Linguists indicate these relative pitches by the following sign, *hana* (a flower) or *koneko* (a kitten).

[4] For example, the first phrase of the song '*Genkotsu yama no tanuki san*' is pronounced '*Genkotsu yama no tanuki san*' (horizontal line indicates the higher tone). When the phrase is sung, the relative pitch relation is maintained as shown in Figure 5.4. There is an established theory of the tonal system of '*Warabeuta*' ('traditional Japanese children's song') that was developed by Fumio Koizumi. He explained that the tonal patterns of traditional Japanese children's songs are categorized into two- to four-note melodies, and that each melody has one or two *kaku on* ('nuclea note') (Koizumi, 1960: 107–14). According to this theory, the song '*Genkotsu yama no tanuki san*' is categorized as a four-note melody, composed of: a major second, followed by a major second, followed by a minor third. The final note is the lowest note or the fourth above it.

CHAPTER SIX

John Blacking and the 'Human/ Musical Instrument Interface': Two Plucked Lutes from Afghanistan

John Baily

Blacking's early insights

John Blacking had a long-standing interest in what he later came to term 'the biology of music making'.[1] The roots of this lay in his undergraduate training in anthropology and archaeology at the University of Cambridge. Physical anthropology was an important part of the syllabus. His wife, Zureena Desai, later played an influential role in supporting and informing his interest in the biological aspects of music and dance; she qualified as a doctor in South Africa and was later awarded a PhD in the Faculty of Medicine at Queen's University Belfast.

In two early papers, published in *African Music*, on the Butembo flute and the Nsenga *kalimba* Blacking developed some seminal ideas about the relationship between music structures and the human body. Concerning the Butembo flute, Blacking found that the music was constructed from repeated patterns of fingering, which, coupled with varying degrees of overblowing to obtain upper partials, seemed to generate the melodic sequences of the tunes. He suggested that the shape of the music was influenced by the spatial properties of the instrument (Blacking, 1955). In the case of the *kalimba*, he found that:

> The most significant common factors of the *kalimba* tunes are not their melodic structures, but the recurring patterns of 'fingering' which, combined with different patterns of polyrhythm between the two thumbs, produce a variety of melodies ... [The] tunes ... are variations on a theme, but the theme is physical and not purely musical. (Blacking, 1959b: 6)

From these examples came Blacking's idea that certain aspects of music structure are 'rooted in the human body'. This phrase is actually a very good example of Blacking's ambiguity of expression. Music is obviously 'rooted in the body', in the sense that music requires ears to hear, hands and vocal parts to move, and brains to facilitate these processes. But Blacking obviously meant more than that. He was interested in showing how musical structures are shaped by the interaction between the morphology of a musical instrument and the human body, with its physical structure, physiological control systems, and psychological information-processing capacities.

When I first met Blacking in 1972 I found these to be exciting ideas because they corresponded to certain insights about music-making derived from my own background in experimental psychology.[2]

Responding to visual targets

Responding to visual targets, such as reaching for objects or pointing at them, is one of those highly complex actions which we tend to take for granted as part of our coordinated biological make-up, but it is in fact a highly intelligent process. It is part of the way we think in movement, in a 'non-ego centred mode of thought', by which I mean there is no inner voice that verbalizes what to do and how to do it. Here we encounter the 'thinking body' in the exercise of normal spatially coordinated behaviour. The efficient exercise of this capacity is in itself positively rewarding: skilled action is inherently pleasurable for the performer.

When I first met Blacking I had recently completed a DPhil on human spatial perception and motor control. As a graduate student at the University of Sussex I had constructed an elaborate (and rather sinister) apparatus to measure the accuracy of pointing at visual targets when the hand itself could not be seen. The apparatus also allowed one to time the duration of pointing movements, to contrast between fast 'ballistic' movements, in which all decisions about the movement are made in advance, and slow 'feedback controlled' movements (see Figure 6.1).

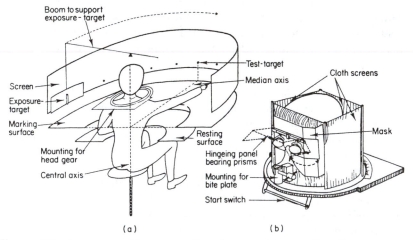

Figure 6.1   Apparatus for measuring visuo-motor coordination

The apparatus included a motor-driven trolley which allowed a human 'subject' (the language is interesting) to point at a target without using the muscles of the arm. Foot switches controlled the left–right movements of the extended arm, and another switch allowed the subject to mark the final position of pointing (see Figure 6.2).

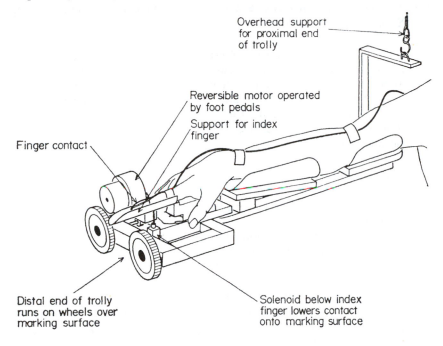

Overhead support
for proximal end
of trolly

Reversible motor operated
by foot pedals

Support for index
finger

Finger contact

Distal end of trolly
runs on wheels over
marking surface

Solenoid below index
finger lowers contact
onto marking surface

Figure 6.2   The passive arm mover

My research involved disturbing the normal relationships between movement and visual perception by 'transforming the visual input' – having people view their arms through a wedge prism which moved everything visually 15° to one side, so that the arm was seen to be in one place and felt (kinaesthetically) to be somewhere else. Pointing behaviour is initially systematically disturbed in this situation but quickly adapts under the appropriate conditions. When the prism is removed and the transformation ends there is again a disturbance in coordination, but now in the opposite direction (Baily, 1972a and b). This sort of research in the 1960s was relevant to early space flight and the issue of human movement under gravity-free conditions. Richard Held at MIT, for example, had argued on the basis of such experiments that human sensorimotor coordination would gradually break down in the absence of gravity. Eventually, he believed, the human sensori-motor system would become totally disorientated and incapable of effective action. These predictions have, of course, proved incorrect. The human capacity to move effectively in the condition of weightlessness is, though, truly remarkable.

'Reading around' my subject in the library of Sussex University I discovered Bruno Nettl's *Theory and Method in Ethnomusicology* (1964) and must have been profoundly influenced by reading Nettl's comments on a passage from Curt Sachs. Sachs had stated:

> The original concepts of vocal and of instrumental music are utterly different. The instrumental impulse is not melody in a 'melodious' sense, but an agile movement of the hands which seems to be under the control of a brain center totally different from that which inspires vocal melody. ... Quick motion is not merely a means to a musical end but almost an end in itself ... the vocal and the instrumental expressions of a tribe are never one in style. They shape two separate arts. (Sachs, 1962: 110)

Nettl commented:

> While we need not accept this theory as applying to all cultures, we must agree that the instrumental and vocal styles of a people often differ greatly. One reason, of course, is the structure of the instruments. *The kinds of things which the human hands can do with an instrument, the kinds of things which random play will emit, may shape the style to a large extent.* (Nettl, 1964: 209, emphasis added)

Nettl's book also directed my attention to Mantle Hood's article 'The Challenge of "Bi-musicality"' which argued that the student of non-Western music should not bypass basic musicianship in the music culture in question, and specifically mentioned acquiring the capacity to hear intervals correctly, and developing memory span in learning pieces aurally. I saw a way of extending my expertise in human sensorimotor coordination into an area in which I had a strong interest as an amateur 'folk, jazz and blues' performer.

After finishing my DPhil I soon had the chance to put these ideas into practice. In 1971 I spent several months in Kathmandu, Nepal, and began, under the tutelage of two young Nepalese graduates of the Bhatkhande College in Lucknow, a practical study of North Indian music which proved invaluable in my later work in Afghanistan. I started to learn to play the tabla, and while I never became a very competent tabla player, I was fascinated by the learning process itself and how it related to my studies of motor skill. Acquiring this new skill allowed me to experience in a very direct way much of what I had read concerning motor learning, the grouping of initially separate components, programming, attention processes and routinization. The tabla tutor that I wrote based on this experience (Baily 1974) explained some of these insights, and put forward some innovative ideas about the verbal representations of movement patterns.

The work with Blacking

This interest in the movement processes underlying musical products was Blacking's and my initial point of contact and a matter on which we agreed to collaborate. We applied to the Social Science Research Council for funding to look at three types of long-necked lute that I had already observed in Afghanistan: the *dutar*, *dambura* and *tanbur*. The SSRC turned down the proposal but invited a resubmission. Eventually we were awarded an SSRC Post-Doctoral Research Fellowship for a project entitled 'A Cross-cultural Study of Music Skills'. According to the abstract of the research application:

> It is proposed to make a cross-cultural study of the music skills involved in playing two types of lute, the Herati <u>dutar</u> and the Irish <u>fiddle</u>. The two music skills will be compared in terms of: (a) the organization of motor patterns in the playing techniques, (b) the acquisition and transmission of the skill, and (c) the social/cultural structures which support the skill. It is hoped to discover how social and cultural factors act upon 'natural' patterns of hand movement and shape the structure of skilled performance.

It is worth reproducing the introductory statement to our proposed investigation because it shows a good deal about the very 'scientific' and highly structuralist approach we were adopting to the study of what we called 'field skills':

> Man's ability to use his hands in a skilful manner to manipulate the environment and to engage in complex operations is one of his most important capacities, and has been a crucial factor in his physical and cultural evolution. This important area of human behaviour has received a good deal of attention from experimental psychologists and others, who have employed a variety of abstract laboratory tasks to isolate and investigate many of the component processes underlying skilled performance. Man, however, is not a laboratory animal, and the laboratory approach hardly does justice to the complexity and richness of the skilled behaviour which he exhibits in his normal everyday life. We will term such everyday skilled activities <u>field</u> skills.
>
> There are two main features of a field skill. Firstly, at the behaviourial level, the skill consists of a basic set of component actions. These make up the motor vocabulary of the skill. The range of possible component actions available to man is large, but the vocabulary of a particular skill consists of a rather limited set drawn from this. Through grouping and sequential ordering, these component actions are elaborated into the motor patterns which are characteristic of the skill. In other words, the component actions of a particular skill are organized into a certain type of structure, which is determined by a set of <u>structural</u> <u>rules</u>. The motor patterns characteristic of the skill are, in a sense, generated from these structural rules. The isolation and definition of its structural rules should be one of the main objectives in the analysis of a field skill.

The second feature of a field skill is that there are a variety of social and cultural factors which impinge upon its performance. These factors determine not only when and where the skilled activity is performed, but how it is performed. They may have a profound effect in shaping the motor patterns which may be observed at the behaviourial level. For this reason, the structure of a field skill cannot be fully appreciated without considering its social and cultural environment. The structural rules underlying a field skill will, to some extent, reflect constraints imposed by gross anatomy, neural wiring within the sensori-motor system, and the psychological processes underlying skilled performance, but they will also reflect social and cultural constraints. It is evident that even such basic activities as walking, standing, sitting and reaching are influenced by social and cultural factors. This influence is more obvious when we consider patterns of movement such as gestures and facial expressions which serve a communicative function. It is difficult to discover what man's 'natural' patterns of movement are until these social and cultural influences on body movement and posture have been estimated.

At present, we can only guess at the impact of social and cultural processes on complex manipulative skills. This problem calls for a cross-cultural study of elaborate and highly structured field skills, in which we try to relate inter-cultural variations in skilled performance with processes in the social/cultural environments. This is the general orientation of the research proposed here. (Blacking and Baily, 1973: 9–10)

The grant application went on to argue that music provides a very profitable area for the study of the organization of motor patterns in skilled manipulative behaviour and outlined one of the key elements of our approach, which was to look at the relationships between the morphology of a musical instrument, the motor patterns which characterize its performance technique, and the structure of the music produced. Whereas Blacking had had the intuitions, I felt that I had the technical knowledge of experimental psychology to analyse more systematically what was going on at the 'human/musical instrument interface'.

In the event, the cross-cultural element of the research was not addressed, for the research on the Irish fiddle was never carried out. The work in Afghanistan had proved very productive. The necessary contrast with the long-necked lute, the *dutar*, was provided by another musical instrument which I found in Afghanistan, the *rubab* (see Figures 6.3 and 6.4).

The *rubab* and the *dutar*

The *rubab* is a short necked double-chambered waisted lute, with three main strings and sets of drone and sympathetic strings. It is the national instrument of Afghanistan and played in many parts of the country, being especially important in the music of Kabul. The *dutar* is a long-necked lute with 10 or 11 sympathetic strings, with tuning pegs along the neck, and is associated

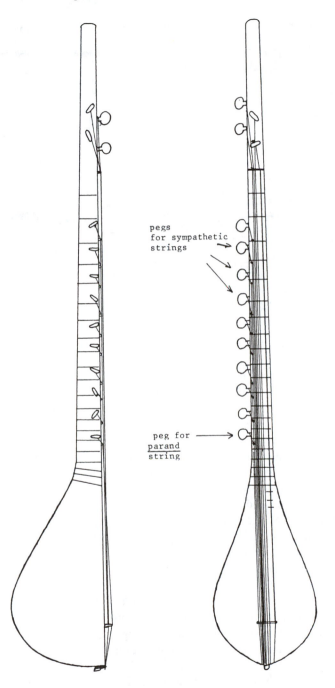

Figure 6.3 The 14-stringed Herati *dutar*

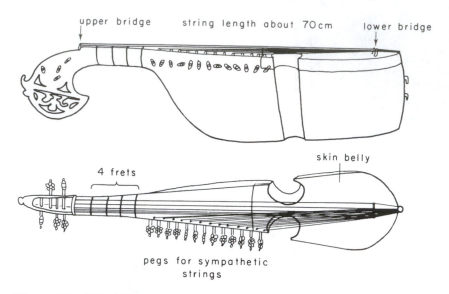

upper bridge   string length about 70 cm   lower bridge

4 frets

skin belly

pegs for sympathetic
strings

Figure 6.4   The Afghan *rubab*

principally with the city of Herat, in western Afghanistan. The 14-stringed
dutar is not an old instrument. It was devised in the early 1960s in order to
adapt the long-necked lute of Herat so that it could play the repertoire of the
rubab, and to allow the Heratis' local instrument to participate in the urban
ensemble of Kabuli music, with the singer accompanied by the hand-blown
harmonium, tabla, *rubab* and other chordophones (Baily, 1976).

The *rubab*'s repertoire embraces a variety of genres. For Afghans, perhaps
the most highly valued *rubab* music is the four-part, or extended, instrumental
piece (*naghma-ye chartuk* or *naghma-ye kashal* – see Baily (1997) for a
collection of such pieces). Figure 6.5 shows a notation for one such piece, in
Rag Kumaj. The notation illustrates the following points about much *rubab*
music: it is melodic rather than harmonic, there is a tendency towards step-wise
scalar melodic movement framed within the octave (similar in many respects to
North Indian music structure), and melodies are constructed around 16-unit
metric cycles. The physical changes made to the *dutar* allowed it to play pieces
of this kind effectively.

We now look at the *rubab* and the *dutar* as keyboards, with which the left
hand of the player interacts. The *rubab* has a fretted range of a nineth, and the
frets are arranged to give an approximately tempered tuning with 12 semitones
to the octave. The *dutar* has a somewhat greater fretted ambitus, extending to a
fourth below the pitch generally taken as tonic. The tuning of the *dutar* is an
octave higher than the *rubab*. From the point of view of left-hand movements
the crucial difference between the two instruments is that whereas the notes on

Figure 6.5 *Naghma-ye kashal* in *Rag Kumaj*

the *rubab* are laid out on three strings, which I call a tiered array, the same notes (an octave higher) are laid out on the *dutar* in a single row, which I call a linear array. The layout of note positions is shown in Figure 6.6, using the *sargam* notation system used by many Afghan musicians. It will be argued that the way in which note positions are laid out, which depends on the morphology of the instrument, has a powerful shaping influence on performance.

Research methods

In retrospect I realize that, from the outset, my methodology relied heavily on learning to perform as a mode of research. But it is a curious fact that no

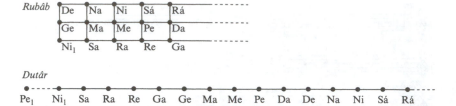

Figure 6.6   The layout of notes on the *rubab* and the *dutar*

mention of this was made in the SSRC grant application. It is as if in the 1970s such an approach might have been deemed to be insufficiently 'scientific' by the SSRC and other funding bodies. Learning to perform was to be regarded as a side-issue, a bonus, but not something to be entertained seriously. Even Hood (1960), in discussing 'the challenge of bi-musicality' did not advocate learning to perform as a method of research: his argument was simply that training in basic musicianship is fundamental to any kind of musical scholarship. Today, I have an entirely different view of the matter and regard learning to perform as a central pillar of ethnomusicological inquiry (Baily, 2001).

I approached learning to play the *dutar* and the *rubab* as a guitarist with an interest in performing modal music, especially North Indian classical music. Nine months before starting my first year of fieldwork in Herat I had obtained a three-stringed *dutar* and made recordings of three *dutar* players in Herat, and used these recordings, plus my own visual observations of the *dutar* players, to teach myself to play. I later discovered that, in some ways, this was not unlike the way most *dutar* players learned, at least initially, through observation and private experimentation (Doubleday and Baily, 1995). Once based in Herat I received more formal instruction from two outstanding *dutar* players, Gada Mohammad and Abdul Karim Herawi (popularly known as Karim Dutari), the acknowledged inventor of the 14-stringed *dutar*.

In due course, as laid down in the SSRC proposal, I constructed a sample of 15 *dutar* players, covering players of both three- and 14-stringed instruments, and looking at three levels of skill (learners, established performers, virtuosos). For the purposes of comparison I recorded them playing a repertoire of five well-known tunes and also filmed the left-hand movements of ten of the musicians playing these pieces in order to investigate patterns of fingering. Thirteen of the 15 *dutar* players also participated in extended recorded interviews.

My approach to the *rubab* was much less systematic. The *rubab* was never intended to be an object of special research but, having encountered the instrument, I was keen to learn to play it. In this I was greatly assisted by two months of lessons in Kabul with Ustad Mohammad Omar, Afghanistan's greatest *rubab* player of recent times. This gave me the basic technique and also introduced me to the type of piece known as *naghma-ye chartuk* (or *naghma-ye kashal*) which was very important in understanding the 'classical' repertoire of the *rubab*. When I moved to Herat I received no further lessons but made a number of recordings, especially of Rahim Khushnawaz, which I used as a source for learning.

My research on the human/musical instrument interface was therefore quite different to that of Blacking. His analyses of Butembo flute and Nsenga *kalimba* music were made from outside, whereas my analyses of the *dutar* and the *rubab* were conducted from the inside, from the perspective of the practical performer grappling with the instruments in question. In that sense I was using myself as an object of investigation. While this approach might seem unduly subjective I was aware that the nineteenth-century polymath scientist Herman von Helmholtz made many of his important discoveries in acoustics and optics through using himself as an experimental 'subject' (Helmholtz, 1967). I knew about his work from my wedge prism experiments. My fieldnotes show that many of my intuitions about the *rubab* and the *dutar* came quite early on in my research, when I was struggling to learn to play these instruments. Now, having played them for 30 years, I am even more certain that the analysis offered below is correct.

Interactions at the interface

The results of the comparison between the *rubab* and the *dutar* are discussed here under three headings:

- the perception of the spatial layout of the keyboard
- how the left hand and its fingers move in relation to the keyboard
- how the right hand activates the melody string(s) to vibrate.

Mapping the Modes

One way of looking at performance on lutes like the *rubab* and the *dutar* is to propose that, in playing a melody, the player generates a sequence of spatial targets and responds to them in turn. The targets are the note positions, the places where you put your fingers to 'stop' the strings. As a keyboard, the tiered array of the *rubab* is an easier spatial framework with which to operate because spatial information is encoded in two dimensions rather than in one.

For example, a very common melodic mode played on both the *rubab* and the *dutar* is *Bairami*, similar in some respects to the Phrygian or E mode. Figure 6.7 shows how the note positions are laid out on the tiered array of the *rubab* and the linear array of the *dutar*.

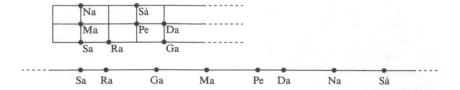

Figure 6.7   The layout of notes for *Bairami* on the *rubab* and the *dutar*

It is easier to 'place' these note positions on the tiered array of the *rubab* than on the linear array of the *dutar*, in the sense of identifying where the notes are located and responding accurately to them. In practical terms, this means that, on the *dutar*, one is more likely to make mistakes – for example, by 'taking' the wrong note. To avoid errors one has to play more slowly on the *dutar* than on the *rubab*, and to concentrate more on the technical placement of each note. The difficulty in locating note positions is compounded by the fact that many different modes are played on the *rubab*, and these often involve different configurations of note positions (Baily, 1981). Consider the note positions for the modes shown in Figure 6.8.

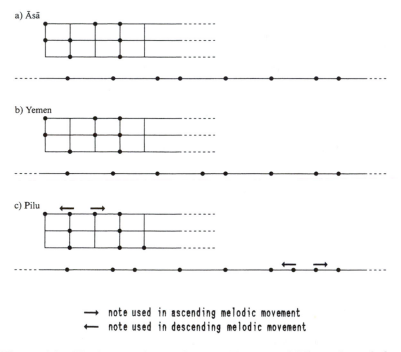

→ note used in ascending melodic movement
← note used in descending melodic movement

Figure 6.8   The layout of notes for *Asa, Yemen* and *Pilu* on the *rubab* and the *dutar*

The different configurations which characterize the various modes are more easily remembered on the two dimensional layout of the tiered array of the *rubab* than on the one-dimensional linear array of the *dutar*. The latter is the more confusing layout with which to work.

In learning to play instruments like the *rubab* and the *dutar*, visual information is very important, and there is no doubt that the keyboard is initially represented cognitively in terms of visual positions in a visual framework. As motor learning proceeds, over a long period of time, the note positions become represented in a more abstract spatial framework that can be apprehended in visual, aural, kinaesthetic and motor terms. But it seems that the *dutar* remains strongly reliant on visual information, as shown by the fact that performance is dramatically disturbed by blindfolding the player.

Finger versus hand movements

A second, but not unrelated, factor concerns the relative accuracy and speed of finger and hand movements. To play an ascending or descending octave scale (that is, a sequence of eight notes framed within the octave) on the *rubab* usually requires only finger movements. The notes required 'fall under the fingers'. In this respect playing the *rubab* is like playing in the first position on the violin – a position which is characteristic of much folk fiddling. In contrast, playing the same scale patterns on the *dutar* requires considerable hand, rather than finger, movements. Changes in the position of the hand are achieved through shoulder and elbow movements. There is a greater demand for visual information to control these movements, whereas finger movements can proceed mainly under kinaesthetic control. Further, finger movements are generally faster and more accurate than hand movements.

The difference between the *rubab* and the *dutar* illustrates the principle of what psychologists used to call stimulus–response compatibility, in the sense of there being a 'good fit' between the layout of a keyboard or control panel and the movements required in dealing with that active surface. The various scalar patterns embodied within the music are more compatible with the tiered array of the *rubab* than with the linear array of the *dutar*. Indeed, it seems very likely that compositions of the *naghma-ye chartuk* (*naghma-ye kashal*) type were originally composed by *rubab* players.

This conclusion about compatibility receives further support when we consider the original *dutar*, from which the 14-stringed instrument developed between 1950 and 1965 (Baily, 1976). The word *dutar* means 'two strings', and the older form of *dutar* was just that, with two strings made of silk or gut, usually tuned a fourth apart. The music played on that kind of *dutar* was structured within tetrachords rather than within octaves, and performance required sequencing rather than playing scalar passages. A very simple example of a sequenced melody is shown in Figure 6.9.

Figure 6.9   Typical sequenced melody

At the level of action, the typical movement pattern for the left hand was to operate in a descending sequence of hand positions, where the fingers operate at each position in 'cluster patterns', using the first, second and third fingers (Baily, 1985: 253), as shown in Figure 6.10.[3]

Figure 6.10   Use of three fingers on the two-stringed *dutar*

Right hand patterns

So far we have discussed the player's left hand. The right hand raises different issues. Both the *rubab* and the *dutar* are played *punteado*, single-string style, with a plectrum. On the *rubab* there is a marked disparity between the downstroke and the upstroke, arising in part from the strongly flexed right-hand position (see Figure 6.11).

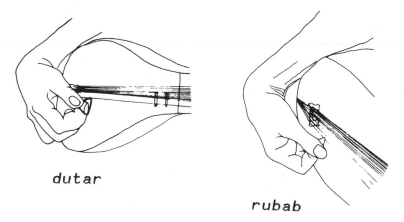

dutar

rubab

Figure 6.11   Right-hand positions for the *dutar* and the *rubab*

The downstroke is strong, with added percussion from the hand itself hitting the skin belly of the instrument as the plectrum strikes the strings. The upstroke is much weaker in amplitude, and acoustically thinner, with no skin sound. Downstroke and upstroke sound very different, and this disparity allows one to create a rich variety of rhythmic patterns by sequencing these two elements according to a simple set of rules when playing the *rubab* (Baily, 1990a, 1991b).

The *rubab*'s complex right-hand technique has been transferred to the *dutar*. Again, the downstroke is stronger and more percussive than the upstroke. The metal plectrum tends to click on the *dutar*'s wooden belly on the downstroke. But now the *dutar* has the advantage in ergonomic terms, since the right hand has to deal with only one melody string rather than with three. This avoids making cross-movements taking the plectrum from one string to another that are required on the *rubab*. In particular, the single melody string of the *dutar* eliminates the technical problem of changing strings after a downstroke and before an immediately succeeding upstroke, which involves interpolating an extra lateral movement between the two (Baily, 1991b: 158).

Conclusions from the comparison between the *rubab* and the *dutar*

The work that I carried out in collaboration with Blacking on the *rubab* and the *dutar* served to identify a number of factors operating at the interface between the human sensorimotor system and a musical instrument. It showed some of the ways in which the interaction between human body and instrument is connected with the structure of the music produced. The research also made us aware of some other factors that need to be taken into consideration:

1. Musical styles vary widely with respect to the degree to which the characteristic motor patterns of their performance techniques embody the constraints imposed by the morphology of the instrument and use movements and sequences of movements that are intrinsically easy for the human sensorimotor system to organize. However, the constraints inherent in a particular spatial layout may be transcended to varying degrees. Baily (1977) argued that the transformation of the Herati *dutar* from a two-stringed instrument of rural folk music to a 14-stringed instrument of urban art and popular music was accompanied by a *decrease* in compatibility and an *increase* in the skill required to play it (measurable in terms of length of time to reach the socially accepted level of musicianly performance).

2. The demonstration of the ergonomic relationships leaves unanswered the question of whether the instrument shapes the music or is selected because it fits pre-existing music. In the case of the 14-stringed *dutar*, the

instrument was modified to equip it to play a repertory seemingly developed with reference to another instrument, the *rubab*. This was, of course, new music for the *dutar*. The alternative possibility, that the instrument shapes the music, would have been more interesting, showing how new music may arise from discovering new ways of moving in relation to the instrument. This idea is implicit in the quote from Nettl (1964: 209) cited earlier in this chapter (see also the quote from Jimi Hendrix in Baily and Driver, 1992: 67).

3. Cases where we can identify a particular instrument exclusively with one kind of music are perhaps somewhat rare. Theories about a close relationship between a morphology and a music run into two kinds of complication:

    (a) Instruments with very different morphologies are used in many societies to play the same music, often brought together in a single ensemble (for example, Irish music, or Iranian music);

    (b) certain instruments, such as the violin, the accordion and the guitar, are used to play a range of very different kinds of music around the world.

4. With respect to the first issue, it remains the case that special relationships between instruments and their music are recognized. One speaks of a 'piper's tune', or of a 'fiddle tune' in Irish music, indicating that these pieces have characteristics which adapt them specially well to the instrument in question. With respect to the second issue, there is clearly a need for cross-cultural studies of instruments such as the violin, accordion and guitar to see how the same morphology is used in radically different ways. A pioneering study of this kind is the analysis of folk blues guitar-playing carried out by Baily and Driver (1992).[4]

The results of the research in Afghanistan were presented at the ASA Conference convened by Blacking in 1975 at Queen's University Belfast on 'The Anthropology of the Body' and published in the conference proceedings (Baily, 1977). The approach to the human/musical instrument interface that Blacking and I pioneered has been adopted by a few other ethnomusicologists, although progress in this potentially fruitful area of cognitive ethnomusicology is hampered by the fact that few ethnomusicologists have any training in experimental psychology.[5] Three studies are worth special mention. Jonathan Stock (1993) has offered an analysis of Chinese *erhu* playing which embodies some of the principles described above. Risto Pekka Pennanen, in his PhD thesis (Pennanen, 1999) has done something similar for the Greek *bouzouki*. Olga Velichkina, in her PhD thesis (Velichkina, 1998), has applied similar ideas to women's panpipe playing in Southern Russia.

Blacking saw ethnomusicology as developing on a broad front, in which its practitioners sought, according to their own individual skills and interests, to 'identify all processes that are relevant to an explanation of musical sound' (Blacking, 1973: 17). What goes on at the body–instrument interface is just one piece of that complex jigsaw that we call music, and Blacking understood the contribution that experimental psychology could make to further our knowledge and understanding of this supreme mystery.

Notes

[1] The term 'biology of music making' was borrowed by Blacking from The Biology of Music Making Inc, a group of medical practitioners in the USA with a strong interest in music. The group organized three international conferences. Blacking attended the second of these, held in Denver in 1987, as a member of the panel convened by Helen Myers on Children's Music (Blacking, 1990).

[2] I first met Blacking in Belfast in 1972, soon after he had been appointed to the Chair of Social Anthropology at Queen's University Belfast. See Baily (1994) for further details.

[3] This 'three-finger three-component action' style of performance is typical of the two Persian long-necked lutes, the *tar* and the *sehtar*.

[4] Bennett and Dawe (2001) offer important insights into the guitar as an instrument of global performance.

[5] The Music Department of Ohio State University is one of the few places where cognitive ethnomusicology is being nurtured. However, it is clear that important insights into the issues discussed here can be had by those without special training in psychology. For example, Bell Yung wrote a very interesting paper on choreographic and kinaesthetic elements in performance on the Chinese seven-string zither as a result of learning to perform on the instrument (see Yung, 1984).

CHAPTER SEVEN

Experiencing the Ballet Body: Pleasure, Pain, Power

Helena Wulff

John Blacking was a pioneer in identifying the body as a focus for anthropological inquiry. His approach to the body placed special attention on dance as a form of non-verbal communication and a medium for creating exceptional bodily experiences for both performers and spectators.[1] In particular, Blacking argued that, in dance, body and mind are ideally united (Blacking, 1977a: 23). His writings have been followed by a growing set of works in a number of disciplines that focus on the body as a site of culture (Turner, 1984; Featherstone et al., 1991) and processes of embodiment (Csordas, 1994a).[2] A major contribution of this line of inquiry is its critique of the classic Cartesian view that posits a separation between body and mind, and prioritizes the mind. Although experiences of the integration of body and mind may indeed be attained during dancing, I shall argue that they take place in a number of shifting and complex ways.

To address this issue, this chapter investigates the ways in which the body is constructed and experienced within the world of Euro-American ballet, since professional dancers, in particular, must do a fair amount of thinking before they are 'able to move *without* thinking' (Blacking, 1977a: 23). The ethnographic material was obtained between 1993 and 1995 from amongst three national classical ballet companies – the Royal Swedish Ballet in Stockholm, the Royal Ballet in London, the American Ballet Theatre in New York – and one contemporary dance company, the Ballett Frankfurt in Frankfurt-am-Main. Since dancers work with their bodies, and they work them extremely hard, the body is central to their conceptual frame. Indeed, there are significant differences between the ways in which the body is conceptualized and experienced amongst professional dancers within the theatre and in society at large outside the theatre. Within the dance world, the body is conceptualized in terms of the dancers' experiences of pleasure, pain and power during performance; dancers also hold particular notions of body types and ideas about the links between mental dispositions and specialist types of movement.

The ethnography of the dance world is set against Blacking's work on Venda dance in southern Africa during the 1950s, focusing in particular on his descriptions of *domba*, the Venda girls' three-part initiation cycle. During *vhusha*, the first phase of initiation, the girls engaged in arduous and painful movement sequences (*ndayo*), while the *domba* dance, an integral part of the final phase of initiation, was clearly pleasurable. In his assessment of the impact of initiation on the girls, Blacking noted that what they remembered most vividly were their experiences during dancing:

> In 1956–8, all who had taken part in the cycle of initiation were agreed that the most important element was the *domba* dance. Concern for the dance outweighed consideration of its extra symbolic significance. Women who had forgotten most of what they might have learnt about the associated symbolism had not forgotten the experience of dancing; they talked of problems of coordinating movements and music, the closeness of other's bodies, the excitement when the dance went well, the transcendence of altered time schedules and the sense of transformation from the physical to the social body that was experienced through contrasting movement styles. (Blacking, 1985a: 86–87)

It is quite likely that it was in light of this observation that Blacking came to conceive of dance as potentially powerful, as it was capable of engendering memorable experiences amongst dancers. Indeed, he wrote that 'the ultimate aim of dancing is to be able to move *without* thinking, to *be* danced' (Blacking, 1977a: 23). And some years later he wrote: 'To be effective in society, dance must mediate between nature and culture in human existence and so be transcendental in context' (Blacking, 1985a: 72).

It is also in terms of the ability of dance to evoke such transcendental states that I understand the power of dance for ballet dancers. During such moments dancers enter into 'optimal states of experience', or that which Csikszentmihalyi (1992: 3) has referred to as 'flow'. It is during these moments that 'mind and body' become fused, and the experience of this integration can be conceptualized as an experience of empowerment. While such theorists as Blacking and Csikszentmihalyi have highlighted the pleasurable dimensions of dance in their understanding of the integration of body and mind, they paid less attention to the impact of bodily pain on memory. Pain, however, is the focus of Foucault's (1979) famous work on the disciplining of bodies. In *Discipline and Punish*, Foucault argues that the impact of bodily discipline produces docile political bodies that, despite their enhanced capablities, can be more easily subordinated. Yet pain is a central aspect of ballet training and practice, and it highlights the complexity in the union of body and mind in dance. I shall be arguing that pain should also be seen as a means of breaking down the Cartesian divide.

Drawing on ethnographic data on the moonlight dance and the rain dance among the Miri, a Nuba group in Sudan, Gerd Bauman (1995: 39) provides a critical discussion of Blacking's idea of the affective power of dance and music performances. Even though the Miri dances promoted heightened experiences, the rain dance only lasted for three minutes at the most; according to the Miri, had it been longer it might have evoked trance. Bauman is not convinced that these short-lived experiences could have a lingering, let alone lasting, effect upon dancers. He does concur, however, that music and dance can produce pleasure, but not that they are necessarily liberating. Bauman suggests that dance and music have a 'dual potential' (1995: 39): they can be liberating, as in the way they were used in the South African independent churches that Blacking (1981) investigated; but they can also be oppressive and a way of maintaining hegemonic authority, as Bloch (1974) has argued.

Here I will develop Bauman's (1995: 39) idea of the 'dual potential' of dance by looking, in the first instance, at how dancers achieve experiences of liberation and personal power that derive from the control they have over their bodies. Then, drawing on Foucault's ideas about bodily discipline, I will discuss the ways in which dance can be a powerful means of controlling bodies – one's own and those of others. These issues will be viewed through a cross-cultural comparison between ballet and Venda dance. This analysis reveals a number of striking similarities in the experiences of pleasure, pain and power brought on by performance in both contexts that supports Blacking's vision of a shared humanity.

European ballet and Venda dance

Ballet is often associated with cultural capital and the elites. This belief does not, however, do justice to the wide range of class, ethnic and racial identities that one finds backstage in the ballet world, neither does it acknowledge the full array of narratives and movements of classical and contemporary ballets. As a matter of fact, ballet dancers see themselves first and foremost as artists and not as a part of the 'high culture' of theatre foyers. There used to be an assumption in the West that ballet was a superior dance form. It is, however, still necessary to state that ballet is but one dance form amongst others, encompassing the different types of art dance, ethnic dance, show dance and social dance. In contemporary stage dance, sections of different dance forms are increasingly being put together into new crossover versions, mixing modern dance with ballet steps and movements from ethnic and social dances.

In his seminal book *How Musical is Man?* (1973), Blacking argued forcefully that the Venda taught him that European 'art' music and 'folk' music are basically the same kinds of music, in that both result from the same mental structures that allow for the manifestation of human musicality. There are, of course, 'distinctions between the surface complexity of different musical styles' (Blacking, 1973: vi), but these may be attributed to differences in social organization. European 'art' music is not to be viewed as the product of an inherently superior musicality, but of a more extensive division of labour, a more developed technological tradition, literacy and systems of musical notation among other factors. Furthermore, as Blacking (1995b) noted elsewhere, there is also 'art' music in African tribal societies and 'folk' music in complex industrial societies. If this distinction is to be of any use at all, it is best viewed in terms of communicative focus: while 'folk' music highlights the social interactions promoted through musical performance, 'art' music draws attention to the aesthetic properties of the music itself. Blacking's observations about the similarities and differences between 'art' music and 'folk' music are equally valid for 'art' dance and 'folk' dance.

When Blacking (1985a: 71–72) wrote about Venda dances, he did not hesitate to compare them to European ballet. It is in a discussion on discursive movements in dance that he noted that such movements were included both in ballet and in such Venda dances as the *tshikona* and the various dances of *domba*. As in ballet, the discursive movements in Venda dance tend to be performed by principal dancers with the 'corps de ballet' as a supportive collective. In noting this, Blacking also informed us that there were such categories as principal dancers and dance collectives in Venda dances. He proceeded with a discussion of the central role of transcendentality in Venda dance to then demonstrate how the Venda dance forms are linked to the larger society. George Balanchine, a choreographer of the New York City Ballet for many years, was equally preoccupied in establishing a link between his dances and the wider social setting when he had the dancers dancing at high speed to reflect the fast pulse in American society (see Wulff, 1998 on national ballet styles).

Venda dances were often circle dances of counter-clockwise movement. According to Blacking, this could be due not only to the limited space available for dancing in the mountainous terrain of the Venda, but also to the centrality the Venda attributed to the circle. In the *domba* dance, the hallmark of the final phase of initiation, the novices formed a tight snake and moved in a circle around a space symbolizing the womb.[3] The steps and the music illustrated the sexual act: ashes from a fire represented the semen that created the foetus in the womb and the bass drum symbolized an unborn baby. By continuously repeating the *domba* dance, a baby was said to grow and be born at the end of initiation. That was also when play songs were sung, and this could produce an elated transcendental state amongst the dancers, as could the 24 hours of ecstatic dancing at the conclusion of the *domba* (Blacking, 1985a). This suggests that there was indeed considerable pleasure involved in the perform-ance of the *domba* dance. The excitement generated by the transcendental states achieved during the *domba* dance also promoted experiences of power, a matter to which I will return.

The *vhusha* dances, on the other hand, were meant to stretch the body. They involved very demanding self-critical exercises called *ndayo* that in fact were so stressful that, when the girls made a mistake or lost their balance, they tended to collapse in pain. In the basic *ndayo* step, the girls moved from a squatting to a crouching position and then shuffled their feet.[4]

In response to Blacking's call for continuous debate (see also Byron, 1995; Baily, 1995), Reily (1998) revisited his extensive field material on the Venda girls' initiation schools (Blacking, 1969a, 1969c–f), and provided a deeper understanding of Venda dance. Her analysis draws on recent anthropological work on ritual orchestration and memory to assess the impact of the initiation schools on Venda women. She uses, in particular, Whitehouse's (1995) demonstration of the impact that the promotion of memorable experiences within the rituals of revival movements in Papua New Guinea has on everyday religious activites. She combines this with Fernandez's (1986) view of ritual as the promotion of experiences of wholeness and suggests that a sense of wholeness is a central aspect of the experience of Venda initiation. It is because of this experience that the girls' recollections of initiation were framed primarily in terms of pleasure.

Initiation was not, however, painless, particularly during the performance of the strenouos *ndayo* movements of *vhusha*. As Blacking noted, '*ndayo* are there to make the girls suffer and honour the old ones' (1969c: 19). Although such pain was meant to prepare the girls for the hardships of womanhood, it was also meant to remind them of the Venda hierarchy. Such an adult show of power was clearly intended to discipline the girls, rendering them competent women in Venda society.

These procedures provide a good example of Foucault's (1979) ideas about the power of discipline as a means of moulding bodies that, while becoming more able, also become more easily controllable. It is often overlooked that one of the important elements of socialization involves the exercise of processes of power and subordination by older generations over younger ones (see Wulff, 1995). Bourdieu's (1977) influential concept of habitus adds to our understanding of the practice of dancing as a mode of inscribing dispositions – that is, perceptions and actions – into the dancer's body, and the crucial point is that these dispositions influence the dancing, as well as the social, life of dancers. Blacking exemplified this not only on an ethnographic level, connecting sections of Venda initiation dance with aspects of the girls' adult social life, but also as a part of his wider interest in the way in which dancers make decisions about movements in performance. He also contemplated how the experience of dancing 'affected people in ways that influenced their decisions outside the immediate dance situation' (Blacking, 1985a: 88), suggesting that new movements can produce mental changes.[5] This was, of course, the aim of the Venda intitaion dances: to promote a mental transformation in the girls, turning them into women: with the onset of the girls' first menstruation the physical changes had already taken place (see also Blacking, 1983a).

Blacking (1985a) comments on the contrasts in the dances used in Venda girls' initiation: the dances progressed from individual steps accompanied by polyphonic vocal and drum sections in the first phases of initiation towards greater uniformity. However, the most salient contrasts were experienced during *ndayo* exercises, which I would suggest is of analytic consequence to my discussion of dancers' experiences of pleasure, pain and power. Here, through juxtaposition, essentially different experiences became interrelated: the intensity of the experience of each *ndayo* depended on its contrast with the previous one. By being instructed to 'move forward on their buttocks without touching the ground with their hands' (Blacking, 1969e: 154), Venda girls were taught about the pain of labour. A pregnant woman thus starts to have 'rumblings in her stomach. ... It burns with pain: but it is nice when it's all over' (Blacking, 1969e: 154). Clearly, the great joy that the arrival of the baby causes is enhanced by the contrast of the relief brought by the end of terrible physical pain. A symbolic birth is, as noted above, an aspect of the grand finale of the *domba* dance which, together with the 24-hour intense dancing, produced transcendental states that also brought experiences of power for the participants.

Disciplined dancers, synchronized bodies

The notion of ritual dance as a mode of oppression brings us back to Foucault's (1979) work on disciplined bodies. While I have already indicated its relevance to dance in the Venda girls' initiation cycle, it is also of analytical significance to ballet. From around the age of ten, ballet dancers spend much of their time disciplining their bodies to perform the movements of ballet, such that they eventually become part of their habitus. These bodily dispositions have a profound impact on the social life of dancers even when they are not dancing. Their impact can be noted in the way in which, during ballet training, dancers also assimilate an old-fashioned decorum of pronounced interactional politeness, particularly when there are inequalities between the parties, such as age, gender or status differences. Dancers also adhere to formal rules of etiquette, such as being on time and dressing smartly, although they avoid expensive-looking, sexually suggestive and ostentatious outfits. Dancers can be said to 'become' the dance, to embody their work, much more intensely than people in occupations in which the body is used less elaborately. Ballet dancers' bodies are their tools and instruments (Wulff, 1998: 102).

Professional ballet dancers are completely dependent on the state of their bodies; they have to be fit at all times. Compared to athletes,[6] who acquire a basic bodily form which they train more intensely before competitions, both young promising dancers and those who are established, but need to confirm their position, constantly have to make an effort to improve. Indeed, dancers abide by the old saying 'You are only as good as your last performance' (Wulff, 1998: 103).

Dancers move in a distinct manner that is different from non-dancers, even when they are *not* dancing. They are very good at non-verbal communication –

something that can cause misinterpretation in interactions between dancers and non-dancers. Through the movements that often accompany their speech, dancers can 'write' sophisticated intertextual messages that are comprehensible to other dancers and ballet people, since they refer to steps or stories related to backstage social contexts, such as amusing incidents that occurred during a performance or a boring rehearsal. Moreover, the physical closeness of dancing, the skin-to-skin contact, leads dancers to stand in close proximity to one another even when they are not dancing, a level of closeness that non-dancers would rarely extend beyond spouses, partners or lovers. Some dancers who are friends, or just enjoy each other's company, may engage in sensual touching and cuddling that would be considered inappropriate in many other contexts (Wulff, 1998: 102, 111). Occasionally, however, the physical closeness of dancing can have sinister consequences, leading to physical aggression amongst dancers. One such instance was the topic of a story I was told by a female senior corps de ballet dancer of the Royal Swedish Ballet, who ended up fighting with a young corps de ballet dancer who did not want to learn the steps that the company was practising. According to the senior dancer, the young dancer was not putting enough effort into learning the steps, so she took her to task in the corridor. In response, the young dancer kicked the senior dancer, which enraged her. The young dancer, however, refused to apologize, and physical aggression ensued. The two women were finally separated by two male dancers who chanced upon them in the corridor. The two dancers remained enemies for a long time after that, but, in the end, they made up, following a common pattern for conflicts and their resolution in the ballet world.

While preparing a new choreography in the studio or learning a role for the first time, many dancers form a mental image of the steps they are to perform, but they have to practise them for some time before – as they say – 'the body understands'. By practising they are able to achieve the right expression and remember the choreographic pattern, although some dancers internalize steps at a faster pace than others. During coaching, dancers may be moved across the studio, since a different spatial perspective can be useful in getting over learning blocks, just as a change in tempo can be helpful.

In reviving productions that were danced a year or so earlier, often, dancers say, 'the head remembers, but not the body'. They also claim that they 'must hear the music to remember the steps'.[7] With the help of the music, dancers are able to recall the steps of a dance for a number of years, having stored them in their 'muscular memory'. My observations indicate that steps can be retained in this way for about five years; after that the memory of a choreography tends to disappear gradually, except among former dancers who become coaches and spend their time teaching steps they know well to young dancers (Wulff, 1998: 103–04).

I witnessed numerous instances indicating the degree to which steps could become inscribed upon the dancers' bodies and called up by the music. Many dancers find it very difficult to refrain from dancing in the wings while another dancer on stage performs a role they have played in another cast. Instead of standing still to await their entry, they 'mark' the steps in synchrony with the dancer on stage (Wulff, 1998: 103–04).

One of the core ideas in the ballet world is the distinction made between a 'good body' or a 'natural talent', on one hand, and 'not having the right mentality', on the other. A dancer with a 'good body' is someone with softness of the limbs and musicality, while the 'right mentality' refers to systematic and dedicated work. Dancers who have 'good bodies' but lack the 'right mentality' are considered idle, and they are also the targets of envy; after all, they do not have to put as much work into their dancing as the majority of dancers. However, these dancers are not likely to make it to the top. The reverse can also happen: dancers who lack the proper physical stature required of leading dancers but possess the 'right mentality' can summon their willpower and put themselves on meticulous schemes of dieting, practice and active thinking about the performance of steps, and thereby come very close to the top (Wulff, 1998: 104). In writing about the importance for athletes and pianists of having certain bodily proportions, Blacking noted that 'a mysterious quality such as determination or will may help a less adequate body to perform better than expected' (1977a: 23).

In the ballet world, such 'thinking dancers',[8] as they are called, deconstruct the choreography and look for solutions to spatial problems in the dancing. A central part of learning how to execute the steps of a choreographic sequence is to know how to prevent injury. 'Thinking dancers' also make an effort, in the studio, practise methods for 'rescuing' mistakes that might occur on stage. These dancers spend a lot of time reading books, listening to tapes and participating in courses on mental training, and are thus very knowledgeable about the effects of diet and training on hormones, stamina and body shape. 'Thinking dancers' tend to practise for longer than their colleagues, both before and after regular working days in studios and workouts, as well as in commercial workouts located outside the theatre. Only a small number of 'thinking dancers' exist – a handful in each company – but they have all astonished choreographers, coaches and colleagues. In time, they attain 'work victories'. Linked to the difference between 'thinking dancers' and dancers who have 'natural talents' or 'good bodies' is the indigenous distinction between 'workhorses' and 'racehorses'. 'Racehorces' are able to elegantly race past the 'workhorses' and soon reach the top without as much effort as the 'workhorses', who remain below them (Wulff, 1998: 104).

There are elaborate conceptualizations in the ballet world concerning body types and movement talents. The ballet body types can be sorted into categories in line with the roles available in classical ballets. One such classical body type is the *soubrette*, a small woman who moves fast; another is the *danseur noble*, a goodlooking male dancer who dances elegantly. As a prince he often dances with a 'lyrical' dancer, the generic classical ballerina. There is also the *demi-caractère*, more commonly known nowadays as the 'character dancer', often male dancers with a pronounced acting talent who are cast in roles such as the Jester in *Swan Lake*. Dancers who have other types of body, or who, because of company politics, are confined to corps work, may flourish if they move to contemporary companies where there is a need for a variety of body types and stage personalities (Wulff, 1998: 102).

Alongside these ideas about classical body types, the ballet world also classifies dancers according to notions of desirable skills. The ability to turn and jump well is valued, and this is why dancers are characterized as 'turners', 'jumpers' or 'pirouetters', even though dancers tend to turn or 'pirouette' better on either the right or the left leg. Those dancers who are unable to perform these movements with ease are negatively identified as 'not turners', 'not pirouetters' or 'not jumpers' (Wulff, 1998: 102–03).

In his exploration of an anthropology of the body, Blacking wrote that 'throughout the world societies attach supreme value to transcendental somatic states and experiences of bodily resonance, or true fellow-feeling' (1977a: 7). This was possibly inspired by Alfred Schutz's (1964: 161, 177) ideas (see Byron, 1995) on how 'mutual tuning-in relationships' are the basis for communication in a 'vivid present'. Although Schutz focused on the interactions involved in music-making, his ideas are also applicable to group dancing, which can also be viewed as instances of 'sharing of the Other's flux of experiences in inner time' and 'experiencing this togetherness as a "We"' (Schutz, 1964: 177).

'We were like one body' is a widespread expression of extraordinary rapport between partners, whether they are lovers or a corps de ballet. Sometimes that rapport encompasses the whole company in big ballet scenes. Dancers' high degree of body consciousness and awareness of other bodies, particularly in motion, lead to issues of proxemics and kinaesthetics (Wulff, 1998 ff). Olsson (1993) uses the term 'proxemic unity' to refer to the closeness which partners or the corps de ballet create on stage when they are 'like one body' and can feel they are in synchrony with one another. Such bodily and mental unity is extended to the off-stage environment. This does not only pertain to the dancers who experienced proxemic unity on stage, for new proxemic unities spring up, like islands of closeness, during backstage rehearsals as well as amongst dancers meeting outside the theatre.

Dancers are extremely good at communicating without direct eye contact – a skill acquired during dancing, which is deployed in interactions at other times. Dancers have a way of scanning what is taking place beside them without turning their heads, thereby applying a kinaesthetic knowledge obtained from ballet. In a dance studio one will commonly encounter two women dancers absorbed in conversation while facing different directions: one may be down on the floor stretching and looking at herself in the mirror while the other is standing up checking her leg as she is lifting it as high as she possibly can. Another typical mode dancers have of relating to people which derives from the forms and spatial orientations of dance is to make their presence known by moving in front of someone without looking at them (Wulff, 1998).

Dancers have a strong sense of the presence of other bodies, especially their movement patterns. This ability obviously comes from dancing with other people in big groups both during rehearsals in the studio and in performance on stage. This sense of the presence of other bodies in motion is transferred to dressing rooms and canteens, where dancers conduct conversations from one side of the room to the other, frequently across the high line of mirrors in the middle of the two rows of dressing-room tables that are blocking their view. The speakers cannot see each other, but they are completely conscious of one another's immediate proximity, which is why their communication takes the form of a ping-pong conversation, with questions and replies back and forth over the rows of mirrors (Wulff, 1998).

The focus on the body in the ballet world also leads to a great deal of talk about what one has eaten. For example, a dancer may explain that she is not doing very well in a morning rehearsal because she had too much for breakfast. A woman dancer can also be heard, as a matter of course, commenting that she is dancing below her standard because she is having her period.

Habitus of pain

There is an air of 'cultural artefact' surrounding classical ballet, as this dance form is sometimes dismissed as 'unnatural', even by dancers themselves. When modern dance emerged in the early twentieth century, with barefoot dancers, loose-fitting costumes and large swinging movements, this was celebrated as 'natural' and 'healthy' (Kendall, 1979: 17–31), unlike classical ballet, with its characteristic tight tutus, narrow pointe shoes and precise movements.[9] Since then, injuries have become a monumental problem in the dance world – both amongst modern dancers and ballet dancers.[10] The risk of having to endure career delays brought on by injury or, even worse, to be forced to leave the ballet world prematurely is always there. When this occurs, it creates traumas both among the injured dancers and those who are still dancing. Injuries tend to happen in rehearsals, sometimes in daily class, but most dramatically on-stage in performance. No one glorifies injuries; they cause too much pain, especially the really bad ones that can even be disabling. But there is a ranking of injuries, according to which injuries that occur in performance are placed at the top. There is an analogy here with soldiers that are wounded in war, or with football players injured in national league matches, suggesting that there is a certain heroism attached to them (Wulff,

1998). Injuries that happen outside the theatre, however, as when a dancer is injured on holiday, lack this prestige.

The growth of studies on the body and embodiment has drawn some attention to the social and cultural meanings of physical pain. DelVecchio Good *et al.* (1992) argue that, although pain occurs in the body, it is intersubjective and also comes about through connections with society and local worlds. Ethnographic studies, such as Wacquant's (1995a) on boxers and Palmer's (1996) on competitive cyclists, observe that the physical torment that is an integral element of these practices makes boxing and competitive cycling seem alien and cruel to outsiders. This is clearly the case with ballet dancing, too. In daily life backstage, the body is discussed most of the time in terms of pain from injuries.

In ballet, men and women perform different steps to some extent, and this means that there is a certain variation in the injuries that affect them. Men lift the women, even carry them sometimes, and are expected to jump higher than women, who are taught to stay longer in balance, but above all dance on pointe. Back injuries are thus more common among men, while women have many knee and foot injuries. When I was doing fieldwork, stress fractures and sprained ankles, as well as spurs in ankles and muscle ruptures, occurred frequently (Wulff, 1998).

Attributing the social construction of pain amongst pianists to the political economy of the concert market, Alford and Szanto (1996) discuss the idea that pain is a necessary element when learning a virtuoso technique. Yet, this pain tends to be denied. In the ballet world it is considered unethical to cast or promote dancers while they are injured. This leads some dancers, who know that they are on the verge of being offered leading roles or solo sections, to conceal their injuries and rehearse, and even perform, on painkillers, anaesthetic creams or injections. This can impair the injured person and may force the dancer to stop dancing in mid-performance (Wulff, 1998).

There are dancers who only suffer the occasional slight injury, but virtually all dancers are injured – and in pain – much of the time. As with pianists – and with the Venda girls who were exposed to pain in their initiation dances – pain is considered necessary to 'make it' as a ballet dancer. According to a psychological study on dancers and pain tolerance, dancers have a higher pain threshold than a control group (Tajet-Foxell and Rose, 1995: 34), although there may be individual and contextual pain tolerance thresholds. It is common for dancers to experience pleasure when they exert themselves so hard that they feel pain – at least as long as it makes them fitter and they enjoy the mirror image of themselves, until they cannot cope with the pain any more. I witnessed quite a few injuries occur, with some dancers being sent to hospital; but there was never an emergency when the first aid equipment, which is close at hand in studios and backstage, was needed. Neither did I see the first aid rooms in use. They were built for dancers, opera singers, stage technicians and other personnel who work in the hazardous backstage area at Covent Garden in London and at the Kennedy Center in Washington, DC (Wulff, 1998).

As if all this physical pain were not enough, there is also a great deal of mental pain in the ballet world, and sometimes, of course, the two are interrelated. Physical pain from an injury can cause mental pain because it stops a dancer from dancing. Mental pain, such as worry over new casting or doing well enough in an upcoming première, can cause physical pain. The latter is, however, usually of a rather diffuse nature and can be described by dancers as 'my whole body is aching'. When they go to the company physical therapist for treatment such as a massage, they also get an opportunity for gossip and intimate conversation. By acting as confidantes, physical therapists provide mental remedy, as well as physical treatment.

Some mental pain is caused by the stress, and occasional harassment and humiliation, that the old-fashioned ballet pedagogy and coaching styles continue to create. Instead of brilliant dancing, this pedagogy may lead to low self-confidence and even anorexia. Women dancers breaking down in tears in the studio as a result of being pushed too hard by unsympathetic coaches is not uncommon. But there are also often tears in the wings or in the dressing rooms after an unsatisfactory performance. This custom of expressing mental pain in public through crying also takes place over disappointing casting and the lack of an expected promotion.

The reward: transcendental states of flow

Within the ballet world pain is a part of the daily life and work of dancers; something dancers take for granted. But dance is also a source of pleasure. In the words of a principal woman dancer at the Royal Swedish Ballet:

> It doesn't happen too often. I love it when you feel that everything just works. You feel that you can say what you want to say, usually the technique works as well. I think that is what gets me going – a quest for that atmosphere, when you can create that very special atmosphere – that's why I put up with the pain.

In the television series, *Dancing*, John Blacking (1987–88) suggested that 'perhaps the greatest secret of dancing is to enter another world, that world of ecstasy and freedom which has made dance both welcomed and feared in different societies'. In this 'world of ecstasy and freedom', people are transported into heightened experiences of delight that are transformative. Both ballet revelations and experiences of transcendence are of this nature, yet they need to be distinguished from one another. Ballet revelations usually spring up during childhood among ballet pupils, but they may occur among adults as well, generally in experiences of *watching* ballet or dance either in the theatre or on television. It was not only classical ballet productions that created ballet revelations for the dancers in this study, but also other dance genres, such as show dance with Fred Astaire and the musical, *Fame*. Some dancers experienced ballet revelations when they were watching guest performances. This was the case with one of the male corps de ballet dancers at the American Ballet Theatre who came from Kiev in the Ukraine. The 'Iron Curtain' was still in existence, and he had already been in ballet school for a few years when he saw a performance of *Romeo and Juliet* by the Winnipeg Ballet on a tour to Kiev. The dancer described the experience of sitting in the audience and his impressions of the Canadian company:

> It was so much better than the ones in Russia. At the end of the ballet I was crying! It was so good! I was shocked! Before they had told us that Russians were the best dancers, but this was even better! They were really into their ballet!

In effect, ballet revelations are formative. The memory of these rapturous moments is long-lasting and may lead to a professional career in dance or a lifelong love of dance. But revelations also hit accidental theatregoers (Wulff, 1998). Even though ballet revelations remain as vivid memories for most dancers, it is, however, the other type of heightened experience, the transcendental states of flow while *dancing*, which dancers refer to spontaneously over and over again.

Dancers discuss their ability to move and control their bodies far beyond the regular movement patterns of dance, and occasionally they attain a state of flow (Csikszentmihalyi, 1990), an optimal experience when action and consciousness fuse. This is what Blacking (1977a, 1985a) referred to as a transcendental state or a peak experience. Moments of flow or transcendence – when dancers are totally in control of their bodies and thereby experience a sense of power – are the rewards. This is the incentive for struggling with seemingly endless hardships, such as constant practising and the endurance of pain, even though most dancers never attain fame (Wulff, 1998).

Flow can happen in daily training and rehearsal, but occurs most importantly in performance (Wulff, 1998). It is during these rare moments that body and mind are united and dancers really are 'able to move *without* thinking'. In the words of a woman soloist at the Royal Swedish Ballet: 'When I forget about what I'm doing, that's when I relax. When it's in my body, when I know that my body is going to do it for me. I don't have to think!'

Many dancers talk about this state using such statements as 'this is when it works', 'there are no stops or ends, there is a fluidity' or 'it's as if somebody else has taken over and you're just there for the ride!'. It is common to describe flow in terms of freedom and flying, such as in this description by Adam Cooper, principal dancer with the Royal Ballet who gained world fame as a male swan in Matthew Bourne's contemporary version of *Swan Lake*:

You feel like you are completely free, everything feels so *natural*! You're
surrounded by this music, everything feels so right. You just don't want to stop!
You have to control yourself. You feel like flying!

According to a woman principal at the American Ballet Theatre, 'You don't
stop where your body ends!'. Flow is when dancers forget the technique and
the dancing becomes effortless.

I heard many stories about dancers being asked unexpectedly to perform a
leading role at short notice. It could be a role that they had learnt but not yet
performed, or even a role they had performed many times, but were asked to
take over halfway through a performance because someone had just been
injured on stage. Out of the stress that this sudden opportunity generated, many
dancers moved into a second state, into flow. In such instances it was the
contrast with the feeling of pain, the mental pain of stress in this case, that
accentutated the pleasure of the heightened state brought on by dance. The
atmosphere that was portrayed on stage during such moments tended to be
rapturous, but dancers did not talk about being carried away while their
character was dying on stage. Regardless of the atmosphere, flow struck
unpredictably and only occasionally. States of flow could not be called up but,
when they arrived, dancers reached into that zone where things that were not
present during rehearsal began to happen. This is when ballet art is created.

Conclusion: the ballet body and the Venda body united

This chapter has explored what it feels like to dance. By comparing ballet with
Venda dance, I have been able to show that memorable experiences of pleasure
and power in dancing – transcendental states of flow – grow out of previous
experiences of pain. These notions of pleasure, pain and power can also be
investigated in relation to audiences at ballet performances; they too can go
through such experiences as they watch ballet. But audiences do not usually
take part in the dance, at least not at classical ballet performances, which makes
their experiences somewhat different from those of the dancers. In
contemporary ballet and dance, however, it can happen that spectators are
asked to come on stage – a circumstance which usually adds to the experience
of pleasure for them. Blacking wrote about how the final climax in the *domba*
dance was watched by many spectators who sometimes could take part in the
dancing and so 'feelings of generalized excitement and satisfaction grew'
(1985a: 84). The pleasure increased at the graduation celebration, which
attracted Venda from different parts of the country.

Building on Blacking's insights, Andrée Grau concurs that the achievement
of heightened experiences is the purpose of dancing, and she reminds us that
they do not happen during every performance. Nonetheless, it is in such

moments of effervescence that 'occasionally allow cultural boundaries to be transcended and dance to be "understood" even when the cultural context is not' (Grau, 1995: 47). In the television series, *Dancing*, Blacking (1987–88)[11] suggested that 'dance transcends cultural particulars at the level of personal expression. Aesthetic communication can therefore provide an alternative', and that 'dance can unite what words too often divide'.

Blacking (1977a, 1983a, 1985a) regarded language as being inadequate for conveying feelings.[12] He kept returning to the point that the essence of the dance experience cannot be adequately translated into words. For Blacking, it was important to move away from ideas about the subconscious when it came to explaining dance experiences. Instead, he saw 'another kind of reasoning' taking place – one which is coherent with the non-verbal form of dance:

> It is not that people abandon reason for emotion when they dance, but that they often introduce another kind of reasoning, whose grammar and content are most effectively, though not exclusively, expressed in non-verbal language. (Blacking, 1985a: 67)

One question which follows from this is to what extent does this 'grammar and content' correspond to reason and emotion as we recognize these entities outside dancing, *or* does dance have the potential to create *new* experiential categories? This is at least what choreographer William Forsythe is aiming at by working with 'an open form that generates new possibilities' - that is, vertiginous spaces and atmospheres (Wulff, 1998: 45), some of which have been identified as 'punk on pointe' (Gilpin, 1993: 105). Watching Forsythe's work, I have indeed been touched by atmospheres – heart-piercing, hilarous, mocking – that I did not know existed. As I write this, I concede to my inability to represent the entire experience of those moments in a text. So a text about dance, whether a journalistic, artistic or scholarly account (and any combination thereof), has to be a new synthesis, an interpretation, sometimes taking the form of a new piece of art.

There is an emphasis in Blacking's writings on what happens during and after dancing, while my ethnography of the ballet world focuses on the preparation for ballet as a career, on the rehearsal process, as well as the performance in itself. Blacking was quite articulate about the fact that dance and movement may have an impact on social life outside the dance context, especially after the dance. During the Venda initiation cycle, for instance, dancing is linked to lessons about womanhood. In classical ballet, the precise steps, postures and proxemics of the dance forms affect the ways in which dancers move and interact with other people outside the studio, even outside the theatre. The movement patterns of ballet dancers are characterized by bodily closeness and expressive gestures shaped by the lines and language of classical ballet.

Drawing on Blacking's (1977a: 23) observations, I began this chapter by referring to the amount of thinking that ballet dancers have to do before they are 'able to move *without* thinking, to *be* danced'. Even though soon after I arrived at the Royal Ballet a hardened male corps de ballet dancer had told me that 'they knock your brains out here', thinking is very much a part of learning how to dance ballet. What this dancer meant was, of course, that dancers are not encouraged to think for themselves, to be original, thereby avoiding confrontations with the ballet management. Obviously, however, it is not only the 'thinking dancers' who engage in thinking, even if they do it more systematically than their colleagues. This particular thinking tends to take place in rehearsals that entail active thinking about how a particular choreography is structured and how best to perform it, including considering measures to avoid injury.

Both in Venda dance and ballet, physical and mental pain is debilitating, whereas pleasure in the form of transcendental states allows for an experience of empowerment. In ballet performances such experiences can generate recognition and fame for individual dancers and thus translate into the achievement of powerful positions in the ballet world. The dynamics of moments of transcendence, of flow, have been at the centre of this chapter. In ballet such moments are the reward for the pain of injuries and excruciating ballet discipline. When pain is replaced by pleasure in Venda dance, moments of flow are what make the initiation work. Such moments are fondly remembered afterwards, just as the memory of moments of flow are cherished in the ballet world. Both types of flow promote a sense of wholeness. And even when flow is evoked in different cultural contexts, the experience of transcendence seems to be quite similar. This, therefore, is where the ballet body and the Venda body unite in a shared experience of humanity across time and geographical distance.

Acknowledgements

I never met John Blacking, but since this collection is a tribute to his legacy, I find it appropriate to note that there is no doubt that he made a momentous impression on many people I *have* met – both colleagues and informants. As a colleague and teacher he clearly had an ability to release people's talents and capacities, and to provide them with intellectual inspiration. And, during my fieldwork on dance in Ireland, one dancer, choreographer, composer and dance writer after the other in Belfast and Dublin have paused and looked at me enquiring with enthusiasm, 'Did you meet John Blacking?'. This has touched me deeply. Having grown up in the ballet world (see Wulff, 1997, 1998, 2000), I sympathize with someone who 'remained a musician at heart, despite the wide variety of his academic interests and accomplishments' (Byron, 1995: 28). I wish I had met John Blacking.

Notes

[1] Some parts of this chapter are revised versions derived from Wulff (1998), especially the section titled 'Ballet body work'.

[2] For some of the work in the upsurge in literature on the body within anthropology and sociology, see Synnott (1993), Howes (1991), and Lutz and White (1986). A pioneer in this area, Douglas (1970, 1978), produced classic antropological work on the body as a social and natural symbol. Scheper-Hughes's and Lock's (1987) prolegomenon to the body in medical anthropology is widely cited. Csordas (1995) has provided a phenomenological discussion of embodiment. Such feminist anthropologists as Martin (1987) have analysed the body in terms of reproduction in a patriarchal order. There is also an ethnographic study by Wacquant (1995b) on boxers in Chicago, in which the sportsmen's bodies are presented as a form of capital. Brownell (1995) connects gender, body and nationalism with sport in China.

[3] Blacking provides numerous photographs of the *domba* dance as well as film footage. For still photos, see Blacking (1969f: 250–51; 1973); for film footage, see Blacking (2001 [1980]; 1998: ../VideoClips/DombaFilm.html).

[4] For still images of the *ndayo*, see Blacking (1969c: 32–35); for film footage, see Blacking (2001 [1980]; 1998: ../VideoClips/V_VC07.html-../V_VC_25.html).

[5] Blacking (1985a) refers to the Alexander principle that now is used quite extensively in the rehabilitation of injured dancers in the ballet world. Also, business corporations have taken to the Alexander principle in order to reduce stress among employees.

[6] For a discussion on sport and Irish dance in terms of character-building as a part of nation-building, see Wulff (2003). On sport, dance and the body, see also Archetti and Dyck (2003).

[7] This obviously does not work when dancers dance to silence in parts of, or throughout, contemporary pieces. Then they rely on a separate structure of counting.

[8] Wacquant (1992: 247) notes that boxers see their trade as 'a "thinking man's game" that they frequently liken to chess'.

[9] See Wulff (2002) on ballet costumes as cultural commodities.

[10] See Koutedakis *et al.* (1996). For a report on dance injuries, see Brinson and Dick (1996).

[11] Blacking (1987–88) wrote and presented the six-part television series *Dancing*, which is a speedy journey, a kaleidoscopic explosion of contrasting dance forms and dance-like activites. It opens with a visit to a ballet rehearsal: a young woman dancer in a calf-long delicate white skirt over a leotard and tights is dancing on pointe with a young man. A woman coach is keeping them on track and time through measured calls. The *pas de deux* is accompanied by a piano.

[12] Scarry (1985) makes the same point about pain, arguing that pain cannot be described adequately in language.

CHAPTER EIGHT

Creating a Musical Space for Experiencing the Other-Self Within

Rebecca Sager

Music's power to create transcendent experience is evidenced worldwide. While music can be a mere diversion or simple pleasure, some music seems to lie at the very heart of what it means to be human. In a revolutionary gesture, John Blacking placed this transcendent power of music at the core of his social theories (1983b; 1995c). He conceived of music and other aesthetic forms not as marginal to scientific inquiry but rather as the fulcrum of human psychology and sociocultural formation. In his theory, music's motivational force links 'self' to 'other', to 'other self', to spirit possession; music links not only individual sensation and emotion to social experience and discourse, but also individual growth to national politics.

Blacking insisted that transcendent states were natural, normal and even necessary for the full development of a human being. In Blacking's vision, music's power to foster human development and social well-being was largely contingent upon experiences of the 'other self' – a 'transcendent state of self' (n.d.a: 12; 1985c). He would argue that it was through the intense experience of transcendence that people could best realize their full potential, both in terms of their personal growth as well as their relationships with others. Blacking's theories have proven rich with interpretive potential, not just for his own work with the Venda, but also for my research in Haitian Vodou singing. In Haitian Vodou, singing can encourage the formation of individual and social identities that lead to Vodou spirits manifesting in the form of possession trances – what can be seen as an experience of the 'other self' within. Whereas many ritual studies focused upon music's symbolic power to trigger trance states, Blacking led the exploration of music's semantic power as a *total musical experience* that creates what he called a world of 'virtual time' and what I submit is more akin to a complete musical space, in which to experience the transcendent state of the 'other self'.

Self and other: Blacking's identity theory

A full exegesis of the 'other self' concept requires an examination of its integral position in Blacking's theory of personal and sociocultural identity. Figure 8.1 aligns the main categories of identity discussed in Blacking's published and unpublished writings.[1] The diagram is somewhat structural in its conception, but note Blacking's initiation of transformative categories (labelled 'a') linking the individual to society and cultural tradition, and blurring the very distinctions between self and society set up in the anthropological discourse that Blacking inherited.

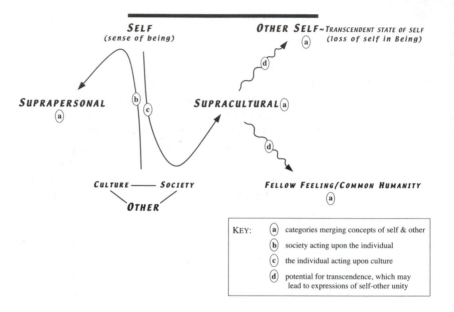

Figure 8.1   Interaction of personal and sociocultural identity categories

Suprapersonal

'Suprapersonal' is a term suggested by Blacking in handwritten annotations he made of Durkheim's *The Elementary Forms of the Religious Life* (1915 [1912]) (these annotations can be found in the Belfast archive). As we know, Durkheim postulates the idea of 'collective consciousness', of which science and morals are a part. Science and morals imply that the individual is capable of raising himself above his own peculiar point of view and living an *impersonal* life (Durkheim, 1915 [1912]: 445). After noting this, Blacking commented, 'Although Durkheim uses the word "impersonal" in this and similar contexts, I think that "suprapersonal" gives a better idea of the concept he is expressing' (Blacking, n.d.b).

The concept of the suprapersonal or impersonal aspect of the self is one way conceptualizing the presence of the opinions and values of others in society within an individual. '… In a word, there is something impersonal in us because there is something social in all of us' (Durkheim, 1915 [1912]: 446). Durkheim postulated an 'antagonistic', 'conflictual', even 'violent' relationship between the person and the internalized, 'impersonal moral law' and 'impersonal reason' that 'incarnates' itself in the individual, whereas Blacking had a decidedly more positive view of the relation of self to society. Certainly there could be a conflict of interest when actions that benefit society come at the expense of the individual or vice versa. However, the crux of Blacking's identity theory is that, in some societies, like that of the Venda, there is a coherent system of ideas about self and society that links personal and sociocultural identity together in such a way that the individual benefits from selfless action. Blacking asserts that the Venda system of personal and social identity has found the '*balance* that must exist between personal and corporate power' (1985c: 45, emphasis added.)

Venda music provides a perfect example of the balance achievable between self-satisfaction and communal concern:

> The polyrhythmic and polyphonic principles of musical performance [characteristic of Venda music] ensured that self-satisfaction could not be gained by self-seeking, but that the best musical results were obtained when all participants combined the maximum of individual skill and fellow-feeling in the realization and elaboration of a basic musical pattern. Pleasing others and pleasing oneself in musical performance were two interrelated aspects of the same activity. (Blacking, 1983b: 61)

Blacking was careful to insist that these rhythmic principles were not simply 'musical gimmicks' but rather constructed the deeply shared values of Venda culture:

> … they express concepts of individuality in community, and of social, temporal, and spatial balance … [T]he players are their own conductors and yet at the same time submit to the rhythm of an invisible conductor. This is the kind of shared experience which the Venda seek and express in their music making. (Blacking, 1973: 29–30).

Suprapersonal phenomena would include any behaviour performed in an enculturated manner – that is, as a consequence of the actor's experience and learning in society. For example, the 'invisible conductor' which Blacking mentions above is a suprapersonal phenomenon that allows an individual to entrain musically and socially in the proper way to bring about music that is deeply satisfying. While it may be difficult to see enculturation as anything but a form of coercion, the incorporation of society and culture into the individual psyche should not be conceived of as passive, since the suprapersonal often originates from one's wilful participation in society and culture, even as those actions are socially informed.

Related to the 'suprapersonal' concept is Blacking's definition of 'experience'. In terms of anthropological terminology, 'experience' is a very present and practice-oriented way of saying 'culture'. Experience is what our minds are made of, since experience inevitably results in neural nets, memory, associations, learning, habits and innovations. In handwritten notes for a speech to the Newman Society in Belfast (1975), titled 'The Anthropology of Religious Experience', Blacking begins by establishing the difference between 'experience' and 'sensation'. '*Sensations* are unique to [a] person, time and place; not really susceptible to analysis'. Experience, on the other hand, is 'cumulative and shared' and therefore social; it creates the link between others and the self. Experience is 'described in language, acted out in company ...', experiences are shared 'either between people (love, joy) or by different people (childbirth, death) ... Experience need not be couched in words, but it must be repeated and in a sense shared'[2]; (Blacking, 1975: 1), punctuation mine, emphasis in original. This rather public definition of 'experience' nevertheless presupposes that our 'shared' experiences affect our inner-sensations. We are socialized or enculturated even at the emotional level (see Blacking, 1985c: 47). Since music can engage the emotions while coordinating interaction between self and others, the power of musical experience is that it may bring about an individual's full emotional development and social integration.

Although the individual may feel many sensations imperceptible to, and not analysable by, others, a great many sensations are felt in regard to others. Quite often, Blacking would cite a Venda proverb: *muthu ndi muthu nga vhanwe* ('Man is man because of his associations with other men') (Blacking, 1973: 28; also 1983b: 56,60; 1985c: 45). 'Self could only be realized through others' (1985c: 45), because 'people become human through social interaction and the richness of personal relationships' (1983b: 60). For the Venda, being a good singer was one way of exhibiting social responsibility, which 'was an indispensable condition of personal identity' (1983b: 56).

> Since the public and the private self, and even the vision of what the self could or should be, are products of social interaction, the structure of every aspect of the self will reflect in various ways the processes of that interaction. Thus music, which is a product of the processes which constitute the realization of the self, will reflect all aspects of the self. (Blacking, 1995a [1969]: 33).

Thus, Venda music was 'an experience of becoming' (Blacking, 1973: 28).

One of the shortcomings of Western cultures is that they have a rather egoistic concept of self when compared to other cultures, such as the Venda (for example, see Blacking, 1983b: 50 and his citation of Robbins [1973]). As a corrective, Blacking proposed that 'the most powerful emotions ... *transcend the self'* rather than *focus on the self* (Blacking, 1983b: 52, emphasis added). Consequently, '... there is a need for a less egoistic concept of self than that generally provided by Euro-American ethno-psychology' (1983b: 47). Blacking asserted in 1983 that current identity theory was, in effect, 'only a theory of situational identity, in which people are said to use various degrees of personal and socio-cultural identity for a variety of purposes, but not in such a way that a single notion of identity can be said to link the different spheres of action and motives for them' (n.d.a: 3). To alleviate this problem, Blacking suggests that we should look at identity (both social and individual) 'in terms of fellow-feeling and growth motivation rather than [egoistic] self seeking' (1983b: 55).

In Blacking's writings, the reference to 'growth motivation' is related to 'self-actualization' – an idea that Blacking attributes to Maslow's book *Motivation and Personality* (1954).[3] Self-actualization is described as 'the full use and exploitation of talents, capacities, potentialities, etc. Such [self-actualizing] people seem to be fulfilling themselves and to be doing the best that they are capable of doing' (Maslow, 1954: 200–01). Maslow suggests that people are motivated by many things, one of which is the '... need for self-actualization or self-fulfillment of the idiosyncratic and species-wide potentialities of the individual person' (Maslow, 1954: p. 2) This 'need' for self-fulfilment is probably what Blacking meant by 'growth motivation'. Blacking took it as a given that humans were naturally motivated to grow into their full potential.

Although growth motivation and self-actualization seem focused on the self, they do take account of others as well, as we see in Blacking's report of Venda culture: 'Children were ... considered to be active ... in their own development, but their self-actualization called for the exercise of cooperation, kindness, neighbourliness, and compassion as well as the acquisition of skills' (1985c: 45). Blacking also considered the experience of the 'other self' to be self-actualizing.

'Fellow-feeling', another term Blacking used in discussing the influence of others on the self, may be defined as an awareness and sensitivity to other people, to the 'other self', and to the world of nature (see Blacking, 1983b, 1985c). It is the 'pleasure of association with neighbours and kinsfolk' that was one of the goals of Venda music (Blacking, 1985c: 51).

One aspect of fellow-feeling is 'bodily resonance' or 'bodily empathy' – the sensation and awareness of synchronicity with the physical movements of others around one in a music situation. Blacking referred to this as 'the experience of "falling into phase" that players shared' (1983b: 57). 'Each player had to hold fast to his/her part, and the collective effort produced both new cultural forms for the ears of performers and listeners and a richer, bodily experience for the participants' (1983b: 57). Bodily resonance seems to relate to 'groove' (see Keil and Feld, 1994) and entrainment – the process of one rhythm adjusting to fit another (see Kelly, 1988) – that are felt by the body both as an emotional connection and the physical sensation of coordinated motion (after all, music is made through motion). 'Thus, sensuous, bodily experience was a consequence of correct musical performance … and a correct musical performance was a way of feeling' (Blacking, 1983: 57).

Supracultural

Blacking moved far beyond Durkheim's vision of culture when he wrote: 'Cultures are not creative; only individuals are creative' (1983b: 55). He argued that 'men are more remarkable and capable creatures than most societies ever allow them to be. This is not the fault of culture itself, but the fault of man, who mistakes the means of culture for the end, and so lives *for* culture and not *beyond* culture' (1973: 7). The idea of living beyond culture is the core theme of the 'supracultural' concept. 'Supracultural' activity is that which passes 'beyond restricted worlds of culturally defined reality' by reworking received cultural forms in an inspired act of individual creativity so that something greatly affective is brought forth (1985c: 44).

While considering the rules of Venda music performance, Blacking describes how certain combinations of musical sounds seem to exceed normal expectations. Of the 'dozens of permutations and combinations that occur … some are more or less acceptable to everyone at the time of performance, and others are much more than that: they are positively transcendental in their effects on audience and performers' (1981: 189). By using one's imagination to chisel away at the received forms of tradition, the resulting supracultural expression could not only transform and enrich the established tradition, but also have a transcendental effect upon those involved (see Blacking, 1985c: 44).

In Blacking's view, transcendent states are often made possible through social music-making, dance or other aesthetically-oriented activities. According to Blacking's identity theory, the transcendent experience that occurs in the social environment 'generates such deep commitment to the people and/or institutions and activities associated with the experience that a strong, personal sense of direction motivates decision-making in a wide range of institutional contexts' (Blacking, 1983b: 52). Although 'music can be used for all sorts of social and political purposes as a kind of totemic emblem … it is only affecting and effective *as music* when it is internalized as a bodily response to a set of cultural symbols' (1983b: 52, emphasis in original). When music is emotionally effecting, it reinforces group identity because 'people's commitment' to the group is 'reinforced by the impact of the music on their senses' (1983b: 52). The emotional tie resulting from the intense pleasure of transcendent experience serves as a primary force motivating[4] the individual to act on behalf of those institutions that facilitated the experience. When individual creativity combines with traditional patterns of music performance to make those motivating musical moments happen, the very nature of the self is tied to the very nature of culture and society (see Figure 8.2). Not only does transcendent experience link the self to society, but it also serves as the primary occasion for experiencing the 'other self' within.

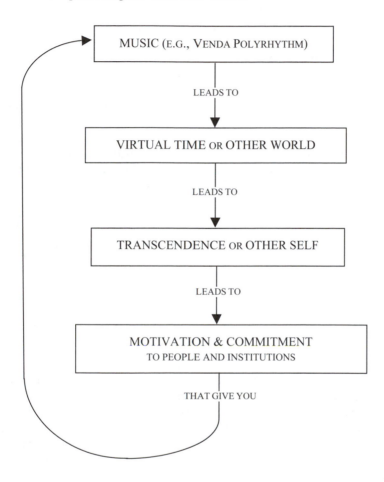

Figure 8.2   Flowchart of motivation through music

Another form of transcendence is the world of 'virtual time' created by music (Blacking, 1967: 17). I believe it was the philosopher Susanne Langer who first used the term 'virtual time' to refer to the quality of time passing more slowly or more quickly than ontological time (that is, clock time) (Langer, 1953: 109). Later, in 1969, Blacking wrote: 'We may say that ordinary daily experience takes place in a world of *actual time*. The essential quality of music is its power to create another world of *virtual time*' (1995a [1969]: 34, emphasis in original). Music offers the possibility of stepping out of ordinary, daily social rhythms and into rhythmic relationships mediated by music. When this happens, music becomes the interface for social entrainment (see the discussion of 'fellow-feeling' above), and, in this way, music provides for a transcendence of the ordinary social order.

Creating a 'special world of time' is what distinguishes music from non-music for the Venda (see Blacking, 1973: 48). It is time, and not melody, which defines Venda music, so it is not surprising that Blacking emphasized the element of time as that which sets apart the transcendent from the ordinary. Transcendence occurs through the 'virtual time' of music because 'we often experience greater intensity of living when our normal time values are upset' (Blacking, 1973: 52).

> It is because music can create a world of virtual time that Mahler has said that it may lead to 'the 'other world'—the world in which things are no longer subject to time and space' (Bonavia 1956, p. 204). Likewise, Hindemith speaks of 'victory over external forces and a final allegiance to spiritual sovereignty' (Wilson 1962, p. 135); and the Balinese speak of 'the other mind' as a state of being which can be reached through dancing and music (de Zoete 1953, 12f). They [the 'other world', 'spiritual sovereignty', the 'other mind'] refer to states in which people become keenly aware of the true nature of their being, of the 'other self' within themselves and other human beings, and of their relationship with the world around them. (Blacking, 1995a [1969]: 34).

The 'other self'

So, what is the 'other self', exactly? The other self is the memory or prospect of self in the experience of transcendence, also referred to as the 'internal other' (Blacking, 1983b: 52). In fact, the connection in Blacking's writings between the concept of the 'other self' and the concept of transcendent experience is so strong that when we read the phrase, 'other self', we can nearly always interchange it with the phrase 'transcendent experience'. To quote Blacking: 'the other self ... was invoked by the transcendent state of the self' (1973: 44–45; 1983b: 57; 1985c).

Blacking states on several occasions that the memory of one's self in a transcendent state, as well as the anticipation of again achieving transcendence, are important components of the 'other self'. Thus, for Blacking, the concept of the 'other self' is tied to one's sense of who one is at different points in time, and this time-sense relates to one's awareness that one has not always been the same. Any normal 'self' is aware of time, past and future. In this regard, one's identity actually consists of many other senses of self. One of those very remarkable moments of having a different sense of self is during transcendent experiences – the 'loss of self in Being' (Fromm cited in Blacking, 1973: 52). It could be said that the knowledge of the self in transcendent experience *is* the 'other self'. This awareness of transcendence, the experience of the 'other self', Blacking argues, is highly motivating – one desires to relive that euphoric experience. As a consistent motivating force, Blacking is able to place the 'other self' at the core of his identity theory.

Although transcendence is universally sought and achievable, the other self can be 'defined' in different ways in different contexts, as a matter of 'interpretation of the "otherness"' one feels (Blacking, 1983b: 57). For example, as Blacking describes the situation, all the participants of *ngoma* might have experienced transcendence and experienced their 'other self'; but 'their consequent actions were constrained by their interpretation of the "otherness" that they felt' (1983b: 57). Types of 'otherness' included 'common group identity' and 'fellow-feeling which transcended normal sociability' (1983b: 57). Only for those who were in their own homes, could the 'other self' be *defined as* their ancestor spirit, and therefore their experience of the 'other self' was *translated into* possession by their ancestor spirit. '[T]he crucial difference between people's responses [to music] lay in the definition of the other self who was invoked by the transcendent state of the self' (1983b: 58). As Blacking thought of it, it wasn't necessary for the 'other self'' to be translated into a culturally recognizable form, such as an ancestor spirit: 'Having feelings through music could be *an end in itself* or a means to an end, depending on the context of the feelings and the person having them' (1995a [1969]: 177, emphasis added).

For the Venda, ancestor possession was a 'very personal manifestation ... of transcendental experience' compared to *tshikona* where transcendence was associated not with one's own ancestor spirits, but 'with the world around [the performers], in which "the other self" within themselves ... communicated with time past and future' (Blacking, 1983b: 50). Here, Blacking invokes the 'virtual time' concept, implying that in this transcendent state of the 'other self', people may sense not just a 'loss of self in Being', but a loss of time in eternity (see Huxley, 1946: 312 concerning his concept of the 'timeless Now', cited by Blacking).

Blacking's publications frequently allude to his ideas about transcendence, 'virtual time', and the 'other self', and he often used them to build new theoretical models, even though he often had little corroborating evidence for the existence of these phenomena. One easily notices the conjectural nature of the sources noted by Blacking in support of these concepts, drawn from the amateur ethnographer de Zoete, philosophers Dewey and Langer, the theologian Huxley, humanistic psychologists Maslow and Fromm, and biographies of Stravinsky, Mahler (by Bonavia), and Hindemith (by Wilson). The most compelling evidence for Blacking's ideas comes from his own rigorous musical and ethnographic analyses of the Venda.

It is not clear just where Blacking derived the idea that the self and other could be so closely related as to become a state of consciousness. Despite obvious influences, Blacking's 'other self' concept comes neither from the Venda, nor from Western anthropology nor from philosophy. The 'other self' is suggested by Venda cosmology that places a reincarnated ancestral spirit within every newborn in a cumulative 'cycle of existence'. Blacking describes the other self as the 'real self' of the ancestor spirit 'return[ing] to earthly society' (1995c: 178–79). But there is no evidence that the term 'other self' is derived from the Venda. Furthermore, the 'other self' was clearly meant to be a universal concept, of which the Venda have a unique variant. Durkheim's idea of the 'impersonal' suggests the idea of otherness being internalized into the self, but neither this nor Blacking's own 'suprapersonal' concept is what he meant by the 'other self'. Robbins's entry on identity (Robbins, 1973 cited extensively by Blacking [1983b]), is suggestive, because Robbins discusses ideas about the 'folk concept of the soul' with which Blacking was surely familiar, including Tylor's description of the soul as 'the second self' and G.H. Mead's as 'the double'. De Zoete's mention of the Balinese concept of the 'other mind,' in the introduction to *The Other Mind: A Study of Dance in South India* (1953), appears in the first printing of Blacking's idea. But since de Zoete offers nothing more specific than that the 'other mind' is also attained through music and dance, we cannot deduce more than a nominal similarity. What becomes clear from examining Blacking's notes, publications and sources is that ideas of 'otherness' within the self – whether in the form of 'impersonal reason', an ancestral spirit, a soul, or an 'other mind' – were attendant in Blacking's intellectual environs.

What Blacking seems to have found in these sources were encouraging glimmers of affirmation for his burgeoning philosophical proposition, which I suspect he arrived at inductively, based on his own experience first as a musician and second as an anthropologist. I get the sense that Blacking developed the 'other self' idea 'creatively' (in his own sense of the word) by piecing together his experience and these reports of other creative individuals he met or about whom he read.

Despite the inconclusive evidence, Blacking was so convinced of the existence of the 'other self' that he called for scholars to make it central to their investigations of identity theory (1983b); he implored educators (1985c) to teach children music in a way that would ensure their experience of the 'other self'. In no less than four important publications (1973, 1983b, 1985c, 1995c [1985],) he asserted that experiencing the 'other self' was the key to fully realizing one's potential.

The case of Haitian Vodou singing and spirit possession[5]

Blacking's theory of music and identity, and especially his concept of the 'other self', relate in very useful ways to the analysis of the social significance of Haitian Vodou singing and spirit possession. Illuminating similarities between a diverse world of comparable musical experiences, his theory forms a bridge between local cultural practices, values and knowledge and ethnomusicology's more unitarian world-view.

Vodou is not a religion, but a way of life; Vodou governs how people relate to nature, to other people and to the spiritual realm. The term 'Vodou' refers to this culture, as well as to spirits, and to the festivals and music supplicating its spirits. In Vodou, spirit possession represents the embodiment of an idealized 'Other-self within' in so far as Vodou's highest social ideals originate from the spirits and are imparted during spirit possession. (Here, I capitalize 'Other' to emphasize that this 'other' is an ideal type (*a la* Weber) with a privileged position in Vodou cosmology and social order.) The 'otherness' I intend by the term 'Other-self within' is akin to what Blacking meant by the term 'supra-personal': the presence of others' ideas and values internalized within the individual psyche. I propose that the Other-self within, as expressed during transcendence in a Vodou music and ritual context, is a manifestation of the highest values imaginable by the person being possessed. It is a sort of projection, if you will, of one's deepest religious or spiritual values into a dramatic, physical form. Within the narrow confines of a small family-based community of Vodou practitioners, this concept works very well. Yet it is possible that the same concept could partly account for the variations between spirits in different regions of Haiti, as well as changes in nation, name and attributes of the same spirit in different communities, the variations evident within every possession and the diverse ends that spirits serve – from the noble and just to the perverse and sinister. While it is conceivable that all possessions may be partly explained with regard to the needs and values of the people involved, I can only confirm the attribution of such values to the spirits themselves within the confines of the family group I worked with.

My idea of the Other-self within is not explicitly expressed by the *sèvitè*—the people who serve the spirits – but rather derives from a widely held social principle of *respè* – literally 'respect' – in which selves and others are identified according to their role in complex interrelationships of giving and receiving care. *Respè* is a model for social interaction where a person who *can* provide others with protection, education, material needs, or healing is *obligated* to do so. The one being nurtured is *obligated* to show deference and respect to the caregiver. *Respè* is a primary cultural value in Haiti, regardless of whether you practise – Vodou or not. Social hierarchies are maintained through displays of respect or deference as, for example, when a visitor kisses the eldest female before greeting the others. In Haiti the saying 'It is for the younger to respect their elders, but for elders to protect the younger' applies to all social classes and religious affiliations. Disregarding the expectations of the *respè–proteje* system is considered to be abandoning those who rely on you.

When *respè* or protection are not reciprocated, social dysfunction results. Such is the case in Haiti, which has the worst standard of living in the western hemisphere (only ranking higher than areas embroiled in violent civil war). The intense poverty, hunger, suffering and political marginalization of Haiti's *klas pòv*[6] ('poor masses') is a replication of patterns of exploitation and degradation of human life normalized during slavery and systematically replicated after independence by Haiti's wealthy elite. The Catholic Church's attacks on Vodou have helped shore up the elite's economic exploitation of the *klas pòv*. Over the last century, fundamental Protestants have joined in the hotly moralistic rhetoric to condemn Vodou as Satanic.

Whereas antagonism toward Vodou once was largely a class issue, today it strongly divides the *klas pòv* (see especially Beauvoir and Dominique, 1988). Some people convert to Protestant sects as a consequence of their desperation, for Protestant-run schools provide daily meals and the possibility of college education in the United States. Protestant worship is also attractive because it allows for experiences of the 'other self' and expressions of high morality. Notwithstanding the benefits, conversions are fraught with problems, not just for the immediate family who may remain committed to Vodou, but also for society, since the vicious anti-Vodou rhetoric has paralysed the collective power of Haiti's large *klas pòv* more effectively than anything the ruling elite has ever perpetrated by law or taxation. At the same time, corruption is systemic from national politics down to the local parish: no leader seems above succumbing to the temptation to exploit an impoverished and vulnerable population.

My research centred on the household of a Vodou *sèvitè* named Lilyàn, whose patron spirit is Jean Dantor. Lilyàn believes that human suffering in Haiti is due to a lack of education in the ways of *respè*, which results in a lack of compassion, wisdom and charity. Or as the spirit, Jean Dantor, summarized the problem, human suffering is caused by *move moun* – bad people. 'Humanity is crippled', and 'everyone suffers', says Lilyàn. Haitian society is turned on its head[7] – caught up in a confusion of behavioural standards of which the principle of *respè* is merely one strategy tempering fervent individualism. Within this kind of confusion, any religious or cultural system finds difficulty in maintaining a coherent system of ideas about personal and sociocultural identity. Yet, despite antagonistic and dysfunctional Haitian social and political arrangements, within many family units the *respè* model continues to serve as a coherent system of ideas about self and others – both human and spirit and the natural environment.

Within the principle of duty and respect, as interpreted in the Vodou practised in Lilyàn's household, spirits can be seen as the ultimate caregivers involved in a *sèvitè*'s life. Believed to be omniscient and omnipresent, Vodou spirits have the greatest capacity to fulfil the obligations of a caretaker: they are aware of more, they have greater wisdom, they have a greater capacity for forgiveness, greater compassion and a greater ability to protect as well as discipline (usually by withdrawing protection). In this sense, spirits are the ideal type of the significant Other.

Respè as a personal quest

I have not observed or recorded Lilyàn during her private times of *respè*. But she readily discusses these times and describes them as being a time of personal devotion set aside from the busy shuffle of work. She says that to practise *respè* is to just sit, quietly listening for the guidance of the spirits. Lilyàn preferred to hold our interviews in a relatively calm and quiet place. She seemed intent on making me understand what *respè* was, and what importance it had for her by demonstrating these principles in her style of speaking and singing. And I understood our discussions to be in a mode not unlike her own devotional times.

The renditions of songs that Lilyàn recorded during these discussions were freer, slower, more elaborate, more extended and more embellished in comparison to those typical of the ceremonies (where other family members generally led the singing). Singing this way emulates Lilyàn's comprehension of the spirits's ideals of *respè*, *sajès* and *sansibilite* – where *sajès* means not only wisdom but also good behaviour, and *sansibilite* means compassion *and* awareness – for awareness of another's suffering is a prerequisite for recognizing their need.[8] Even when Lilyàn talks about these ideals, she uses a calm, slower and lower-pitched voice. As she tells me about *respè*, her speaking and singing style are iconic of her practice of *respè* in which being still and attentive is necessary to listen for the spirits's direction.

In Vodou tradition it is believed that spirits give the songs to people, and the songs are a rich source of esoteric knowledge. Indeed, compared to speech, a song's musical parameters conveying emotional attitude are largely fixed, preordained by the composition's rhythm and melodic contours as well as the performance tradition which are themselves preordained by the Vodou spirits. In this respect, songs tend to enforce a particular attitude towards the topic of the words being sung. This may cause a singer to realign her own attitude to that conveyed by the song and the singing style. Because, in Vodou, the songs are taught to people by spirits – sometimes in dreams, but also during possessions – and because spirits sing while they are in human form, the emotional meaning expressed in the composition and performance aligns directly with the very ideals that the spirits intend to teach humans through singing the song. In other words, what is to be learned through singing Vodou songs is not the meaning of the words per se but, rather, the emotional meaning conveyed by how the words are expressed musically. These meanings are grasped through 'living with the song' – by repeatedly singing the song in accord with its performance tradition. In fact, only after I learned to sing these songs myself did I begin to apprehend the expressive stereotypes at play. Through repetition, in the course of daily but also ceremonial enculturation, comes an embodiment of the habits of this expressive practice. Consequently, *singing well gradually and effectively imparts the spirits's moral lessons.*

An example of this principle became evident one day when Lilyàn brought me to a beautiful place in the mountains atop cliffs that tumbled into the sea far below. This was Lilyàn's family's property, although just the foundations of several homes remained after having been destroyed in 1986 during the tumultuous aftermath of Jean-Claude Duvalier's brutal dictatorship. This period is referred to as the *dechoukaj* ('uprooting') when Duvalier's supporters and his private militia, the *Tonton Makout,* were targeted for revenge. But typical of Haitian history, the political instability also inspired the persecution of Vodou *sèvitè*. During the anti-superstition campaign sanctioned by the Roman Catholic archbishop in 1986, many prominent Vodou *sèvitè* were murdered and their properties plundered (see Beauvoir and Dominique 1988).

Today, Lilyàn lives instead on her husband's family property. During a recording session there, on 19 July 1998 Lilyàn sang the song '*Paren Ogoun*' and described the *dechoukaj* at length. The song is about people who hate Vodou spirits and tells of the spirit Ogoun's continued protection of them despite the persecution of his followers. Another layer of meaning comes from knowing that Ogoun is considered as a warrior general; the pacifistic quality of this song reveals a depth to Ogoun's personality rarely recognized. Rather than expressing vengeance or anger in return for hatred, Lilyàn's performance expressed an adoption of the spirit Ogoun's attitude of tolerance. The performance conveyed her centring in *respè* to such an extent that even the word '*rayi*' ('to hate') was sung in a calm tempo and low range characteristic of *respè*. This performance style was consistent throughout all other recordings I collected of Lilyàn singing this song. Even when Lilyàn led this song during *seremoni*, accompanied by other singers and a battery of percussion, the tempo remained relatively slow, and – though more metrically constant – any rhythmic feel was thwarted by elongated nasal consonants, rubato and sliding between the notes. It was only in comparison to all the other instances of Lilyàn's discourse about anger that I had recorded and analysed that I came to realize how extraordinary this musical setting is. The musical setting is largely responsible for communicating the very moral lesson of the song – the spirit's message of forgiveness. Understanding this song means singing it in a way that embodies the values of the Other-self within, which in this case is Ogoun and his genuine regard for others – including his persecutors.

Paren Ogoun	Parent Ogou
Ou pap genyen ze	You haven't got eyes
Pou nou gade sa ye	for you to see what it is
Sa yap fe nou	they are doing for you
Di ou met rayi nou	You can hate us
Men se ou wa we.	but it is us you will see.
Apres Bondye lesen lezany	After God, the saints, the *zany*
Nap viv ake ou	we are living with you

Festival singing and socialization

In keeping with domestic Vodou tradition, Lilyàn hosts an annual celebration for her family's master spirit, Jean Dantor. Jean Dantor is associated with the Catholic saint, John the Baptist, and the Vodou festival coincides with the Catholic feast day by starting on 23 June and continuing over seven or eight days. Attended by nearly 80 relatives, neighbours and friends of all ages, the festival relies heavily on everyone's cooperation from cooking and cleaning to singing throughout many nights. Every year the festival varies according to the family's financial means. The year I conducted my research, Lilyàn's family had sustained significant financial losses; difficulties in recovering were compounded by her fifth pregnancy and the deteriorating national economic situation.

According to Lilyàn's eldest son, it is a beautiful thing to have a Vodou festival in your home. Preparations include making home repairs and improvements, decorating, shopping, baking and finally, bathing and donning your best clothes. In between the *seremoni*s, after getting a couple of hours' sleep, adults hang-out telling jokes (*yo chita blage*), recounting stories, discussing problems, and possbly watching World Cup soccer on television, while lively youngsters run and play games with cousins and neighbours.

For the *seremoni*, all the Vodou spirits will in turn be shown *respè* with songs, and their favourite perfumes, foods and beverages are placed on a centre table. Lilyàn hires drummers to accompany the singing and dancing to create a festive atmosphere.

Each song is *monte* – begun – by a singer who is mature in terms of musical and spiritual knowledge; after the introduction, the other participants respond by singing the *ede*, which literally means 'help'. Helping is obligatory for anyone feasting in the yard, and participants may be publicly admonished by the organizers if they are not singing enthusiastically enough. Once the *ede* and the drumming enter, the leader confines her personal expression to the regular patterns of song that facilitate participation, while the lead part might alternate between two or three experienced singers. The act of singing well in this way models the highest social values of cooperation, mutual support and respect that are the core values expressed in the Vodou song repertoire. The performance of these ideal social relations creates an atmosphere of social harmony necessary for spirit possession: 'spirits will not come where there is fighting or arguing' (Lilyàn, personal communication). If the participants sing the *ede* and have a good time dancing, the spirits will not only be enticed to come to the *fèt* ('party') but will stay longer. The energy they invest in their work is rewarded by the transcendence which the participants may personally experience, as well as by the benefits imparted by the spirits who join the festivities in physical form. 'It's at these times', explains Lilyàn, 'that the spirits can tell you secrets about the future, and it is the spirits who show us how to share; it is they who show us how to live'.[9]

Performance of possession

Once possession occurs, there are noticeable stylistic differences in the musical expression of the Other-self within. The point of the singing differs as well. Spirits sing for a number of reasons, for example, to call other spirits, to teach a new song, to educate and to *pran plezi* ('have fun'). During festivals, a spirit has the prerogative to take over leading the songs. Musical analyses reveal that spirits introduce extreme variations in both the melodies and texts of the songs. Spirits can halt the ritual progression by taking over the singing; ultimately the master spirit of the family mediates between the other spirits' and the family's agenda. When a spirit is working, people know to hold their response, and not sing *ede,* as this only prolongs the work and delays the point in time when people can start asking for the spirit's help or counsel.

In comparing performances of Lilyàn as herself and as possessed by the family's master spirit, Jean Dantor, the most noticeable difference is the spirit's constant switching between singing and speaking – often mid-phrase. Jean Dantor also consistently sings at a pitch about a perfect fourth higher than Lilyàn and uses a vocal timbre coloured by constriction at the top of the throat. Other notable differences are frequent and extreme timbre changes, and more exaggerated dynamic changes that are not characteristic of Lilyàn's singing.

Through the differences in singing style, Jean Dantor asserts total control over the ceremonial discourse. Having established himself as the focus of everyone's attention, Jean directly admonished one family member for having two sexual partners, criticized a close family friend for loving money too much and supervised the butchering and distribution of a ram sacrificed earlier in the morning.

Below is an excerpt of a speech and song that Jean Dantor (in possession of Lilyàn) performed during an evening visit to Lilyàn's household. The content concerns the cause of human suffering and his assurance that those whose greed causes suffering will never escape the consequences: they and their own children for generations to come will suffer in kind. The song poignantly reinforces the message of Jean Dantor's speech. In the song, the spirit Ziya admonishes human behaviour saying that humans are guilty of bringing misery upon themselves.[10]

Jean Dantor speaking:

Men se yo ki tourne vin peye sa ankò.	They are the ones who have to turn back and pay for that still.
Si yo tout pou sa kite di pa bon,	If they would quit, say it is not right,
wi y pa te ban lè mouri	yes they should not make you suffer/die
tout ou es ap fe mouri.	of all of those responsible for deaths.
Eske pou pa jwenn youn menm	Is it that you won't find even one
pou rete nan menm kondisyon-an?	who will stay in these same conditions?
Pou sèneryen sèneryen	They who are totally unconcerned about
petit-a petit-o peyi-sa.	the children, the country's children.
Tout sa ki sèneryen	All these who are totally uncaring
se petit-a petit-o	it is the children, their children
ki peye sa, y pa sa?	who pay for it, isn't it so?

Someone speaks:

Peyi a tombe.	The country is falling.

Jean Dantor, singing:

Ziya, Ziya alawe	Ziya, Ziya oh!

Jean Dantor speaking:

Ma prale, wi.	I'm going to leave.

Another person says:

Jean, ou pa ka ale,	Jean, you can't leave,
m pa genyen de mo adye.	you haven't said farewell to me.

Jean Dantor, singing again:

Rele Ziya alawe	Call Ziya oh!

Jean Dantor speaking:

Retire flè yo pita.	Better yet, remove those flowers.

The semantic differences communicated in *how* the spirit manipulates timbre, contour and timing, as well as differences in discourse style, help to identify the voice being heard as that of a spirit. In so doing, the differences give the spirit's singing and speaking the additional moral authority necessary to most effectively discipline, teach, protect and heal the community and its individuals. It is largely through Jean Dantor's singing that he fulfils his own spiritual obligation on behalf of the family (in terms of the ritual work he must perform at the ceremonies) as the ideal caregiver in the Haitian *respè-proteje* complex. As the extract above shows, Jean Dantor (the spirit) interspersed singing lines of this song (for example, '*Ziya, Ziya, alawe*') into his conversation with people gathered at the *kraze-tab* ritual. At the conclusion of this conversation the spirit Jean Dantor and the people gathered at the *kraze-tab* began to sing the song together. The opening lyrics and the song structure are set out below:

monte:

Rele Ziya men alawe
Pech a later-yo
Di mande later-o
Nou move pou tet-a-nou

Rele pech a later nou move
Ver di tel a-yo nou mechan-an ey
M sezi anmwaye, map pral alawè
Ver di tel a-yo nou mechan an nou
*   pou tet-a-nou*

ede:

Ziya, Ziya alawe
Ziya, Ziya alawe
Ziya, Ziya alawe
Pech a latè ou mechan menm pou
*   tet-a-nou*

lead:

Anba later nou move
Inverti ter-a-yo nou mechan-an-ye

Ma pral Ziya ma pral alawe
Kretyen-yo nou mechan pou tet-a-
nou

beginning:

Call Ziya, here is *alawe*
Sinners of the world
Demanding the world
You're bad for your own sake

Call sinners of the world you are foul
Turn, tell some of them you are evil
I'm totally dismayed, I'm going *alawe*
Turn, tell some you're wicked to your
    own selves!

help:

Ziya, Ziya *alawe*
Ziya, Ziya *alawe*
Ziya, Ziya *alawe*
Sinners of the world you are bad even to
    your own selves

lead:

You down on eaarth are foul-tempered
Turning the world upside down, you are
    wicked,
I am going Ziya I am going *alawe*
Everyone is greedy, but at your own
    expense
etc.

Singing Vodou songs in Lilyàn's home, whether as personal devotion or in *seremoni* to call the spirits, is an important means of internalizing good moral behaviour, values and motivations. The internalization or 'embodiment' of Vodou's spirit-derived ideals occurs just as all forms of cultural acquisition do: through the internalization into ourselves of others' words, acts, opinions and evaluations. *Sansib* – aware and compassionate people – are, in particular, most familiar with this 'suprapersonal' presence or morality within their psyche.

These same individuals achieve full integration with this Other-self within when they translate the 'other self' felt during transcendent music experiences as a manifestation of a Vodou spirit.

While from my perspective, the moral values of participants strongly influence their interpretation of the Other-self within, in Lilyàn's family this is thought about from the spirit's perspective: they believe that spirits only manifest on those people of the best moral character. This is because spirits simply fill a *vesèl*, meaning they are constrained in their physical manifestation by the limitations of the human body, the singing voice and the moral and intellectual development of the person they possess. Therefore, the interpretation of the 'other self' in the performance of possession is contingent on the performer's 'suprapersonal' awareness – that is, their internalized social values.

In comparison with the conflicting value systems informing everyday social interaction (described above), there is a remarkable coherence with the musical system underlying Vodou singing as seen from the *monte-ede* structure, the modal organization of melodic movement and the recurring patterns of the expressive stereotypes. For Vodou practitioners, participating in the recreation of these patterns of sound creates a public display of shared musical values that can only be achieved in the Vodou festival environment.[11] Participation in a redundant aesthetic form like Vodou singing can facilitate the kind of social interaction that leads to feelings of social solidarity and belonging.

Many people participating in the ceremonies do not share Lilyàn's level of understanding, just as they do not share her introspective devotional practice nor her acts of charity nor practice of healing. Many family members are not particularly concerned with the spiritual or mystical aspects of Vodou; for them, these ceremonies have significance primarily as a family gathering. Everyone comes because it is fun and uplifting; most arrive with intentions to help show *respè,* hoping for the favour of the spirits in return, while a few seek personal enlightenment or edification. Like Blacking suggests for *ngoma*, not all within a Vodou *seremoni* interpret their other selves in the same way. Some may be exuberant and express joy, while a few may express their 'other selves' as possession by a Vodou spirit – an Other-self within. For all who are committed to the social principles embodied in Vodou song, singing has the potential to be absolutely transcendent.

The total musical experience

A thorough examination of the transcendent effects of music would be incomplete without a full assessment of music's various semiotic qualities that are instrumental in creating a musical space for experiencing the other-self within. Music's semantic power ultimately resides in the *total musical experience,* the sum of all musical affects or effects, whether they be referential or non-referential – that is, certain emotional, physiological and cognitive responses not necessarily involving symbolic meaning.

Within the disciplines of philosophy and musicology, the field of music semiology has primarily focused on how music can be meaningful in referential ways: as a symbolic system (much as language is a symbolic system); by referring to its own self (in terms of the expectations of a style or the internal structure); as an expression of emotions; for the associations it evokes; or as an icon (for example, of music's associated institutions or social events, as a marker of identity, or the arrival of a point in a ritual sequence – see Blacking (1973: 49–50)). Within this semiotic tradition, many studies of music in ritual have focused upon music's symbolic power to trigger trance states. But I propose that the non-referential attributes of music are largely responsible for creating a total musical experience through which people can feel what Blacking calls a transcendent state of self – the 'other self'.

Through publication (for example, Blacking, 1995c [1985]), teaching, and conference participation, Blacking contributed to what has become a basic tenant of ethnomusicology: that proper context and enculturation are essential for music's effectiveness at the onset of possession trance. Although there is an extensive body of ethnographic evidence regarding music's role in transcendent experiences, the 'unanalysable' nature of such experiences (in that they are profound not just in the realm of observable *experience,* but especially in the realm of inner *sensation*) means they still elude precise scientific description and complete comprehension in terms of human psychology. As a result, many of our ideas about the role of music and trance remain conjectural.

One of Blacking's contributions to the study of music and trance was his observation that music is effective in inducing transcendent states that are not exclusively interpreted as possession trance. For example, he often asserted that, in Venda *ngoma* ceremonies, all the participants could be deeply moved by a good music performance and all appeared to have the same intense musical experience, even though only those in their own home would be possessed (Blacking, 1995c [1985]: 178). By claiming that, for the Venda, transcendence was always the aim of music-making, Blacking turned his focus away from possession trance per se. At another point, Blacking wrote about 'the effectiveness of [a] particular *style* of music' (1995c [1985]: 178, emphasis added), which, to me, suggests that he believed that music's effectiveness is not derived exclusively from symbols embedded in particular pieces or musical motives, but rather from the totality of behaviours and tradition ordering the sounds that constitute a style (perhaps we could call this a 'supra-referential' meaning). Finally, Blacking commented that 'musical experience itself was a kind of possession' (1995c [1985]: 180; see also 1973: 48) and that intense musical experience could be an end in itself (1995c [1985]: 177; 1983b: 57) rather than something that needed to culminate in a possession trance. Music's capacity to fully engross human consciousness was not merely to serve as an impetus for transcendent experience; instead, an intense musical experience was the very sensation of transcendence itself.

It is a fact well established by scientifically modelled research that there are 'inevitable physiological responses to music' (see Blacking, 1983b: 48), but it appears that trance is *not* one of those responses. For example, rhythmic drumming affects any normal person at the precognitive level of brain stem functioning, but this effect is obviously an insufficient trigger for the onset of trance. If it were, as Rouget so effectively argued against Neher's (and similar) studies, then most of Africa would be in trance all the time (Rouget, 1977a: 234; 1985). In a review of the extant studies in music psychology, Patrick McMullen (1996: 387) reports no success in psychologists' endeavours to establish consistent links between musical stimuli and affective response.

This is not to say that a physiological response to rhythm is irrelevant to the total musical experience. Blacking himself often stated that, although the proper context was necessary for possession, 'ultimately, [possession] depended on a proper, rhythmically steady performance of the music ...' (Blacking, 1983b: 57; see also 1973: 44–45; 1985c). McMullen has advocated that inquiries be redirected to ask how musical experience generates less specific effects, such as generalized aesthetic response and 'activation' or arousal at different psychological, physiological or behavioural levels (see McMullen, 1996: 390–91). Whether noticed consciously or not, music's effect on the body (in terms of changes in blood circulation, blood pressure, respiration, cardiac contractions, immune system and so on) contributes to the effect of a total musical experience.

In light of this discussion, further progress in our understanding of the transcendent effects of music demands a thorough examination of the role of music's non-referential qualities. Although my assertions remain conjectural, intuition leads me to hypothesize that the ubiquitous, non-referential qualities of musical experience are instrumental in creating transcendent experience. To develop this hypothesis, I will consider the physiological phenomena involved in time perception, sound localization and gesture–motor perception. The objective is to assess the effectiveness of these modes of perception in creating a total musical experience with the potential to engender a sense of a virtual world of time, activity and space in which a person may achieve a transcendent state of self.

Non-referential meaning

As discussed above, Blacking's mention of 'virtual time' was often accompanied by an entourage of metaphors for extraordinary, 'otherly' experiences: 'the other world', 'inner-world', 'other mind', and especially, the 'other self'. In *Music and Trance*, Rouget speaks in a similar fashion about musical sounds marking out a space, proposing that music's sort of crystallization of time has the role of maintaining a certain continuity of 'being-in-the-world' that is related to possession trance experience (Rouget 1985: 121–24). (Not surprisingly, these comments are found in Rouget's discussion of the psychological affects of music.) As we make music, being 'in time' with other humans engenders in us a particular sense of being in the world. Blacking referred to this phenomenon as 'bodily resonance' or 'bodily empathy'.

Blacking asserted the non-referential impact of music's 'virtual time' on transcendent experience in statements such as: 'The rhythm of music per se can transport us in a variety of ways, from tapping our feet to falling into a state of trance or giving vent to anger' (Blacking, 1995a [1969]: 34). In the frame of 'virtual time', music has the potential to mediate not only social entrainment (as discussed above), but all dimensions of time flow, including memory, as well as continuation and expectations – a form of projection into the musical future – based on our knowledge and past experiences of music structures (see Lipscomb, 1996: 139).

Music psychology research has established that '[h]earing is a primary sense through which we create a stable, inner world of time' (Hodges, 1996a: 45). This ability originated millions of years ago, at a time when it is believed that mammals hunted at night. It was an adaptive advantage for mammals to perceive sounds occurring across time as indications of approaching or retreating prey or predators and most importantly, to 'detect their exact direction of movement, entirely in the dark' (Hodges, 1996a: 45). Hodges contends that this ability to hear sequences of sound over time 'as connected patterns of movements in space' is one of the necessary cognitive facilities for comprehending musical contours, motives, and structures (Hodges, 1996a: 45 citing Campbell 1986: 263–64).

Timing cues are also largely responsible for creating our sense of the type of space we inhabit as well as the precise location of sounds in our environment. This psychological phenomenon is known as 'sound localization'. The auditory system of mammals can discern the tiny discrepancies between the time it takes a sound to reach one ear as compared to the other, as well as differences in the arrival time of sound waves reverberating off objects in our environment (Lipscomb and Hodges, 1996: 84). Using these minute discrepancies in arrival time, we are able to gain not only a general sense of our immediate landscape, but also come to know the direction and velocity of things moving around us, even if these movements are far away and out of view (Risset and Wessel, 1999: 142). Considering the importance of sound for creating our most basic sense of being in the world, it should not be surprising that sudden deprivation of acoustic information is highly disorienting. A stunning example of this came from Roger Darcy, an acoustic architect, who designed an anechoic chamber to be dead silent. When he entered his own creation to test it, he lost his balance and crumpled to the floor (personal communication). Roger's anecdote confirms how necessary, basic and automatic our use of acoustic phenomena is for placing ourselves in our world.

Not only is our sense of hearing our most pervasive sense – for even in sleep, the body responds to sounds not consciously perceived (Lipscomb and Hodges, 1996: 124) – it also appears that sound localization is an automatic function of the auditory system (Risset and Wessel, 1999: 142). Sound localization results in a mental map of our spatial environs, created from our perception of the movement, quality and intensity of sounds surrounding us. When I became aware that sound always represents movement in our environment, I realized that musical sounds must also react with this innate function of the auditory system to create the perception of a world of objects out of view, but nevertheless rising, falling, advancing and retreating, with velocity and depth. Such perceived musical movements would be mapped on to our associations with similar movements experienced in nature. If musical sounds can create a musical 'space', then what might be the results on the meaning of the music, or the quality of experience of the music, when it becomes subject to this innate function?

Although acoustic phenomena are automatically processed for location, I believe that experience and education can enhance the effects of spatialization, just as the awareness that an acoustic phenomenon in music will cause musical sounds to be interpreted spatially in ways different from other environmental phenomena. (Likewise, interpretations will be made according to the listener's development and cultural priming to attend to, or disregard, the effect.) When music dominates our hearing, or at least the focus of our attention, the phenomenon of sound localization results in our feeling part of a musical space that engages the totality of our being for as long as the music lasts. Obviously orchestral music and electro-acoustic music are involved in intentionally placing sounds in space, either with techniques of orchestration or by electronic sound diffusion. Nevertheless, even the musical contours of a solo voice can construct a world of shape and form and time which can transport us out of ordinary, non-musical experience.

Another factor potentially aiding in the construction of a complete musical reality is the involvement of the motor cortex in music perception. Although not yet clearly understood, research is being carried out to determine 'how the gestural experience of producing a sound in a physical world interacts with its perception' (Rissett and Wessel, 1999: 42, citing Cadoz *et al.*, 1984, 1993). Sundberg concluded that people 'seem to interpret [vocal] sounds in terms of how the voice organ was used in producing the sounds' (Sundberg, 1999: 210). Blacking similarly reported that, for the Venda, 'music sounds were always associated with a rhythmical stirring of the body, and I remember an old, blind, master musician criticising a performance on one of my tape recordings on the grounds that the drummers could not have been moving their shoulders and arms correctly' (Blacking, 1983b: 57). Frank Weins, my piano teacher at university, could *hear* whether I was playing with the proper technique and taught me to do the same.

The bottom line is that music perception involves senses other than hearing, such as the feeling of our body in motion (see also Hodges, 1996b: 256, 261–62; Keil and Feld, 1994; note also the above discussion of 'fellow-feeling' and 'bodily resonance'). If listening can engage the motor cortex because we imagine how a sound was physically produced, then it is possible that listening to music (and not even participating) can become totalizing by involving all of our capacities for sensation, action or being in the world, including physical motion (even if we are not physically producing the sound).

By comparison, singing to oneself more strongly involves the body in motion than does merely listening. It seems especially likely that a singer, such as Lilyàn, can absorb herself in her song with a physical commitment so deep that her singing becomes totally engrossing as she imposes on herself not just a musical space and a virtual time, but also a tradition of vocal gestures. In doing so, she may not only connect not with the traditions embodied in her 'suprapersonal' self, but she may also express her emotions and become 'possessed by the music itself' or potentially experience her 'other-self' as the Vodou spirit Jean Dantor, or Paren Ogoun.

With regard to music in religious practice, perhaps it is this totalizing experience of being in a *musical space* that helps convince us that a world is possible beyond what we see and touch. Some people may hold religious beliefs because the experience of music creating another world convinces them that a world beyond what they see is possible. Such an assertion is not new. Blacking himself wrote: 'Musical performances provided experimental proof of the spiritual nature of the universe ...' (Blacking, 1995a [1969]: 180). A person's sense of 'musical space' that may create the perception of an 'other world' is not simply an experiential frame that could be duplicated by any other artistic medium. If music's transcendent affects are uniquely due to how its sonic properties are perceived and interpreted by the human auditory system, then it is not merely rhetorical to suggest that *music is truly an incomparable aesthetic form*. This is not to say that all musics are equal in their aesthetic capacity. As Blacking put it, 'There is a difference between music that is occasional and music that enhances human consciousness, music that is simply for having and *music that is for being*' (1973: 50, emphasis added).

I have overstated the case for non-referential meaning in order to swing a conceptual pendulum back to the centre, because these effects have not received the same consideration as referential meanings of music. But while 'referential' and 'non-referential' may be convenient labels for recognizable aspects of experience, there is no proof that they are separable or independent. I suspect that all types of musical meaning are largely unified through emotional association and are contingent upon memory; while one aspect of meaning may mask another, one may also enhance the other for the full transcendent effect of the total musical experience. The focus of further research in this area should be to determine exactly how referential and non-referential meanings work in tandem. Social experience, physical sensation, emotion and symbolism *all* relate and are needed to make the most sense of our being in the world. The more we understand about how music is meaningful, the more resolved we must be that we can never fully know, in specific terms, what music means to an individual at any given moment. Yet, it will be through our continued research into the interaction between our variously labelled semantic experiences of music that we may ultimately understand the significance of music as something people care so deeply about that music motivates action and commitment in other spheres of life.

Conclusion

In Blacking's theory the 'other self' is related to a transcendent state of self which may be interpreted in numerous ways. Blacking places the definition of the other self somewhere between the awareness of oneself in a state of transcendence and the interpretation of the other self found in that state. For the hosts of a Venda *ngoma* ceremony, one definition of that other self may be the 'real self', which is the ancestral spirit that was reincarnated in that person upon their birth.

In relation to my own research, I have been thinking of the 'other self' as being expressed through the manifestation of a Vodou spirit. I have also embellished Blacking's model by thinking about the Vodou spirit as being a manifestation of the best caretaker imaginable within the Haitian *respè–proteje* model of ideal social relations. This 'suprapersonal' Other-self within could be thought of simply as a generic term for all the various manifestations of the 'other self' in Vodou's complex cosmology, in the sense that any manifestation of a Vodou spirit, regardless of name, is an embodiment of what the person being possessed has learned and can imagine to be of highest social value. The efficacy of and need for different representations (such as the more violent, revolutionary *Petwo* versus the more staid *Rada*) is never doubted in social terms, but the morality of the spiritual representation could be questioned in universalist terms. Finally, these 'other selves' expressed in Vodou possession trance, have a different social status than ordinary people, and they communicate this difference in the way in which they communicate musically, and their social authority is enhanced thereby.

The most valuable part of this endeavour for me has been to contemplate how the other is a part of the self, and how selves are aware of their own internal otherness. It is perhaps less remarkable to contemplate the *other* in the self than to really understand the *self as other*. In accomplishing this, Blacking transformed the landscape of identity theory and proved the central role of musical experience in creating the transcendent states that meld the self and the other in common humanity.

Notes

[1] I am grateful to the School of Anthropological Studies of Queen's University Belfast for their invitation to conduct research in the John Blacking Archive, and especially to Suzel Ana Reily for her hospitality. The Belfast collection contained many items of value in my search for the origins and meaning of the 'other self' concept. Files from John's early period of lecturing, publishing and letter-writing in South Africa, while at Pittsburg as well as at Queen's, provided me with a unique insight of his intellectual progression on concepts such as universals, biological foundations of behaviour, the meaning of music, and music's transformative power.

[2] Blacking states that even a single religious conversion experience is cumulative in that it requires preparation and is translated into action related to culture. (After this comment, Blacking wrote: 'cf Jung on St. Paul'. He indicated no specific reference.) Although Blacking does not use 'experience' exclusively to refer to what is socially shared, this shade of meaning is often in play. It helps to understand this, because often Blacking expresses the relation of self to society through simply using the words 'sensation' or 'feeling' to refer to what is personal, and 'experience' for what is social.

[3] The term 'self-actualization' was apparently first coined by Kurt Goldstein (Maslow, 1954: 91).

[4] Motivation is central to Blacking's theory of identity. This focus is clearly influenced by Tomkins's (1964) assertion that '*affects are the primary motives of men*' (1964: vii, emphasis in original), as well as Robbins's (1973) review article on identity which states that current concepts of culture lack a theory of motivation, which the identity concept could provide.

[5] I wish to thank the Wenner-Gren Foundation for Anthropological Research for underwriting the fieldwork upon which this discussion is based.

[6] In discussing class politics in Haiti, Averill writes:

> The term *klas* in Haiti does not refer to a position determined strictly by relationship to the means of production, but admits numerous criteria, including family background, geographic origins, wealth, education, phenotype, and comportment ... At the most superficial level, Haitians divide the country into two basic status groups: those with access to power and money (*lelit*, the elite) and those without (*pèp* or *mas*, the people or masses) ... [or] more often *rich* (rich) and *pòv* or *malere* (the poor or poverty stricken). (Averill, 1997: 3)

The *klas pòv*, or *pèp*, includes 'rural peasants, *abitan*, urban *proletaria, klas ouvriye* (urban working class), and structurally unemployed slum dwellers, *lounpen* (from lumpen proletariat)' (Averill, 1997: 4).

[7] The exact *kreyòl* phrases that Lilyàn used to describe Haiti's social problems include '*tout moun soufri*', '*lezòm enfimè*', and '*sosyete tet anba*'.

[8] Lilyàn said: '... *se respe ki manke ki fe we lezòm fin anfimyè, ou fin ak goum antre-yo, yo vin bay lajan plis anpotans ke san ... moun ki ap goume pou lajan ...*'. (personal communication, 1998).

[9] '*Se lè sa o y ka bay yon kek sekre ... Se yo yo menm ki montre nou koman pou pataje, se yo menm ki montre nou koman pou nou viv*' (Lilyàn, personal communication, 1998).

[10] There's irony in the fact that Ziya herself is a spirit known for wreaking havoc and disorder; children are removed from her presence to keep them safe (Lilyàn, personal communication, 1998).

[11] I mean this comment to be taken in comparison with individual singing where the sharing does not occur. There are many arenas for 'public displays of shared musical values' in Haiti. Vodou music in particular has been an historically significant presence in many Haitian popular musics (see Averill, 1997). Since the 1980s, *mizik rasin*—roots music predominantly based on Vodou music—has become an important genre of popular music. Richard Morse, leader of RAM, a *mizik rasin* band, tells me that he has witnessed possessions at *mizik rasin* concerts, and the exuberance displayed at Vodou festivals and *mizik rasin* concerts is not unparalleled to the reactions of fans at dances I have attended in the north by the local bands *Tropicana* or *Septenrional*.

CHAPTER NINE

Bach in a Venda Mirror: John Blacking and Historical Musicology

Britta Sweers

> We need ... waste little time with Blacking's rather portentous claim that only after understanding Venda music of the Transvaal has he been able to understand Western music properly. One is glad for Blacking; but he has not done anything to help *us* with Western music, however much he may have helped us with the repertory of Venda children's songs. (Kerman, 1985a: 167)

In *How Musical is Man?* John Blacking presents a fascinating analysis of the relationship between music, social behaviour and thought patterns within the South African Venda society. By emphasizing that the meaning of music cannot be derived merely from musical analysis, but rather that it is the construction of a specific sociocultural context, Blacking's study set the agenda for ethnomusicology well beyond the early 1970s when it was first published. Furthermore, it provides an exemplary reflexive account of how a Western ethnomusicologist's world-view came to be challenged by an encounter with a different musical system. Yet, the American musicologist Joseph Kerman would probably not have paid much attention to Blacking's work in his critique *Contemplating Music* (1985a) had Blacking not presented Venda music as a means of understanding *all* music cultures, including Western art music. If Blacking had to resort to the remote Venda to achieve an adequate understanding of his own culture, might Kerman not be right in viewing Blacking's perspective as highly idiosyncratic and of little interest to the wider world of music scholarship? Blacking's general claim thus leads to a relatively simple question: can ethnomusicology, conceived as the musicology of the other, be of use to historical studies that focus on Western cultures and, if so, how?

Ethnomusicology, particularly in the United States, has grown dramatically in the wake of the increasing popularity of 'world music'. In an effort to secure their position within academia in light of this development, music departments that traditionally focused almost exclusively on historical musicology have started to incorporate ethnomusicologists and popular music scholars into their staff. Furthermore, with the emergence of so-called 'New Musicology', theoretical issues have gained prominence, although, again, this has not always been motivated by a perceived need for reformation. This has also been the case in Germany where the major historical musicological society, *Die*

Gesellschaft für Musikforschung, drew up a memorandum in 1998 to demonstrate the discipline's innovative and interdisciplinary orientations. Facing severe financial cuts and increasing doubts about its practical use within political circles, musicology found itself being regarded by some as little more than a decorative appendage, referred to as an *Orchideenfach* ('orchid discipline'). In an effort to respond to this view, the memorandum underlined the field's importance, by citing research undertaken within ethnomusicology, systematic musicology and popular music studies. It is worth noting, however, that these disciplines were only given marginal acknowledgement, with historical musicology taking the foreground; indeed, a subsequent critical analysis of the teaching of musicology in Germany by Jan Hemming, Brigitte Markuse and Wolfgang Marx (2000) revealed that interdisciplinary approaches, as well as non-historical disciplines, only make up a small portion of the academic course curricula.[1] Generally speaking, within academia, a thorough examination and practical realization of the possibilities ethnomusicology could offer to musicology have only been undertaken by a few historical scholars, most notably Peter Jefferey (1992), who developed a comprehensive perspective in the study of Gregorian plainchant by employing methods for intercultural comparison.

In contrast to Germany, where ethnomusicology is only taught in a few universities, attempts at forging new orientations within historical musicology have already been part of the larger critical discourses among Anglo-American ethnomusicologists. In 'New Musicologies, Old Musicologies: Ethnomusicology and the Study of Western Music', for example, Jonathan Stock (1998: 42) has provided a detailed analysis of the fundamental principles separating the two disciplines, while also suggesting possible areas of overlap. He pointed out, for instance, that historical musicology has generally focused on Western music (particularly on individual performers/composers), the notated musical material and its reconstruction, while ethnomusicology has focused on the non-Western world, addressing such issues as culture, the complex of conceptualization–behaviour–sound, performance/musical events, transmission and change. Yet, recently, historical musicology has also started to turn its attention to the sociocultural factors surrounding music, and ethnomusicology has begun to discover the musics of the West as a field of research. In order to contribute to this discussion, I shall focus on debates within the European early music scene. In particular, I am interested in looking at how ethno-musicological perspectives might contribute to the development of performance practices within early music.

Ethnomusicology: the 'other' and humanity

Consciously or unconsciously, Joseph Kerman's polemic criticism of the counterpunctual role of the Venda in Blacking's work highlighted a major internal contradiction in the conceptualization of ethnomusicology: on the one hand, it claims to contribute to the general understanding of humanity and, on the other, it continues to be perceived as the discipline that studies 'the musical other'.

In the second edition of the *New Grove Dictionary of Music and Musicians*, Carole Pegg (2001: 367) defines ethnomusicology as 'the study of social and cultural aspects of music and dance in local and global contexts', suggesting close links between ethnomusicology and the fields of social and cultural anthropology. The term 'anthropology' was originally coined in Germany around 1500 to describe a humanistic science that was set as a counterpart to theology. This comprehensive orientation was still evident in the theoretical writings of Johann Gottfried Herder, who, in *Ideen zur Philosophie der Geschichte der Menschheit* (1787–91), attempted one of the broadest-ever portrayals of humanity by compiling a vast array of available knowledge about the nature, the culture and the history of humankind.[2]

As in this monumental project, the desire to understand the nature of humanity through the collection of vast bodies of data from the most diverse of sources has probably always been suffused with – if not dominated by – a fascination with cultural difference, and this is just as true of anthropology as it is of ethnomusicology. Yet, conceptualizing 'the other' has been a complex endeavour. Philosophically speaking, anything that deviates from one's own conceptions and norms is perceived as different; this also includes the various musics that occur within one's own cultural area but stand outside one's immediate social networks. As the social and cultural distance increases between one's own cultural heritage and that of the other, the other's cultural universe comes to be perceived increasingly as foreign. This need not be because it stands outside one's own (Western) cultural sphere, such as the Tuvinian *chöömey* singing from Mongolia, but also because it is based on radically different value systems. For example, in contrast to the preference for clear, clean sounds in Western art music, the Shona strive to achieve rich, buzzing sounds; therefore, they attach bottle caps or shells to the resonators of their *mbiras* (see Berliner, 1981). The need to identify difference is also reflected in such expressions as 'exotic' and 'alien' that were used within academia well into the early twentieth century. Although the academic world has all but abandoned such subjective expressions for the incomprehensible, the fascination with the other has remained.

This is especially evident in the term 'ethnomusicology' and other terms employing the 'ethno' prefix, such as 'ethnology' – a prefix that places the emphasis squarely on otherness. In classical Greek, '*ethnos*' was the term for the other, and it was used to refer to the non-Greek peoples with different traditions, economic systems and religions that were considered inferior to Greek high culture. Otherness is accentuated even more by some of the other terms employed in ethnomusicology and its sister disciplines, such as 'non-Western' or 'non-European'. Within the Anglo-American axis, the very canon of ethnomusicology focuses on the non-Western, comprised, as it is, of the polyrhythms of sub-Saharan Africa, the classical traditions of India and the Indonesian gamelan orchestras. By adopting this canon and using it as the basis for the teaching curricula and textbooks of the discipline, the emphasis on the other is further propagated to each new generation of students that enrolls in ethnomusicology programmes. As Bruno Nettl has pointed out (1999: 305), this common ground is necessary to enable scholars with different research areas to communicate with one another. However, the focus on the other as a self-contained cultural entity can lead the discipline away from its broader humanistic project.

In the central reference book *Ethnomusicology: An Introduction*, Helen Myers (1992c) claims that the three main areas of study within ethnomusicology are: (1) oral traditions, (2) the high art musics of Asia and the Arab World and (3) folk musics. Within each of these research domains, different aspects of the other are highlighted: the focus on societies with oral traditions emphasizes the qualitative other that has been shaped by different sociocultural factors; by concentrating on Asian and Arab art music, geographic distance is stressed; and the studies of folk musics underline their distance to art music.

Generally speaking, the differences in the characteristics of the musical systems also relate to particular theoretical approaches. First, among the non-literate peoples of the non-Western world a 'culturalist' paradigm is common, and these 'musical others' tend to receive anthropological treatments, an orientation that is especially apparent in American ethnomusicology. Second, the classical (literate) traditions of the non-Western world, such as those of China and India, tend to lead to (historical) musicological orientations, since their highly developed music notation systems and theories make them appear to be closer to the West than the non-literate cultures that can only be investigated through extensive fieldwork. Finally, folk musics, the musics of the 'others within', stand in an intermediate position. Often linked to nationalist agendas, folk musics have been the focus of some ethno-musicological schools (for example, those of Scandinavia and Eastern Europe among others); however, in other academic contexts, folk musics have been entirely ignored. This, for example, is the case with English folk music: it has been disregarded by historical musicologists whose main focus resides in the study of art musics, as well as by ethnomusicologists, perhaps because of its proximity to Western cultures.

It is no surprise, then, that, regardless of its various theoretical orientations, to some outsiders, ethnomusicology appears as the study of the musics of the other. Indeed, in the *Random House Webster's College Dictionary* (1991: 459), ethnomusicology is defined as 'the study of folk or native music, especially of

non-western cultures, and its relationship to the society to which it belongs'.[3]
Although Kerman must have read some of Blacking's writings, his perception
of the field of ethnomusicology remained superficial, reduced to the study of
the other; consequently, he dismissed it as inadequate for his new 'critical
musicology' (Kerman, 1985a: 174). Blacking, more than any of the other major
ethnomusicologists of his time, had a very clear humanist agenda, which is
evident in the distinctions he made between music (sound as cultural product),
music-making (the social in performance), and musicality (musical capacity as
a human universal), giving the discipline a comprehensive scope. Why did
Kerman ignore this orientation? Was it because his criticism was directed at an
entirely different issue? As he pointed out, his critical musicology aimed to
study the 'meaning and value of art works' rather than the meaning of a musical
genre to its culture and the value of a musical activity to its society (Kerman,
1985a: 16), which Blacking saw as the aim of ethnomusicology. Yet, one might
still wonder why Kerman overlooked the possibilities that Blacking's humanist
approach could offer to historical musicology when he emphasized that his
'interest in ethnomusicology amounts largely to an interest in what it can bring
to the study of Western music' (Kerman, 1985a: 167). From Kerman's
viewpoint, this was limited to ethnomusicological contributions to the study of
oral transmission and to the conceptualization of modes. Could his misgivings
have derived from the fact that Blacking's theories were often strongly linked
to his ethnographic material? Indeed, Kerman did acknowledge the value of
Blacking's work to those wanting to learn something about African music.
However, a look at the discipline's development could have given Kerman an
understanding of how ethnomusicology has always been much more than a
series of holiday trips presented as expeditions for the collection of a few
incoherent field recordings.

Comparative musicology: the other in global perspective

One could argue that already in the 1920s and 1930s the German school of
comparative musicology combined the concerns of both ethnomusicology and
historical musicology by using ethnographic findings as a means of filling the
gaps in the written history of Western music. This approach was based on the
assumption that, throughout the world, the process of musical development
entailed a unified sequence of stages, as if it followed the laws of nature: it was
assumed that the 'simpler' the music, the stricter the rules that determined its
creation. Influenced by the ideas known as *Kulturkreislehre* ('theory of culture
circles'), while drawing on a large body of data derived from the ethnographic
expeditions of the late nineteenth century, comparative musicology divided the
world into large areas based on shared cultural features. These 'culture circles'
were then correlated to characteristics found in Western art music and were

then organized into chronological sequences that were meant to represent the various stages in the development of that type of music. This is the stance taken by Curt Sachs in *Geist und Werden der Musikinstrumente* (1929); he noted analogies between certain archaeological findings and the instruments used by so-called 'primitive' populations. He then went on to investigate performance practices, which led him to the conclusion that the polyphony of the Fuegians and Pygmies represented the level of development of 'our prehistoric ancestors' (Sachs, 1943: 23).

The last major study within this theoretical framework was undertaken in the 1930s by Marius Schneider who systematized the general observations of his predecessors by developing a detailed linear model of the prehistoric development of European polyphonic art music. Schneider claimed that the structural parallels between early organum and Caucasian polyphonic singing were far too striking to be completely coincidental. Therefore, in *Geschichte der Mehrstimmigkeit* (1968 [1934]), he organized the non-Western cultures of the world into four large development stages based on differences in their tonal systems and polyphonic forms. Bach's polyphonic art was placed at the summit of the system, the various (unintentional) forms of heterophony to be found around the world were placed at the lowest level of the scale, while sub-Saharan Africa, with its extremely complex polyphony and homophonic forms, was said to represent the highest level. Eventually, the theoretical foundations of *Kulturkreislehre* were dismissed within academia, as researchers came to realize that similar musical characteristics could derive from quite distinct creative processes and that these could only be ascertained through an investigation that contemplated the cultural context surrounding the music in question.

A mirror in the other: a view from *How Musical is Man?*

One of the most significant findings in ethnomusicology since the Second World War was the recognition that sound material alone is insufficient to achieve an adequate understanding of music. As John Blacking exemplified in *How Musical is Man?*, a music historian who looks only at recorded material might interpret the occurrence of five-, six- and seven-tone scales in Venda culture as the manifestation of a transitional stage, in which the music was moving from a pentatonic system to a more complex heptatonic one. A closer look at the sociocultural factors surrounding the musical life of the Venda, however, reveals that they had used heptatonic xylophones and reed pipes long before they adopted the pentatonic reed pipes from their southern neighbours, the Pedi. For Blacking, therefore, behaviour and conceptualization constituted spheres to be investigated by the ethnomusicologist:

I am interested in Venda music more as the product of human minds in Venda culture and society than as a stage in the history of world music. In asking how musical is man, I am obviously concerned with all aspects of the origins of music, but not with speculative origins, or even with origins which a foreign historian thinks he can detect, but which are not recognized by the creators of the music. The origins of music that concern me are those which are to be found in the psychology and in the cultural and social environment of its creators, in the assembly of processes that generate the patterns of sound. (Blacking, 1973: 58)

Blacking clearly realized that the sociocultural study of other musics has the potential to generate reflection upon one's own (Western) musical thinking. In an encounter with very different cultural assumptions, one's commonsense notions can be relativized.[4] As ethnomusicologists have noted, not all musical systems are based on harmony and melody, as in the West, and not every culture operates according to the Western idea of professional musicianship. Indeed, Blacking noted that amongst the Venda, social, physical and musical activities were so closely interwoven that all the members of the society were musicians. Likewise, when comparing the role of personal emotional expression in Western and in Venda music, he observed that, in the West, individual expression is rated above technical mastery, whereas the Venda appreciate technical precision and it is regarded as the physical expression of feeling.

Kerman's portrayal of Blacking suggests that Blacking turned to African music because he was unable to find a place in his own culture. However, Blacking was in fact strongly rooted in the Western art music tradition. As Byron pointed out, 'the English choral and organ traditions were as much a part of his everyday school life as reading and writing; music was in the air at home and at school. At ten, he gave his first solo keyboard performance, a recital of Giles Farnaby pieces on his father's virginal' (1995: 2). During fieldwork Blacking listened to Alban Berg's *Wozzek* and the compositions of Anton Webern, and in the introduction to *How Musical is Man?* he described himself as a 'musician who [became] a professional anthropologist' (Blacking, 1973: v). Blacking continued to give piano recitals throughout his life, and he also founded and conducted the university choir in Witwatersrand; furthermore, he gave regular recitals at Queen's University Belfast almost up to his death.

The critiques he formulated toward his own cultural heritage derived from the way in which it was continuously challenged by his experiences during fieldwork. But Blacking's objectives transcended the critical reflection of Western music culture; he aimed at a much broader project than that for which Kerman gave him credit, by emphasizing that an understanding of the musical universe of the Venda was only a first step in the process of ultimately achieving an understanding of human musical behaviour in general.

There is, however, an inherent contradiction to this project: if, from a cultural relativist perspective, music can only be understood in terms of the culture to which it belongs, how can ethnomusicologists, as outsiders, claim to understand the musics they study? This question gains yet greater relevance when considered in relation to the view that the distance between the observer and the observed plays a critical role in the collection of a reliable body of data during fieldwork (see Bohlman, 1991b; Nettl, 1983). It has been taken almost as a given within academia that this distance is what guarantees scientific objectivity, and, despite the challenges to this view,[5] it has provided a justification for the presence of Western anthropologists and ethnomusicologists in non-Western cultures. Because the fieldworker consciously distances him- or herself from the culture under investigation, it is assumed that he or she can maintain greater neutrality, for nothing is taken for granted and all actions and value judgements have to be questioned. Consequently, sociocultural patterns that are beyond the consciousness of cultural insiders, confined, as they are, to an *etic* perspective, can be identified and verbalized by an outsider's *emic* scientific perception. Yet, to gain a true *etic* understanding, the researcher must be able to give up his or her 'objective', distanciated perspective and then take it up again for the *emic* verbalization process. This means that such ethnographic research can involve a difficult balancing act that, when carefully undertaken, can produce fascinating results. This has been demonstrated by Ruth M. Stone's (1982) multi-layered analysis of music making of the Kpelle of West Africa. Stone moved toward the other not only by using and translating the performers' language and phrases, but also by translating their time conception and hierarchical structures into Western perception, thereby offering access to their culture for outsiders as well.

Nevertheless, a radical interpretation of cultural relativism presents a challenge to any possibility of a foreign ethnomusicologist gaining an insider's understanding of another musical culture. How, then, one might ask, are we to account for the depth that Stone achieved in her *etic* understanding of Kpelle music? This was a question that also perplexed John Blacking, and he responded to it by positing a common basis to human musicality that allows for the transcendence of cultural difference:

> Music that was exciting to the contemporaries of Mozart and Beethoven is still exciting, although we do not share their culture and society. ... Many of us are thrilled by *koto* music from Japan, *sitar* music from India. I do not say that we receive the music in exactly the same way as the players ..., but our own experiences suggest there are some possibilities of cross-cultural communication. (Blacking, 1973: 108f)

For Blacking, the solution to this contradiction was to be found in bodily experience – 'that which is in the human body and which is universal to all men' (Blacking, 1973: 111) – which might allow one to approach the deep structures of music: the hidden factors which generate their external or surface features. Even though two people might not perceive music in exactly the same way, 'to feel with the body is probably as close as anyone can ever get to resonating with another person' (1973: 111). This also applies to music from other epochs; for instance, Blacking suggested that one might come closer to Debussy through the bodily experience of trying to find out how he held his hands and body when playing the piano. Hence, this problem not only addresses the encounter with different cultures, but suggests that any music can – and should – be investigated from an ethnomusicological perspective, including traditions with which one may have grown up.

Yet, as Bruno Nettl (1989b: 1) has observed, despite the recognition among ethnomusicologists that one's own musical heritage can be legitimately embraced as a research topic, only a few Western ethnomusicologists have tried to investigate their own culture. One of the most common arguments is that an objective approach – which is necessary for the study of other cultures – is difficult to achieve in this kind of research:

> ... it is taken for granted that only in studying a culture foreign to himself can a scholar muster sufficient objectivity. By studying his own culture, he may be conditioned to too many prejudices and personal associations to be properly objective – so many ethnomusicologists believe. Thus one may envision Western music being investigated in ethnomusicological fashion by African or Asian scholars, while Westerners could continue to specialize in non-Western cultures. (Nettl, 1964: 8)

It would seem, then, that Kerman's critique is once again vindicated, since ethnomusicologists continuously reinforce the image that their discipline constitutes the study of the music of the other, focusing primarily on the investigation of oral traditions and the art musics of Asia and North Africa. Although over the past two or three decades there has been an increase in the number of studies focusing on processes of acculturation and of studies undertaken within Western urban societies, there is still a strong emphasis on the musical other, while the study of Western music has remained neglected.

Ethnomusicologists entering their own cultures

Voicing the view of many ethnomusicologists, Nettl (1964: 12) has pointed out that historical musicology has often been accused of operating within a very limited scope and methodology, despite the large musical variety in the West. However, ethnomusicological studies of Western music are similarly rare, despite their potential for enormously enhancing the discipline's scope and validity. Likewise, historical musicology could be enriched by new, more comprehensive perspectives. This has led such ethnomusicologists as Bruno Nettl and Philip Bohlman not only to note the absence of ethnomusicologists in the traditional domain of the historical musicologist, but also to conduct several seminal investigations of their own Western culture. What is significant about their approach is that it challenges the assumption that one must be a cultural outsider in order to observe the field from a distanciated perspective. Yet, before embarking upon the ethnomusicological investigation of Western music, both Nettl and Bohlman had undertaken research among musical others. It could be argued that this prior fieldwork experience was an important – and perhaps even indispensable – precondition for the new project, allowing them to view their own cultural heritage from a new perspective.[6] Nettl and Bohlman thus both put themselves in the position of a distanciated *emic* observer (in Nettl's case, a fictitious visitor from Mars), and, from that standpoint, they strove to unravel the cultural assumptions underlying the musical universe under investigation. At the same time, however, they could take up the insider's *etic* viewpoint to validate their observations.

When Bohlman took a stroll through the streets of modern Vienna, he did not perceive it as the city of Mozart and Schubert, but as a fascinating mixture of various present-day cultures that include Viennese coffee-house music, Hungarian dance bands, as well as Peruvian street musicians. Only when viewed in a historical context does Vienna become the capital of classical music, the place where a major portion of the Western canonical repertoire was composed.

That researchers do not necessarily have to be outsiders is also confirmed in Bruno Nettl's (1989b) article 'Mozart and the Ethnomusicological Study of Western Culture'. To verify the methods of his discipline, he embarked upon the new project by addressing the same questions that he had dealt with in his study of the musical concepts of the Blackfoot Indians (1989a). In an effort to understand the main underlying concepts of the Western 'musical universe', he adopted anthropological field methods and chose a reasonably small socio-cultural unit for his investigation: an American school of music. By taking the role of a Martian, Nettl achieves the critical distance that enables him to present the commonsense notions of the music students as a culture-specific conceptual world. Within the music school, interest centres on composed music, and composers are venerated almost as though they were sacred beings. The 'Martian' is especially struck by the hierarchical ordering of composers and by the dominant role of a very small number of them, the so-called 'great masters', such as Bach, Mozart and Beethoven. These figures have a high rate of appearance on concert programmes and their names are familiar in the wider society. Furthermore, a large number of scholars have devoted their entire lives to the study of one of these composers and his (as most are male) music, confirming the degree to which they are esteemed both within and outside academia. Nettl goes on to describe a number of ritual elements that take place within the Western concert context that involve both musicians and audiences, such as the choice of outfits, programme patterns and behavioural structures, and, although these observations might initially be considered rather trivial, they are actually very revealing of the reverence with which the music is held. Thus, such an approach can provide an important basis for a more balanced understanding of Western musical culture.

To us, it seems natural that a Western symphony orchestra performs Western European music in Boston as well as in Rio de Janeiro, Tokyo and Jerusalem. Yet, in his investigation of the German house-concert among European-Jewish communities in Israel, Bohlman (1991a) warns us not to forget the historical and contextual specificities of the musical event. Even though a Beethoven string quartet may be played anywhere in the world, this does not automatically imply that it also has the same functions and is perceived in the same way from one setting to the next. Although these quartets, like the works of all the great masters, could be said to exist as absolute music, in that they can be separated from any specific geographical location and their sonic structure can be identified in a diversity of settings, they do not constitute neutral entities. Rather, their meanings can – and do – change from one context to the next. This becomes evident when one notes the controversial reception of Richard Wagner in Israel.

Ethnomusicologists visiting historical cultures

Although active fieldwork cannot be undertaken as part of a project involving the study of a Western historical context, ethnomusicological methods can still be applied in such research. Given the ethnomusicological sensibility for the other, an ethnomusicologist who is undertaking the study of a Western historical musical universe might begin by focusing on 'the other of the past'. Although the interest in the musical other found its clearest expression in the exoticism of Debussy and Ravel around the turn of the twentieth century, one need only look at sources from the sixteenth to eighteenth centuries to see that this interest was not a new phenomenon. As becomes evident from J.J. Quantz's *Versuch einer Anweisung die Flöte traversiere zu spielen* (1752), for instance, in the baroque era, the contrast between French, Italian and German performance styles was not only the object of observation, but also a matter of theoretical reflection.[7] Other sources show that there were circles at the time that were extremely curious about other musics. For example, a fascinated Telemann, who lived in the Polish region of Zary from 1705 to 1708, did not restrict his musical ear exclusively to court life; indeed, after a stay in Krakow, he described the Polish traditions he encountered as music of 'barbarian beauty' (Koch, 1982).

Systematic descriptions of 'foreign musics' were already appearing in the eighteenth century. Jean-Jacques Rousseau notated examples of Chinese and American musics in his *Dictionnaire de musique* published in 1767, while

William Jones published his study, *On the Musical Modes of the Hindoos*, as early as 1784.[8] Only recently have music scholars been turning to these early works as serious objects of research. While ethnomusicologists often lacked the tools and the theoretical background to undertake historical studies, historical musicologists have tended to be unprepared to deal with traditional musics. However, in his investigation of Charles Fonton's 'Essai sur la musique orientale' (1751), Amnon Shiloah (1991) has demonstrated how these works may be a key to achieving a more nuanced understanding of these eras. As one of the earliest European descriptions of Turkish music, Fonton's study is not only of historical interest for ethnomusicologists, it is also a reflection on the musical thinking of the eighteenth century. This becomes evident in the way in which Fonton presents the inadequacies of Western notation and the ethnocentrism of his time.

Ethnomusicology in historical musicology

In ethnomusicology the marker of otherness has been geographic distance, but a distanciated gaze can also be achieved through temporal differentiation. Thus, one could argue that the object of research within historical musicology is also constituted by the musics of other cultures. The distance separating the present from the medieval, the baroque or the romantic ages is not only evident in such external characteristics as instruments, notation and repertoire, but also, and more crucially, in the complexities of the historical circumstances that have shaped the mentalities of the past and the present. Nearly two decades before Bohlman (1991a), Blacking (1973: 67) had warned against the dehistoricization of classical Western music. The occurrence of identical musical figures in Benjamin Britten's *War Requiem* and Gustav Mahler's *Lied von der Erde* might raise the same feelings among audiences today, yet it should not be presumed that these musical figures also had their current meanings for listeners at the time of their composition, since the pieces were composed under different sociocultural conditions. While Mahler's setting of Chinese lyrics (recomposed by Hans Bethke) aimed to portray a philosophical *Weltschmerz*, Britten's *War Requiem* from 1961 referred to impressions of the Second World War, created, as it was, for the rededication of bomb-damaged Coventry Cathedral. As Blacking pointed out, the notion of a unified Western musical tradition needs to be challenged, for besides the temporal discontinuities within the canon, one must also consider the discrepancies between different musical genres, as well as regional diversities:

> The musical conventions of the eighteenth century stand between the Gibbons madrigal and the Tchaikovsky symphony [no. 6] ... . And so I find it hard to accept that there has been a continuous musical tradition between England in

1612 and Russia in 1893, in which certain musical figures have had corresponding emotional connotations. The only justification ... would be that the emotional significance of certain intervals arises from fundamental features of human physiology and psychology. (Blacking, 1973: 68)

Yet Blacking went on to say that, amongst the Venda, the patterns of intervals are more important than the precise pitches of the notes, thereby showing how their musical system challenges any assumptions regarding universal musical meanings. However, the idea that historical cultures can be understood by a modern researcher remains grounded on the assumption that there are certain human universals that are equally valid from a historical perspective. Nonetheless, an awareness of the 'historical other' has been slow to emerge within historical musicology. This is not simply because it will take time for the firmly grounded dehistoricized orientation within Western music history to dissolve, but also because the consequences of this new perspective go far beyond a mere revision of previous musicological studies. From a distanciated perspective it is likely that other musical genres that previously were consciously ignored, such as popular musics and folk musics, would begin to attract the researchers' gaze.[9] For example, in terms of musical artistry, the simple, yet entertaining songs of the *Musicalische Kurtzweil* (*Musical Amusement*), published by the relatively unknown composer Erasmus Widmann (1572–1634) in 1611, cannot compete with the art music of his contemporary, Heinrich Schütz. However, Widmann's songs provide a particularly revealing window into the mentality of the era. Their texts depict everyday life and use vernacular language, with themes that revolve around drinking, war, student life and marriage troubles; the tunes draw on regional folksongs. Yet, within academia, the study of 'small masters' (*Kleinmeister*) such as Widmann has been highly undervalued, even trivialized, in relation to the investigation of such giants as Bach, Mozart and Wagner. Consequently, this rich material has remained neglected within music scholarship.

The emergence of a new sensitivity within historical musicology became especially evident with the rise of what has come to be known as 'New Musicology', an orientation that was at least partly instigated by Joseph Kerman's general critique in *Contemplating Music* (1985a). It is not, however, possible as yet to fully assess the theoretical directions being generated by 'New Musicology'. Rather than a critical self-reflection, Kerman's critique of the focus on music analysis was aimed primarily at the distinction made within American academia between musicology and music theory (Cook and Everist, 1999: x), while the calls for a more relativistic approach were often combined with a strong pessimism regarding the possibilities for historical cross-cultural understanding. Within the ongoing debates regarding the focus and methods of musicology, Nicholas Cook and Mark Everist, in their preface to *Rethinking Music*, claim that '[i]t would not be entirely unreasonable to complain that the

New Musicology deconstructed everything except the disciplinary identity of musicology' (1999: ix). Likewise, in his seminal article, 'The Web of Culture: A context for Musicology', Gary Tomlinson (1984: 362) concluded that the endeavour to '*converse* with other cultures and other times' serves as the basis for all the branches of musicology, even though he doubted that such a multi-layered approach would become the norm:

> The web is a construction of the historian, taking shape and gaining coherence from the reciprocal (and rich and haphazard) interaction of his evolving assumptions with his increasingly meaningful data, the events he selects for inclusion in the context. (Tomlinson, 1984: 357)

The change of perspective became most obvious in the now established terminology of 'gender studies'. Female researchers had been present in ethnomusicology and ethnographic research from early on; the English folksong researcher Maud Karpeles (1885–1976) as well as the American field collectors Frances Densemore (1876–1957) and Alice C. Fletcher (1838–1923) are only a few names that can be mentioned here.[10] Although female repertoires had been collected right from the very first collections, a sensitivity to gender issues did not emerge within ethnomusicology until the mid-1970s; nevertheless, this was a decade earlier than in historical musicology.

Within historical musicology, one of the main figures to bring gender awareness into her research was Susan McClary. Interestingly, in adopting this stance she drew directly from the major tenets of ethnomusicology:

> Because the musical images produced by people foreign to us are usually opaque, discouraging us from thinking that we can hear straight through to universal meanings, we tend to be aware that there are many levels of social mediation involved in the production of other music … . The project of critical musicology (of which feminism would be an important branch) would be to examine the ways in which different musics articulate the priorities and values of various communities. (McClary, 1991: 26)

Along with gender issues, in her early work McClary attempted to take account of differences in mentalities and sociocultural legacies, as in her analysis of the differences between female and male rhetoric in Monteverdi's *Orfeo* (McClary, 1991, ch. 2). According to McClary, the significant changes in seventeenth-century private social life and behaviour were also reflected in the style of rhetoric in music, with rhetoric being an element of male education. Orfeo is likewise an excellent rhetorician, while female rhetoric is only expressed as seduction and lament. Unfortunately, however, this comprehensive perspective would eventually give way to a far more radical feminist orientation, often going as far as to attribute gendered significances to each single chord in a piece derived from the canon. In her analysis of Bizet's opera

Carmen, for example, McClary represents the nineteenth-century aesthetic fascination for ethnic topics *solely* as a projection of male sexual fantasies. One could argue, therefore, that this perspective is just as radical as the previous, male-dominated one; she is superimposing her own readings upon a distant historical era, without the backing of contemporary sources to validate her positions.

Although gender studies have generated points of contact within the various fields of music scholarship, it is still not possible to speak of a true integration of ethnomusicological methods and historical musicology. Along with its broader sociocultural perspective, ethnomusicology can also offer a vast array of methodological and theoretical resources to the new historical approach taking shape within musicology. However, as Jonathan Stock (1998) has emphasized, these possibilities have rarely been explored. One reason for this is that many musicology departments simply do not have the necessary expertise in ethnomusicology within their staff; yet, as Stock (1998: 46) further notes, as long as historical musicology resists the idea that Western music can be investigated on an equal footing with other music cultures, a true change will not occur.

There are, however, positive signs that transformations within the conceptual framework of the discipline are under way. One example of this is Nicholas Cook's study *Music: A Very Short Introduction* (1998), which portrays a broad twentieth-century musical landscape in which an orchestra interpreting a Beethoven symphony is discussed in conjunction with such pop stars as the Spice Girls within the context of the modern mass media. Another comprehensive approach was undertaken by the editors of *The Garland Encyclopaedia of World Music*; in the volume dedicated to Europe (Rice, Porter and Goertze, 2000), for example, Western classical music is presented in the larger context of a complex network, consisting of numerous regional folk, popular and art musics, and it also discusses the main conceptual orientations of European high culture, such as the strong historical perspective and the focus on single composers. Although the chapter titled 'History of European Art Music' (Schulenberg, 2000) might seem superficial to classically trained researchers, it places the music within a contextual framework. The music is located in what Mark Slobin (1993) calls the 'supercultural sphere' (that is, part of the international Western educational canon and high art culture), but it is not presented as the only music of importance within the complex landscape of numerous micro-cultures, musical styles and contexts.

In rethinking new approaches within historical musicology, one runs the risk of overemphasizing the perspectives of other disciplines, such as popular music studies. While this may generate a shift in perspective, it may not be helpful in achieving a deeper understanding of the multi-layered meanings of Western art music. Yet, the book *Rethinking Music*, edited by Nicholas Cook and Mark Everist (1999), for example, already points to a more balanced structure, consisting, as it does, of chapters written by both historical musicologists and ethnomusicologists. In this way, the book not only opens up larger dimensions (for example, by looking at musical text in general or the institutionalization of musicology), but also presents new ways of looking at seemingly long-established topics, such as Beethoven's symphonies that are, for instance, analysed from the perspective of performance practice.

Approaching the 'historical other': ethnomusicological contributions to early music studies

While musicology is still struggling to establish new perspectives, performance studies have already made head-roads towards an integration of ethnomusicological approaches. This is particularly true in early music studies, especially in baroque music performance. Despite Mendelssohn turning his attention to Bach's *St. Matthew's Passion* in 1929 and instigating a baroque revival movement amongst his contemporaries, during the late eighteenth and early nineteenth centuries baroque music was generally perceived as alien, and it had no presence in performance programmes. Moreover, in contrast to other historical styles, subsequent periods were also rather condescending towards the baroque era, perceiving it as overornamented and pompous. Indeed, this view is embodied in the name given to the period: 'baroque'. Coined around 1750, the term was probably adapted from the Portuguese *barroco/a* (lit. 'irregularly shaped pearl') and conflated with the medieval Latin *baroco* that described a kind of obfuscating syllogism (Costello, 1991).

During the 1960s and 1970s a few scholars and performers began turning to the pre-romantic periods of European music, establishing what came to be known as the early music scene. This movement was confronted with the problem of how to approach the historical other, for, as researchers engaged in more detailed studies of early performance practices, they felt themselves becoming increasingly alienated from the distant norms and behavioural patterns of the historical cultures they were investigating. This was also reflected in the criticisms levelled against the scene. Due to the rougher sound colours, quieter instruments and seemingly exaggerated playing techniques – epitomized, perhaps, by Frans Brüggen's recorder-playing in the *Messa di Voces* – the performers were often accused of musical extremism. Although to classically trained ears, the overt effect of these performance practices verged on the exotic, they were based on reconstructions derived from a diversity of historical sources, including a range of early instruments, iconographic representations and written scores as well as theoretical treatises and other sources that could provide clues about tuning, playing techniques and phrasing.

Within the German early music scene during the 1970s, two quite distinct trends emerged, although both took extreme positions: one of these trends became so dominated by a fascination for exotic sounds that it started to neglect the historical sources, while the other took an extreme stance in its aim for 'authenticity' in the reconstruction of technical details, despite the fact that this route often resulted in rather musically dull performances. The position represented by Stefan Kunze (1983) pointed to the limitations in the historical sources. While quite a bit of primary material of the era is available for investigation, it is limited in what it reveals about the audience's aesthetic attitudes and listening habits. The employment of basic ethnomusicological methods of investigation, such as participant-observation and interviews, cannot be undertaken in the study of the historical other. Thus, the degree to which it is possible to achieve an inner, *etic*, level of understanding of the period is limited by the researcher's inability to become separated from a twentieth/twenty-first century mindset. Furthermore, because one must also assume a considerable disunity of musical reception even within a given era, any attempt to reproduce the musical sound of early music and the reception of that sound at the time for audiences today will only amount to a partial realization of the project.

But why even strive for 'authenticity'? We know the precise size of Bach's choir, but, as Theodor W. Adorno (1955) asks, was Bach actually happy with such a small choir? And would he be satisfied with a modern 'authentic' performance with its limited instrumentation? According to Adorno, one should read the 'objective', notated music independently of its original context, and perform it in an adequate modern language. From this perspective, the performance practices of early music in the nineteenth century are much more consistent with the aesthetics of their time than those of the modern early music scene, because they set the old music to a language comprehensible for modern listeners (for example, as orchestral arrangements or with romantic instrumentation).

Alternatively, could the other in this music also imply something else? One of the most interesting studies in the field of early music is Jan Reichow's (1984a–c) three-part article *'Ich muss meine Spielart gantz anders ändern...'* ('I Must Completely Alter my Performance Practice') – title that derives from the exclamation used by the composer Johann Gottfried Schwanberger (1737/40–1804) when he first heard a performance by Johann Sebastian Bach. Reichow re-examines the various trends within early music studies, and asks, for instance, what Mozart could have meant when he wrote that music should be performed with expression, taste, feeling and fire:

> Is it not possible that upon hearing his music played by one of our best orchestras, he may have been so horrified as to exclaim: 'How cold and piercing! Don't you hear that the all-decisive dimension is missing?' (Mozart, quoted in Reichow 1984a: 15).[11]

According to Reichow, the problem does not reside in the effort to understand a different and incomprehensible culture, but in the absence of a willingness to seriously undertake such a task with respect to the historical other. In 1974 Ulrich Dibelius published a critical article titled 'Alte Instrumente machen noch keine Alte Musik' ('Old Instruments Alone do not make Early Music') which accused musicians of having neglected the actual music by focusing mainly on the recreation of a historic–exotic sound. It is, of course, important to attend to the expressive aspects of music, but, as Reichow points out, this should not be considered as a licence for total freedom in performance practice. As any ethnomusicologist knows, the act of strumming on Indian instruments does not automatically produce Indian music – not only because Indian music is based on its own musical vocabulary with which performers of Indian music must be familiar, but also because the music articulates with a specific sociocultural background. Similarly, an effective performance of historical music can only be achieved if it attends to the language, the thinking and the sensibilities of the era that it represents. Thus, an early music instrumentation, a profound knowledge of the historical sources and their background, and personal interpretation must all coalesce in the performance space.

Thus, as Reichow concludes, rather than ignoring the other, we should consciously try to move towards him or her. As the fieldwork experience of ethnomusicologists such as Blacking has demonstrated, there are mechanisms that allow for a better understanding of the other. And even if one finds the historical mentality excessively alien, it is still possible for one to become acquainted with the musical vocabulary and the behavioural patterns of the time and achieve a comprehension of the culture at that level. Reichow is not only concerned with the creation of 'authentic sound', but also with an adequate use of existing resources to create a highly expressive music, arguing that this is what Mozart would have wanted. He thus takes the instruments as an invitation for innovation, adding a new perspective to the current body of cultural knowledge. In this he follows a trend established by previous generations of musicians, such as Schwanberger, whom he quotes claiming:

> ... that I am able to generate a vivid imagine of Bach playing the organ at the Thomaskirche in Leipzig, with all its exoticism, while an enchanted contemporary musician reacted to it by exclaiming: 'I have never heard anything quite like this before; I must now completely alter my playing style...'. (Schwanberger, Leipzig, 12 November 1727, quoted in Reichow 1984a: 16)[12]

Old instruments may be inferior to our modern ones, and it may be that Bach would have liked to have had a larger choir. Yet the resources of the past offer new possibilities precisely because of the specificities of their limitations. Historical music derives its special power from the way in which it combines old instruments, knowledge of the sources (including an understanding of the contemporary thinking and feeling) *and* personal interpretation. However, this approach requires new ways of dealing with the primary sources, which should not be restricted to the preparation of source editions and catalogues, as some historical musicologists seem to think. This work is necessary, but it has become an end in itself, thereby loosening the connection between the sources and the actual period performance practices. Only rarely have musicologists looked at the major cultural factors underlying the music, precisely the types of issue that form the staple of ethnomusicological fieldwork.

That some aspects of ethnomusicological inquiry have indeed been adopted by historical musicology becomes clearly evident in the coverage of the British scene's major publication, *Early Music*. From its very first volumes, the journal has published several articles of mutual interest to ethnomusicologists and historical musicologists. In 'Domenico Scarlatti and Spanish Folk Music' (1976), for example, author and harpsichordist Jane Clark, who accompanied a Spanish folk dance group, pointed to the obvious influence of Andalusian folk music on Scarlatti's sonatas: K 490(2) contains rhythmic devices common to the *saeta*; K 492 shows an affinity with the *buleria*; and K 421 employs chromatic flamenco passages. These observations not only add to a more precise picture of what is usually more generally described as Spanish elements in Scarlatti's music, but they might also even point towards a different chronological ordering in the composition of the sonatas.

In 1996, *Early Music* went a step further by publishing an issue that was not only completely dedicated to ethnomusicological topics, but the contributions themselves were all written by ethnomusicologists. By asking whether there is also early music in cultures other than the West, the authors added new dimensions to our perceptions of history within music. As Richard Widdess pointed out in the editorial:

> In the West the past often seems to be a distant country, of which we catch occasional, tantalizing glimpses between skyscrapers of modern life; part of the attraction of early music surely is that it can transport us vividly, if temporarily, to that country. (Widdess, 1996: 373)

Widdess goes on to tell us that South Indian musicians claim that their music is up to 4000 years old. Through this observation Widdess highlights the way in which the focus on 'authenticity' in the performance of historical music may constitute cultural retrogression. Instead, musicians might more fruitfully look upon current performance practices as a continuation of the past, in a manner analogous to that witnessed in the Changu Naranyan temple in the Kathmandu Valley, that makes active use of artefacts that are more than 1500 years old. Henry Stobart's (1996) article, 'The Llama's Flute', adds a global perspective to the investigation of Western historical music. Not only did Stobart emphasize the similarities between the Bolivian *pinkillu* flutes and Spanish renaissance recorders, but he also shows how, despite the disasters of the European invasion, the recorder – an instrument that played a central role in Spanish church music – was adapted to Andean crop-growing rituals by evoking the devils that came to be associated with the white foreigners.

The one area in which the integration of ethnomusicological methods has made the greatest headway is in the study of Gregorian plainchant. Although this music had been notated and handed down from the sixth century onwards, the sources are formalized mnemonic aids, as the actual transmission was oral. Thus, the study of this music requires a highly specialized literary background, including knowledge of theology and cultural history, on the one hand, and a clear understanding of oral transmission processes, on the other. Such research should also include the reconstruction of the sociocultural context of the music and the incorporation of intercultural comparisons of the techniques of oral transmission, drawing on data acquired through modern fieldwork methods. That such a comprehensive approach can lead to significant new insights was clearly demonstrated by Peter Jefferey's study, *Re-Envisioning Past Musical Cultures* (1992) which illustrates the oral element within Gregorian plainchant through a close investigation of regional oral traditions – for instance, in the area of the Byzantine church in Dalmatia, Armenia and Georgia. Furthermore, instead of merely focusing on editorial issues, Jefferey also located the music socioculturally by reconstructing the daily life of the monks who performed the music, and he has even placed it in a larger context by describing Gregorian plainchant as one style among many others, such as the art and entertainment musics of the era.

Intercultural comparison can also be helpful in the reconstruction of historical performance styles. The lack of historical sound samples does not mean that researchers must restrict themselves to notated material. One can learn quite a bit from the playing styles of Roumanian or Irish fiddlers, which need not be restricted to clumsy comparisons.

This approach has already been applied successfully in the teaching of early music at the Folkwanghochschule in Duisburg, Germany.[13] One problem that arises when approaching singing styles is that one cannot fall back on period instruments, such as seventeenth-century violas da gamba. Historical treatises reveal that the baroque vocal style was characterized by vibrato-less singing. From the viewpoint of the present belcanto style, with its relatively low chest voice, it seems difficult to imagine how a loud voice projection across long phrases could have been achieved without vibrato. In order to see how this may have been possible, students at Duisburg have started looking at song traditions in various cultural areas that have not been influenced by the belcanto art, such as Norwegian *kulokkar,* Bulgarian 'open-throated' singing or Andalusian flamenco. These various singing styles, which are all distinguished by a higher larynx position and thus a higher chest voice, do not only allow for a loud, vibrato-free voice projection well into late adulthood, but also for precisely intoned singing during very quick passages – something that is not possible in the belcanto style. However, the objective here is not to imitate the Bulgarian vocal style as such, but rather to look to such alternative techniques for assistance in the interpretation of historical sources.[14]

New perspectives for historical musicology

In this overview of the possible points of intersection between historical musicology and ethnomusicology, I have only been able to discuss a small selection of the approaches that have developed out of a confrontation with the other. It is doubtful whether ethnomusicology will ever replace historical musicology completely, or even that it will aspire to do so. Nevertheless, there is no doubt that ethnomusicology can provide an extremely enriching complement to historical musicology, providing a specific method for viewing music through the eyes of an other. Hopefully, it has also become obvious that the implications of such a perspective go far beyond the methodological, since a distanciated perspective on the other may lead historical musicologists to interrogate the role of their field in modern society. In this way, the field may reach the stage envisioned by Gilbert Chase in 1972 in his publication, *Perspectives in Musicology*: 'I maintain that the term musicology should have the same sort of breadth, scope, and depth that the term anthropology has in social sciences' (Chase, 1972: 219).

Joseph Kerman did not believe that Blacking's perspective on the Venda could be helpful for an understanding of our own music. For Blacking, however, the study of the Venda provided a mirror that reflected his perceptions of his own musical culture, thus allowing him to step out of his subconsciously-held Western perspectives. Likewise, an understanding of the musical value systems of distant centuries helps us to reflect back upon our own, present-day culture, which we should want to understand better, be it from ethnomusicological or historical musicological perspectives. And this is the reason why Blacking's research on the Venda is so important for Western music studies.

Notes

[1] Of the 47 German universities investigated in 1998, only 6 per cent of teaching involved ethnomusicology, with two-thirds of the classes taking place in only five universities. See also Sweers (2000).

[2] In Germany this approach would later separate into two major disciplines, the culturally-oriented direction called *Ethnologie*, and the physical studies, summarized as *Anthropologie*, which became a part of biology. In the United States, in contrast, 'anthropology' became the collective term for the four major areas of anthropology – cultural anthropology, archaeology, ethnolinguistics and physical anthropology.

[3] The emphasis on the study of the other is also reflected in other dictionaries: Although *Merriam-Webster's Collegiate Dictionary* (10th edn, 1994) also includes ethnomusicology as 'the study of music in a sociocultural context', the first entry is nevertheless 'the study of music that is outside the European art tradition'.

[4] In his introduction to *Ethnologie*, Hans Fischer (1992) has argued that one reason why students are attracted to anthropology is that it provides them with a means of gaining a better understanding of their own lifestyle and culture.

[5] Compare the various articles in the *Journal of Indian Musicology* and *Journal of the Madras Music Academy* from the 1970s. For a more recent discussion, see Witzleben (1997).

[6] This idea has served as the basis for the development of the ethnomusicology programme at the University of Bamberg. To ensure that the German students do not focus exclusively on the study of foreign cultures and that the foreign students do not limit their projects to the investigation of their own cultural backgrounds, all students are required to conduct two field research projects – one in their chosen field and another in the local surroundings.

[7] This perception was still evident in the classical era: for instance, the German writer and theorist Johann Joachim Engel (1741–1801), whose plays were, in his day, almost more famous than those of Goethe and Schiller, analysed the difference between Italian and French gestures in his study *Ideen zu einer Mimik* (1785–86).

[8] There are a number of earlier examples, although many of these documents lack a systematic scientific background. For example, in his *Harmonices Mundi* (1619: 153), Johannes Kepler provided the transcription of a Turkish melody he had heard at the court in Prague as a counterexample to his conception of harmony.

[9] Suppan (1973) could be viewed as an early German example of this.

[10] See also Sarkissian in Myers (1992d) and Richard Keeling (1989).

[11] '*Wäre es nicht denkbar, daß er, wenn er seine Musik mit einem unserer Spitzenorchester erleben würde, entsetzt ausrufen würde: "Wie kalt und schneidend: Hört Ihr denn nicht, daß das Entscheidende fehlt?!"*'

[12] '*…daß ich mir Bachs Spiel an der Orgel der Thomaskirche zu Leipzig intensiv vorstelle als eine Möglichkeit, der ein Exotisches anhaftet, während ein zeitgenössischer Musiker eher entgeistert reagierte: ich habe so was noch niemahls gehöret, und ich mus meine Spielart gantz anders ändern ….*

[13] This example is taken, with kind permission, from the teaching concept of Hans-Georg Kramer, lecturer of viola da gamba and early music performance practice at the Folkwanghochschule Duisburg.

[14] Other projects under discussion include the construction of concert programmes that integrate Spanish baroque music with flamenco performance or English renaissance music with English folk music, in an effort to generate a more comprehensible and relativized picture of so-called Western art music.

Bibliography

Adorno, Theodor W. (1955), *Prismen*, Frankfurt: Suhrkamp Verlag.

Agawu, Kofi (1997), 'John Blacking and the Study of African music', *Africa*, **67**(3), 491–99.

Alford Robert R. and Andras Szanto (1996), 'Orpheus Wounded: The Experience of Pain in the Professional Worlds of the Piano', *Theory and Society*, **25**(1), 1–44.

Allen, Lara (1995), 'The Effect of Repressive State Policies on the Development and Demise of Kwela Music: South Africa 1955–65', in Carol Muller (ed.), *Papers Presented at the 10th Symposium on Ethnomusicology*, Grahamstown: International Library of African Music, Rhodes University, pp. 1–4.

Andersson, Muff (1981), *Music in the Mix: The Story of South African Popular Music*, Johannesburg: Raven Press.

Appadurai, Arjun (1991), 'Global Ethnoscapes: Notes and Queries for a Transnational Anthropology', in Richard G. Fox (ed.), *Recapturing Anthropology: Working in the Present*, Santa Fe, CA: School of American Research Press, pp. 191–210.

Archetti, Eduardo and N. Noel Dyck (eds) (2003), *Sport, Dance and Embodied Identities*, Oxford: Berg.

Arima, Daigoro (1951), *Nihonjin no Ongaku* (*The Music of the Japanese*), Tokyo: Meikyokudo.

Asad, Talal (ed.) (1973), *Anthropology and Colonial Encounter*, London: Ithaca Press.

Averill, Gage (1997), *A Day for the Hunter, A Day for the Prey: Music and Power in Haiti*, Chicago: University of Chicago Press.

Baily, John (1972a), 'Adaptation to Prisms: Do Proprioceptive Changes Mediate Adapted Behaviour with Ballistic Arm Movements?' *Quarterly Journal of Experimental Psychology*, **24**, 8–20.

—— (1972b), 'Arm-Body Adaptation with Passive Arm Movements', *Perception and Psychophysics*, **12**, 39–44.

—— (1974), *Krishna Govinda's Rudiments of Tabla Playing*, Brighton: Unicorn Books, with accompanying audio cassette.

—— (1976), 'Recent Changes in the Dutâr of Heart', *Asian Music*, **8**(1), 29–64.

—— (1977), 'Movement Patterns in Playing the Herati Dutâr', in John Blacking (ed.), *The Anthropology of the Body*, London: Academic Press, pp. 275–330.

—— (1981), 'A System of Modes Used in the Urban Music of Afghanistan', *Ethnomusicology*, **25**(i), 1–39.

—— (1985), 'Music Structure and Human Movement', in Peter Howell, Ian Cross and Robert West (eds), *Musical Structure and Cognition*, London: Academic Press, pp. 237–58.

—— (1990a), 'John Blacking and His Place in Ethnomusicology', *Yearbook for Traditional Music*, **22**, xii–xxi.

—— (1990b), 'The Role of Motor Grammar in Musical Performance', in Frank Wilson and Franz Roehmann (eds), *Music and Child Development: Proceedings of the 1987 Denver Conference*, St Louis: MMB Music, pp. 202–13.

—— (1991a), 'John Blacking – Reminiscences', in *Popular Music*, **10**(2), 220–21.

—— (1991b), 'Some Cognitive Aspects of Motor Planning in Musical Performance', *Psychologica Belgica*, **31**(2), pp. 147–62.

—— (1994), *John Blacking: Dialogue with the Ancestors,* John Blacking Memorial Lecture 1991, London: Goldsmiths College.

—— (ed.) (1995), 'Introduction', *Working with Blacking: The Belfast Years, The World of Music*, **37**(2), 4–10.

—— (1997), 'The *Naghma-ye Kashāl* of Afghanistan', *British Journal of Ethnomusicology*, **6**, 117–63.

—— (2001), 'Learning to Perform as a Research Technique in Ethnomusicology', *British Journal of Ethnomusicology*, **10**(2), 85–98.

Baily, John and Andrée Grau (2001), *Domba (1956–1958): A Personal Record of Venda Initiation Rites, Songs and Dances (Study Guide),* Bloomington; IN: SEM.

—— and Peter Driver (1992), 'Spatio-motor Thinking in Playing Folk Blues Guitar', *The World of Music*, **34**(3), 57–71.

Barz, Gregory and Timothy J. Cooley (eds) (1997), *Shadows in the Field: New Perspectives in Ethnomusicology*, New York: Oxford University Press.

Bauman, Gerd (1995), 'Music and Dance: the Royal Road to Affective Culture?', *The World of Music*, 37(2), 31–42.

Beauvoir, Rachel and Didier Dominique (1988), 'Savaloué', unpublished book manuscript.

Bennett, Andy and Kevin Dawe (2001), *Guitar Cultures*, Oxford: Berg.

Berliner, Paul (1981), *The Soul of Mbira*, Berkeley: University of California Press.

Blacking, John (n.d.a), 'Musical Performance and Political Consciousness in the Venda', draft paper to be presented at the Identity: Personal and Social-Cultural Symposium, QUB John Blacking Archive, Box 15.

—— (n.d.b), lecture notes on *The Elementary Forms of the Religious Life* by Emile Durkheim, QUB John Blacking Archive, Lecture Notes S.A. Box.

—— (1954–55), 'Musical Instruments of the Malayan Aborigines', *Federation Museums Journal*, n.s., **1–2**, 35–52.

—— (1955), 'Eight Flute Tunes from Butembo, East Belgian Congo', *African Music*, **1**(2), 24–52.

—— (1957), *The Role of Music amongst the Venda of the Northern Transvaal, Union of South Africa*, Roodeport: International Library of African Music.

—— (1959a), 'Fictitious Kinship amongst Girls of the Venda of Northern Transvaal', *Man*, **59**, 155–58.

—— (1959b), 'Patterns of Nsenga *Kalimba* Music', *African Music*, **2**(4), 26–43.

—— (1959c), 'Problems of Pitch, Pattern and Harmony in the Ocarina Music of the Venda', *African Music*, **2**(4), 15–23.

—— (1961), 'The Social Value of Venda Riddles', *African Studies*, **20**, 1–32.

—— (1962), 'Musical Expeditions of the Venda', *African Music*, **3**(1), 54–72.

—— (1964a), *Black Background: The Childhood of a South African Girl*, London and New York: Abelard Schuman.

—— (1964b), 'Some Effects of Migrant Labour on Rural Africans', *Black Sash*.

—— (1964c), 'The Cultural Foundations of the Music of the Venda', unpublished D. Litt dissertation, Witwatersrand University.

—— (1965), 'The Role of Music in the Culture of the Venda of the Northern Transvaal', in Mieczyslaw Kolinski, (ed.), *Studies in Ethnomusicology*, 2, New York: Oak Publications, pp. 20–52.

—— (1967), *Venda Children's Songs: A Study in Ethnomusicological Analysis,* Johannesburg: Witwatersrand University Press.

—— (1969a), 'Initiation and the Balance of Power: the Tshikanda Girls' Initiation School of the Venda of the Northern Transvaal', in *Ethnological and Linguistic Studies in Honour of N J van Warmelo*, Pretoria: Department of Bantu Administration and Development, pp. 31–38.

—— (1969b), 'Process and Product in Human Society (Revised Manuscript)', inaugural lecture, Johannesburg: University of the Witwatersrand.

—— (1969c), 'Songs, Dances, Mimes and Symbolism of Venda Girls' Initiation Schools, Part I: *Vhusha*', *African Studies,* **28** (1), 3–35.

—— (1969d), 'Songs, Dances, Mimes and Symbolism of Venda Girls' Initiation Schools, Part II: *Milayo*', *African Studies,* **28**(2), 69–118.

—— (1969e), 'Songs, Dances, Mimes and Symbolism of Venda Girls' Initiation Schools', Part III: *Domba*', *African Studies,* **28** (3), 149–99.

—— (1969f), 'Songs, Dances, Mimes and Symbolism of Venda Girls' Initiation Schools', Part IV: The Great *Domba* Song', *African Studies,* **28**(4), 215–66.

—— (1970a), 'The Myth of Urban Man', in H.L. Watts (ed.), *Focus on Cities*, Durban: University of Natal, pp. 228–38.

—— (1970b), 'Tonal Organization in the Music of Two Venda Initiation Schools', *Ethnomusicology*, **14**(1), 1–54.

—— (1971), 'Deep and Surface Structures in Venda Music', *Yearbook of the International Folk Music Council*, **3**, 91–108.

—— (1973), *How Musical is Man?* Seattle: University of Washington Press.

—— (1975), 'The Anthropology of Religious Experience', lecture notes for a guest lecture to the Newman Society in Belfast, QUB John Blacking Archive, Lecture Notes S.A. Box.

—— (1977a), 'Some Problems of Theory and Method in the Study of Musical Change', *Yearbook of the International Folk Music Council,* **9**, 1–26.

—— (1977b), 'Towards an Anthropology of the Body', in John Blacking, (ed.), *The Anthropology of the Body*, London: Academic Press, pp. 1–28.

—— (ed.) (1977c), *The Anthropology of the Body*, London: Academic Press.

—— (1980a), 'Political and Musical Freedom in the Music of Some Black South African Churches', in Ladislav Holy and Milan Stuchlik (eds), *The Structure of Folk Models*, ASA Monograph, No. 20, London: Academic Press, pp. 35–62.

—— (1980b), 'Purpose, Theory and Practice for the Next Twenty-Five Years in Ethnomusicology', paper presented at the Annual Meeting of the Society for Ethnomusicology, Bloomington, Indiana, USA.

—— (1980c), 'Trends in the Black Music of South Africa, 1959–1969', in Elizabeth May (ed.), *Music of Many Cultures*, Berkeley: University of California Press, pp. 195–215.

—— (1981), 'The Problem of "Ethnic" Perceptions in the Semiotics of Music', in Wendy Steiner (ed.), *The Sign in Music and Literature*, Austin: University of Texas Press, pp. 184–94.

—— (1982), 'Songs and Dances of the Venda People', in David Tunley (ed.), *Music and Dance: Fourth National Symposium of the Musicological Society of Australia*, Nedlands: University of Western Australia, pp. 90–105.

—— (1983a), 'Movement and Meaning: Dance in Social Anthropological Perspective', *Dance Research*, Spring, pp. 89–99.

—— (1983b), 'The Concept of Identity and Folk Concepts of Self: A Venda Case Study', in Anita Jacobson-Widding (ed.), *Identity: Personal and Socio-Cultural*, Stockholm: Almqvist and Wiksell, pp. 47–65.

—— (1985a), 'Movement, Dance, Music, and the Venda Girls' Initiation Cycle', in Paul Spencer (ed.), *Society and the Dance: The Social Anthropology of Process and Performance*, Cambridge: Cambridge University Press, pp. 64–91.

—— (1985b), 'The Context of Venda Possession Music: Reflections on the Effectiveness of Symbols', *Yearbook for Traditional Music*, **17**, 64–87.

—— (1985c), *'Versus gradus novos ad Parnassum musicum: exemplum Africanum'*, in David McAllester (ed.), *Becoming Human through Music: The Wesleyan Symposium on the Perspectives of Social Anthropology in the Teaching and Learning of Music,* Middletown: Wesleyan University, pp. 43–52.

—— (1986), 'Identifying Processes of Musical Change', *The World of Music*, **28**(1), 3–15.

—— (1987), *A Commonsense View of All Music: Reflections on Percy Grainger's Writings on Ethnomusicology and Music Education,* Cambridge: Cambridge University Press.

—— (1987–88), *Dancing*, a series of six *ca.* 30-minute television programmes produced by Ulster Television Ltd, Belfast.

—— (1990), 'Music in Children's Cognitive and Affective Development', in Frank Wilson and Franz Roehmann (eds), *Music and Child Development: Proceedings of the 1987 Denver Conference*, St Louis: MMB Music, pp. 68–78.

—— (1992), 'The Biology of Music-making', in Helen Myers (ed.), *Ethnomusicology: An Introduction*, London: Macmillan, pp. 301–14.

—— (1995a [1969]), 'Expressing Human Experience through Music', *Music, Culture and Experience: Selected Papers of John Blacking,* ed. R. Byron, Chicago: University of Chicago Press, pp. 31–53.

—— (1995b), *Music, Culture and Experience: Selected Papers of John Blacking,* ed. R. Byron, Chicago: University of Chicago Press.

—— (1995c [1985]), 'Reflections on the Effectiveness of Symbols', *Music, Culture and Experience: Selected Papers of John Blacking,* ed. R. Byron, Chicago: University of Chicago Press, pp. 174–97.

—— (1998), *Venda Girls' Initiation Schools,* website produced by S.A. Reily and L. Weinstock for the ERA Project, University of Kent at Canterbury, URL: http://www.qub.ac.uk/VendaGirls/index.html.

—— (2001 [1980]), *Domba: a Personal Record of Venda Initiation Rites, Songs and Dances*, video produced by the Society for Ethnomusicology, A-V Series, No. 2.

Blacking, John and John Baily (1973), 'A Cross-cultural Study of Music Skills', unpublished, SSRC application for a research grant.

—— and Joann Keali'inohomoku (eds) (1979), *The Performing Arts: Music and Dance*, The Hague: Mouton.

Bloch, Maurice (1974), 'Symbols, Song, Dance and Features of Articulation', *European Archives of Sociology*, **15**, 55–81.

Bohlman, Philip V. (1991a), 'Of Yekkes and Chamber Music in Israel: Ethnomusicological Meaning in Western Music History', in Steven Blum, Philip V. Bohlman and Daniel M. Neuman (eds), *Ethnomusicology and Modern Music History,* Urbana and Chicago: University of Illinois Press, pp. 254–67.

—— (1991b), 'Representation and Cultural Critique in the History of Ethnomusicology', in Bruno Nettl and Philip V. Bohlman (eds), *Comparative Musicology and Anthropology of Music*: *Essays on the History of Ethnomusicology*, Chicago: University of Chicago Press, pp. 131–51.

—— (1992), 'Europe: Music in the Life of Modern Vienna', in: Bruno Nettl, *et al.* (eds), *Excursions in World Music*, Englewood Cliffs, NJ: Prentice Hall, pp. 196–231.

Bonavin, F. (91956), *Musicians on Music*, London: Routledge and Kegan Paul.

Bourdieu, Pierre (1977), *Outline of a Theory of Practice*, Cambridge: Cambridge University Press.

Brinson, Peter and Fiona Dick (1996), *Fit to Dance?* London: Calouste Gulbenkian Foundation.

Brook, Barry S., Edward O.D. Downes and Sherman van Solkema (eds) (1972), *Perspectives in Musicology*, New York: Norton.

Brownell, Susan (1995), *Training the Body for China*, Chicago: Chicago University Press.

Bruner, Jerome (1983), *Child's Talk: Learning to Use Language*, Oxford: Oxford University Press.

Byron, Reginald (1995), 'The Ethnomusicology of John Blacking', in John Blacking, *Music, Culture and Experience: Selected Papers of John Blacking*, ed. R. Byron, Chicago: Chicago University Press, pp. 1–28.

Campbell, Jeremy (1986), *Winston Churchill's Afternoon Nap*, New York: Simon and Schuster.

Chakrabarty, Dipesh (1992), 'Provincializing Europe: Postcoloniality and the Critique of History, *Cultural Studies*, **6**(3), 337–57.

Chase, Gilbert (1972), 'American Musicology and the Social Sciences', in Barry S. Brook, Edward O.D. Downes and Sherman van Solkema (eds), *Perspectives in Musicology,* New York: Norton, pp. 202–26.

Clark, Jane (1976), 'Domenico Scarlatti and Spanish Folk Music', *Early Music*, **4**(1), 19–21.

Clifford, James and George E. Marcus (eds) (1986), *Writing Culture: The Poetics and Politics of Ethnography*, Berkeley: University of California Press.

Cohen, Anthony P. (1992), 'Post-fieldwork Fieldwork', *Journal of Anthropological Research*, **11**, 287–313.

Comaroff, Jean (1985), *Body of Power, Spirit of Resistance: The Culture and History of a South African People*, Chicago: Chicago University Press.

—— (1996), 'The Empire's Old Clothes: Fashioning the Colonial Subject,' in David Howes (ed.), *Cross-Cultural Consumption*, London: Routledge, pp. 19–38.

Comaroff, Jean and John L. Comaroff (1989), 'The Colonization of Consciousness in South Africa', *Economy and Society*, **18**(3), 267–96.

Cook, Nicholas (1998), *Music: A Very Short Introduction*, Oxford: Oxford University Press.

Cook, Nicholas and Mark Everist (eds) (1999), *Rethinking Music*, Oxford: Oxford University Press.

Cooke, Derryck (1959), *The Language of Music*, London: Oxford University Press.

Cooley, Timothy (1997), 'Casting Shadows in the Field: An Introduction', in Gregory Barz and Timothy Cooley (eds), *Shadows in the Field: New*

Perspectives for Fieldwork in Ethnomusicology, New York: Oxford University Press, pp. 3–19.

Coombe, Rosemary J. (1997), 'The Properties of Culture and the Possession of Identity: Postcolonial Struggle and the Legal Imagination,' in Bruce Ziff and Pratina V. Rao (eds), *Borrowed Power: Essays on Cultural Appropriation*, New Brunswick: Rutgens University Press, pp. 74–96.

Coplan, David B. (1980), 'Marabi Culture: Continuity and Transformation in African Music in Johannesburg, 1920–1940', *African Urban Studies*, **6**, 49–78.

—— (1982), 'The Urbanisation of African Music: Some Theoretical Observations', *Popular Music*, 2, 113–29.

—— (1985), *In Township Tonight: South Africa's Black City Music and Theatre*, Johannesburg: Ravan Press.

—— (1994), *In the Time of Cannibals: The World Music of South Africa's Basotho Migrants*, Johannesburg: Witwatersrand University Press.

—— (1998), 'Popular Music in South Africa', in Ruth M. Stone (ed.), *The Garland Encyclopedia of World Music: Africa*, London and New York: Garland, pp. 759–80.

Costello, Robert B. (ed) (1991), *Random House Webster's College Dictionary*, New York: Random House.

Csikszentmihalyi, Mihalyi (1990), *Flow*, New York: Harper Perennial.

—— (1992), *Optimal Experience,* Cambridge: Cambridge University Press.

Csordas, Thomas. J. (ed) (1994), *Embodiment and Experience*, Cambridge: Cambridge University Press.

—— (1995), 'Embodiment as a Paradigm for Anthropology', *Ethos*, 18(1), pp. 5–47.

Dahlhaus, Carl (1987), *Schoenberg and the New Music: Essays by Carl Dahlhaus*, trans. D. Puffett and A. Clayton, Cambridge: Cambridge University Press.

Da Matta, Roberto (1984), 'Carnival in multiple planes', in John J. MacAloon (ed.), *Rite, Drama, Festival, Spectacle: Rehearsals toward a Theory of Cultural Performance*, Philadelphia: Institute for the Study of Human Issues, pp. 208–40.

De Carvalho, José Jorge *et al.* (1991), 'John Blacking – Reminiscences', *Popular Music*, **10**(2), 219–20.

De Hen, Ferdinand J. (2000), *Aspecten van muziek en dans in Swaziland*. Brussels: Academie van Overzeese Wetenschappen.

de Zoete, Beryl (1953), *The Other Mind: A Study of Dance in South India*, London: Victor Gollancz Ltd.

Delius, Peter (1989), 'Sebatakgomo: Migrant Organisation, the ANC and the Sekhukhuneland Revolt', *Journal of Southern African Studies*, **15**(4), 581–616.

DelVecchio Good, Mary-Jo, Paul Brodwin, Bryon Good, and Arthur Kleinman (eds) (1992), *Pain as a Human Experience*, Berkeley: University of California Press.

Desmond, Cosmas (1971), *The Discarded People*, Harmondsworth: Penguin.

Dibelius, Ulrich (1974), 'Alte Instrumente machen noch keine Alte Musik', *Musica*, **28**, 319–24.

Doubleday, Veronica and John Baily (1995), 'Patterns of Musical Development among Children in Afghanistan', in Elizabeth Warnock Fernea (ed.), *Children in the Muslim Middle East Today*, Austin: Texas University Press, pp. 431–46.

Douglas, Mary (1970), *Natural Symbols*, New York: Vintage.

—— (1978), *Purity and Danger*, London: Routledge & Kegan Paul.

Du Bois, W.E.B. (1969), *The Souls of Black Folk*, New York: New American Library.

Durkheim, Emile (1915 [1912]), *The Elementary Forms of the Religious Life,* trans. Joseph Ward Swain, London: George Allen and Unwin.

Ebisawa, Bin (ed). (1987), *Oto no Shigusa: Arima Daigoro Ronjyutsu shu* (*Gesture of Sound: The Collected Monographs of Arima*), Tokyo: Ongakunotomo sha.

Engel, Johann J. (1785–86), *Ideen zu einer mimik, Erster und Zeyter Theil*, Berlin: Mylins'sche Buchhandlung.

Erlmann, Veit (1991), *African Stars: Studies in Black South African Performance*, Chicago: University of Chicago Press.

—— (1999), *Music, Modernity and the Global Imagination: South Africa and the West*, Oxford: Oxford University Press.

Evans-Pritchard, E. E. (1962), *Essays in Social Anthropology*, London: Faber.

Fairley, Jan (1991), 'Remembering – John Blacking', *Popular Music*, **10**(2), 115–19.

Featherstone, Mike, Mike Hepsworth and Bryan Turner (eds) (1991) *The Body*, London: Sage.

Feld, Stephen (1982), *Sound and Sentiment: Birds, Weeping, Poetics, and Song in Kaluli Expression*, Philadelphia: University of Pennsylvania Press.

Fernandez, James (1986), 'The Argument of Images and the Experience of Returning to the Whole', in Victor W. Turner and Edward M. Bruner (eds), *The Anthropology of Experience*, Urbana: University of Illinois Press, pp. 159–87.

Fischer, Hans (ed) (1992), *Ethnologie*, Frankfurt am Main: Dietrich Reimer Verlag.

Fonton, Charles (1751) 'Essai sur la monsigne orientale comparée à la musique enropéenne', manuscript, Bibliothéque Natimale, n.a. 4023.

Foucault, Michel (1979), *Discipline and Punish*, New York: Vintage.

Fujita, Fumiko (1989), *Problems of Language, Culture and the Appropriateness of Musical Expression in Japanese Children's Performance.* Tokyo: Academia Music.

—— (1990), 'The Intermediate Performance between Talking and Singing: From Observational Study of Japanese Children's Music Activities in Nursery Schools', in Jack Dobbs (ed.), *Music Education: Facing the Future*, Christchurch, NZ: ISME, pp. 140–46.

—— (1994), 'Ongaku Hyogen' ('Expressive Musical Performance'), Natsuki, in Okamoto *et al.* (eds), *Youji no Seikatsu to Kyoiku* (*The Life of Early Childhood and Eduction*), vol. 4, Tokyo: Iwanami shoten, pp. 176–94.

—— (2003), 'Arima Daigoro no Ongakuron ni mirareru Minzokuongakuteki na Manazashi' ('Ethnomusicological Inquiries found in both Arima's and Blacking's Essays on music'), *Study of Music: Annual Bulletin of the Postgraduate Course of the Kunitachi College of Music*, **15**, 61–81.

Geertz, Clifford (1973), *The Interpretation of Cultures*, New York: Basic Books.

—— (1988), *Works and Lives: The Anthropologist as Author*, Stanford, CT: Stanford University Press.

Gilbert, Janet (1975), Review of John Blacking's *How Musical is Man?*, *Journal of Music Therapy*, **12**, 100–101.

Gilpin, Heidi (1993), 'Static and Uncertain Bodies: Absence and Instability in Movement Performance', *Assaph*, **9**, 95–114.

Glasstone, Richard (1996), *Dulcie Howes*, Cape Town: Human & Rousseau.

Grau, Andrée (1991), 'John Blacking – Reminiscences', in *Popular Music*, **10**(2), 221–28.

—— (1995), 'Dance as Part of the Infrastructure of Social Life', *The World of Music*, **37**(2), 43–59.

Guha, Ranajit (1992), *Elementary Aspects of Peasant Insurgency in Colonial India*, Delhi: Oxford University Press.

Hansen, Deirdre (1981), 'The Music of the Xhosa-speaking People', unpublished PhD thesis, Johannesburg: University of the Witwatersrand.

Harris, Marvin (1987), *Cultural Anthropology*, New York: Harper & Row.

Harrison, Frank (1973), *Time, Place and Music*, Amsterdam: Frits knuf.

Harwood, Dane L. (1976), 'Universals in Music: A Perspective from Cognitive Psychology', *Ethnomusicology*, **20**, 521–33.

Heidegger, Martin (1962), *Being and Time*, trans. J. Macquarrie and E. Robinson, New York: Harper.

Heimes, Klaus F. (1990), 'The Soft Constitution of the Musical Object: Preliminaries to the Formulation of a Philosophy of Music Education in South Africa', *South African Journal of Musicology*, 10, 57–75.

Helmhotlz, Herman von (1967), *Handbuch der Physiolishen Optik*, Vol III, trans. J. P. Southall, New York: Dover.

Hemming, Jan, Brigitte Markuse and Wolfgang Marx (2000), 'Das Studium der Musikwissenschaft in Deutschland – eine statistische Analyse von Lehrangebot und Fachstruktur', *Die Musikforschung*, **53**(4), 366–88.

Herder, John Gottfried G. (1778–79), *Volkslieder*, 3 vols, ed. Heinz Rölleke, Stuttgart: Philipp Reclam jun., 1975.

Herder, Johann G. (1784–91) *Ideen zur Philosophie der Geschichte der Menschheit*, 4 vols, Riga and Leipzig: Hartknoch.

Herndon, Marcia (1975), review of John Blacking's *How Musical is Man? Ethnomusicology*, **19**(2), 143–45.

Herskovits, Melville J. (1952a), 'Introduction', in Sol Tax (ed.), *Acculturation in the Americas: Proceedings and Selected Papers of the 29th International Congress of Americanists*, Chicago: University of Chicago Press, pp. 48–63.

—— (1952b), 'Some Psychological Implications of Afroamerican Studies', in Sol Tax (ed.), *Acculturation in the Americas: Proceedings and Selected Papers of the 29th International Congress of Americanists*, Chicago: University of Chicago Press, pp. 152–60.

—— (1958 [1938]), *Acculturation: The Study of Culture Contact*, Gloucester, MA: Smith.

Hodges, Donald (1996a), 'Human Musicality', in Donald Hodges (ed.), *Handbook of Music Psychology,* 2nd edn, San Antonio: IMR Press, pp. 29–68.

—— (1996b), 'Neuromusical Research: A Review of the Literature', in Donald Hodges (ed.), *Handbook of Music Psychology,* 2nd edn, San Antonio: IMR Press, pp. 197–284.

Hofmeyr, I. (1993), *'We Spend Our Years as a Tale That is Told': Oral Historical Narrative in a South African Chiefdom*, London: James Chorey.

Hood, Mantle (1960), 'The Challenge of "Bi-musicality"', *Ethnomusicology*, **4**(2), 55–59.

—— (1982 [1971]), *The Ethnomusicologist*, Kent: Kent State University Press.

Hornbostel, Erich von (1933), 'The Ethnology of African Sound-instruments', *Africa*, **6**, 129, 277–311.

Howard, Keith (1991), 'John Blacking: An Interview', *Ethnomusicology*, **35**(1), 55–76.

Howes, David (ed.) (1991), *The Varieties of Sensory Experience*, Toronto: University of Toronto Press.

Huskisson, Yvonne (1958), 'The Social and Ceremonial Music of the Pedi', unpublished PhD dissertation, Witwatersrand University.

Huxley, Aldous (1946), *Perennial Philosophy,* London: Chatto and Windus.

James, Deborah (1991), 'Musical Form and Social History: Research Perspectives on Black South African Music', in Joshua Brown, *et al.* (eds), *History from South Africa: Alternative Visions and Practices*, Philadelphia: Temple University Press, pp. 310–18.

—— (1994), 'Basadi ba baeng/The Women are Visiting: Female Migrant Performance From the Northern Transvaal', in Elizabeth Gunner (ed), *Politics and Performance: Theatre, Poetry and Song in Southern Africa*, Johannesburg: Witwatersrand University Press, pp. 81–110.

—— (1997), '"Music of Origin": Class, Social Category and the Performers and Audience of Kiba, a South African Migrant Genre', *Africa*, **67**(3), 454–75.

—— (1999a), 'Bagageöu/Those of my Home: Migrancy, Gender and Ethnicity in the Northern Province, South Africa', *American Ethnologist* , **26**(1), 69–89.

—— (1999b), *Songs of the Women Migrants: Performance and Identity in South Africa*, International African Institute, Edinburgh University Press.

Jefferey, Peter (1992), *Re-envisioning Past Musical Cultures: Ethno-musicology in the Study of Gregorian Chant*, Chicago and London: University of Chicago Press.

Johnston, Thomas (1971), 'The Music of the Shangana-Tsonga', unpublished PhD thesis, Witwatersrand University.

—— (1975), 'Tsonga Music in Cultural Perspective', *Anthropos*, **70**, 761–99.

Jones, William (1784), *On the Musical Modes of the Hindoos*, Calcutta.

Josephson, David (1991), Review of John Blacking's *A Commonsense View of all Music*, *Ethnomusicology*, **35**(2), 263–68.

Kaufman, Robert (1972), 'Shona Urban Music and the Problem of Acculturation', *Yearbook of the International Folk Music Council*, **4**, 47–55.

Keeling, Richard (ed.) (1989), *Women in North American Indian Music: Six Essays*, Bloomington: University of Indiana Press.

Keil, Charles and Steven Feld (1994), *Music Grooves: Essays and Dialogues,* Chicago: University of Chicago Press.

Kelly, Janice (1988), 'Entrainment in Individual and Group Behavior', in Joseph E. McGrath (ed.), *The Social Psychology of Time: New Perspectives*, Newbury Park: Sage, pp. 89–112.

Kendall, Elizabeth (1979), *Where She Danced*, Berkeley: University of California Press.

Kepler, Johannes (1619), *Harmonices Mundi Libri*, V, Linz: Hans Planck.

Kerman, Josef (1985a), *Contemplating Music: Challenges to Musicology*, Cambridge, MA: Harvard University Press.

—— (1985b), *Musicology*, London: Fontana.

Kikkawa, Eishi (1959), *Hogaku Kansho Nyumon* (*Introduction to the Appreciation of Traditional Japanese Music*), Osaka: Sogen sha.

Kippen, James (1990), 'John Blacking (1928–1990): A Personal Obituary', *Ethnomusicology*, **34**(2), 263–70.

Kirby, Percival (1967), 'The Effect of Western Civilisation on Bantu Music', in Isaac Schapera (ed.), *Western Civilisation and the Natives of South Africa*, London: Routledge and Kegan Paul, pp. 131–40.

—— (1968), *The Musical Instruments of the Native Races of South Africa*, Johannesburg: Witwatersrand University Press.

Klor de Alva, J. Jorge (1997), 'Nahua Colonial Discourse and the Appropriation of the (European) Other', in Bruce Ziff and Pratima V. Rao (eds), *Borrowed Power: Essays on Cultural Appropriation*, New Brunswick: Rutgers University Press, pp. 169–92.

Koch, Klaus-Peter (1982), 'Die polnische und die hanakische Musik in Telemanns Werk, Teil 1: Dokumentation', *Magdeburger Telemann-Studien*, **VI**, 6.

Koizumi, Fumio (1960), *Nihon Dento Ongaku no Kenkyu (The Study of Traditional Japanese Music)*, Tokyo: Ongakunotomo sha.

Koutedakis, Yiannis, Paul Pacy, N.C.C. Sharp, and Fiona Dick (1996), 'Is Fitness Necessary for Dancers?' *Dance Research*, Winter, **14**(2), 105–18.

Kowarzik, Wolfdietrich and Justin Stagl (eds) (1993 [1976]), *Grundfragen der Ethnologie – Beiträge zur gegenwärtigen Theorie-Diskussion*, Berlin: Dietrich Reimer Verlag.

Kramer, Cheryce (2000a), 'Music as Cause and Cure of Illness in Nineteenth-century Europe', in Peregrine Horden (ed.), *Music as Medicine*, Aldershot: Ashgate, pp. 338–52.

—— (2000b), 'Soul Music as Exemplified in Nineteenth-century German Psychiatry', in Penelope Gouk (ed.), *Musical Healing in Cultural Contexts*, Aldershot: Ashgate, pp. 137–48.

Krige, J. D. (1937), 'Traditional Origins and Tribal Relationships of the Sotho of the Northern Transvaal' *Bantu Studies*, **XI**(4), 321–57.

Kruger, Jaco (1986), 'Venda Instrumental Music, with Reference to Certain Chordophones and Idiophones', unpublished M.Mus dissertation, University of Cape Town.

—— (1993), 'A Cultural Analysis of Venda Guitar Songs', unpublished Ph.D thesis, Grahamstown: Rhodes University.

—— (1999), '"Singing Psalms with Owls": A Venda Musical History, Part I: *Tshigombela*', *African Music*, **7**(4), 122–46.

—— (1999–2000), 'Of Wizards and Madmen: Venda *Zwilombe*, Part I: "A Wizard of all Good Things"', *South African Journal of Musicology*, **19–20**, 15–31.

—— (2000), '*Mitambo*: Venda Dance Theatre', *South African Theatre Journal*, **14**, 73–96.

—— (2001), 'Playing in the Land of God: Music Performance and Social Resistance in South Africa.' *British Journal of Ethnomusicology*, **10**(2), 1–36.

Kubik, Gerhard (1974), *The Kachamba Brothers' Band: A Study of Neo-Traditional Music in Malawi*, Zambian Papers, 9, Lusaka: University of Zambia.

—— (1979) 'Pattern Perception and Recognition in African Music', in John Blacking and Joann Keali'inohomoku (eds), *The Performing Arts: Music and Dance*, The Hague: Mouton, pp. 221–49.

—— (1985), 'African Music: The Dimension of Cross-cultural Understanding.' *South African Journal of Musicology*, **5**, 1–5.

—— (1989), 'The Southern African Periphery: Banjo Traditions in Zambia and Malawi', *The World of Music*, **31**(1), 3–30.

—— (1999), *Africa and the Blues*, Jackson: University Press of Mississippi.

Kunze, Stefan (1983), 'Musikwissenschaft und musikalische Proxis. Zur Geschichte eines Missverständnisses', in Peter Reidemeister and Veronica Gutmann (eds), *Alte Musik, Praxis und Reflexion*, Winterthur, pp. 115–24.

Lambert, Constant (1934), *Music Ho!*, London: Faber and Faber.

Lang, Paul Henry (1972), 'Musicology and Related Disciplines', in Barry S. Brook, Edward O.D. Downes and Sherman van Solkema (eds), *Perspectives in Musicology*, New York: Norton, pp. 185–201.

Langer, Susanne (1953), *Feeling and Form: A Theory of Art,* New York: Scribner.

Lindahl, Marita (1995), *Inlärning och Erfarand (Experience and Learning).* Göteborg: Göteborg Studies in Educational Sciences, p. 103.

Lipscomb, Scott (1996), 'The Cognitive Organization of Musical Sound', in Donald Hodges, (ed.), *Handbook of Music Psychology,* 2nd edn, San Antonio: IMR Press, pp. 133–75.

Lipscomb, Scott and Donald Hodges (1996), 'Hearing and Music Perception', in Donald Hodges (ed.), *Handbook of Music Psychology,* 2nd edn, San Antonio: IMR Press, pp. 83–131.

List, George (1963), 'The Boundaries of Speech and Song', *Ethnomusicology*, **7**(1) 1–16.

Lutz, Catherine and Geoffrey White (1986), 'The Anthropology of Emotions', *Annual Review of Anthropology*, **15**, 405–36.

McAllester, David P. (1954), *Enemy Way Music,* Cambridge, MA: Peabody Museum.

McClary, Susan (1991), *Feminine Endings: Music, Gender, and Sexuality.* Minneapolis: University of Minnesota Press.

McLeod, Norma and Marcia Herndon (1983), *Field Manual for Ethnomusicology*, Norwood: Norwood Editions.

McMullen, Patrick (1996), 'The Musical Experience and Affective/Aesthetic Responses: A Theoretical Framework for Empirical Research', in Donald Hodges (ed.), *Handbook of Music Psychology,* 2nd edn, San Antonio: IMR Press, pp. 387–400.

Mang, Esther (2000), 'Intermediate Vocalization of the Boundary Between Speech and Songs in Young Children's Vocalization'; paper presented at the Eighteenth International Research Seminar, Salt Lake City, Utah, USA.

Manganaro, Marc (ed.) (1990), *Modernist Anthropology: From Fieldwork to Text*, Princeton: Princeton University Press.

Manuel, Peter (1988), *Popular Musics of the Non-Western World: An Introductory Survey*, Oxford: Oxford University Press.

Martin, Emily (1987), *The Woman in the Body*, Boston: Beacon Press.

Maslow, Abraham (1954), *Motivation and Personality*, New York: Harper.

Mattheson, Johann (1740), *Grundlage einer Ehren-Pforte*, Hamburg.

Mayer, P. and I. Mayer (1971), *Townsmen or Tribesmen*, Cape Town: Oxford University Press.

Merriam, Alan (1964), *The Anthropology of Music*, Evanston: Northwestern University Press.

—— (1969), 'Ethnomusicology Revisited', *Ethnomusicology*, **13**(2), 213–29.

—— (1974), Review of John Blacking's *How Musical is Man?*, *Journal of American Folklore*, **87**, 166–68.

Miller, Terry E. and Japernchni Chonpairot (1994), 'A History of Siamese Music Constructed from Western Documents, 1505–1932', *Crossroads: An Interdisciplinary Journal of Southeast Asian Studies*, **8**(2), 1–192.

Molepo M.M. (1984), 'The Changing Nature of Labour Migration from the Northern Transvaal with Particular reference to Molepo Village c1900–1940', unpublished MA dissertation, University of London, SOAS.

Moore, Jerrold Northrop (1984), *Edward Elgar: A Creative Life*, Oxford: Oxford University Press.

Moore, Sally Falk (1989), 'The Production of Cultural Pluralism as a Process', *Public Culture*, **1**(2), 26–48.

Muller, Carol A. (1999), *Rituals of Fertility and the Sacrifice of Desire: Nazarite Women's Performance in South Africa*, Chicago: University of Chicago Press.

Myers, Helen (1992a), 'Field Technology', in Helen Myers (ed.), *Ethnomusicology: An Introduction*, London: Macmillan, pp. 50–87.

—— (1992b), 'Fieldwork', in Helen Myers (ed.), *Ethnomusicology: An Introduction*, London: Macmillan, pp. 21–49.

—— (1992c), 'Introduction', in Helen Myers (ed.), *Ethnomusicology: An Introduction*, London: Macmillan, pp. 3–15.

—— (1992d), 'Gender and Music', in Helen Myers (ed.), *Ethnomusicology: An Introduction*, London: Macmillan, pp. 337–48.

Nadel, Siegfried F. (1930), 'The Origins of Music'. *The Musical Quarterly*, **16**, 531–46.

Nettl, Bruno (1964), *Theory and Method in Ethnomusicology*, New York: The Free Press of Glencoe.

—— (1983), *The Study of Ethnomusicology: Twenty-nine Issues and Concepts*, Urbana and Chicago: University of Illinois Press.

—— (1985), *The Western Impact on World Music: Change, Adaptation, and Survival*, New York: Schirmer Books.

—— (1989a), *Blackfoot Musical Thought: Comparative Perspectives*, Kent, OH: Kent State University Press.

—— (1989b), 'Mozart and the Ethnomusicological Study of Western Culture (An Essay in Four Movements)', *Yearbook for Traditional Music*, **21**, 1–16.

—— (1999), 'The Institutionalization of Musicology: Perspectives of a North American Ethnomusicologist', Nicolas Cook and Mark Everist (eds) *Rethinking Music*, Oxford: Oxford University Press, pp. 287–310.

O'Hanlon, Rosalind (1988), 'Recovering the Subject: Subaltern Studies and Histories of Resistance in Colonial South Asia', *Modern Asian Studies*, **22**(1), 180–224.

Olsson, Cecilia (1993), *Dansföreställningar*. Lund: Bokbox.

Palmer, Catherine (1996), 'A Life of its Own', unpublished PhD thesis, University of Adelaide.

Parry, Benita (1994), 'Resistance Theory/Theorising Resistance or Two Cheers for Nativism', in Francis Barker, Peter Hulme, and Margaret Iversen (eds), *Colonial Discourse/Postcolonial Theory*, Manchester: Manchester University Press, pp. 172–96.

Pêcheux, Michel (1982), *Language, Semantics and Ideology*, trans. Harbans Nagpal, London: Palgrave Macmillan.

Pegg, Carole (2001), 'Ethnomusicology – I. Introduction'. in Stanley Sadie (ed.) *The New Grove Dictionary of Music and Musicians*, 8, London: Macmillan Publishers, pp. 367–68.

Pennanen, Risto Pekka (1999), *Westernisation and Modernisation in Greek Popular Music*, Tampere: University of Tampere Press.

Perischetti, Vincent (1978), *Twentieth Century Harmony: Creative Aspects and Practice*, London: Faber and Faber.

Picken, Laurence *et al.* (1981–97), *Music from the Tang Court*, vols 1–3 (1981–1985), Oxford: Oxford University Press; vols 4–6 (1987–97), Cambridge: Cambridge University Press.

Pike, Kenneth L. (1948), *Tone Language*, Ann Arbor: The University of Michigan Press.

Post, Jennifer C, Mary Russell Bucknum and Laurel Sercombe (1994), *A Manual for Documentation, Fieldwork, and Preservation*, Bloomington, IN: Society for Ethnomusicology.

Pratt, Mary Louise (1991), 'Arts of the Contact Zone', *Profession*, **91**, 33–40.

—— (1996), 'Transculturation and Autoethnography: Peru 1615/1980', in Francis Barker, Peter Hulme, and Margaret Iversen (eds), *Colonial Discourse/Postcolonial Theory*, Manchester: Manchester University Press, pp. 24–46.

Quantz, Johann Joachim (1752), *Versuch einer Anweisung die Flöte traversiere zu spielen*, Berlin: Johann Friedrich Voß.

Ranger, T.O. (1975), *Dance and Society in Eastern Africa, 1890–1970: The Beni Ngoma*, London: Heinemann.

Reichow, Jan (1984a), 'Ich muss meine Spielart gantz anders ändern ... Part I', *Concerto*, **5**, 15–21.

—— (1984b), 'Ich muss meine Spielart gantz anders ändern ... Part II', *Concerto*, **6**, 19–23.

—— (1984c), 'Ich muss meine Spielart gantz anders ändern ... Part III', *Concerto*, **7**, 18–23.

Reily, Suzel Ana (1998), 'The Ethnographic Enterprise: Venda Girls' Initiation Schools Revisted', *British Journal of Ethnomusicology*, **7**, 45–68.

Rice, Timothy (1994), *May It Fill Your Soul: Experiencing Bulgarian Folk Music*, Chicago: Chicago University Press.

—— (1997) 'Toward a Mediation of Field Methods and Field Experience in Ethnomusicology', in Gregory Barz and Timothy Cooley (eds), *Shadows in the Field: New Perspectives for Fieldwork in Ethnomusicology*, New York: Oxford University Press, pp. 101–20.

Rice, Timothy, James Porter and Chris Goertze (eds.) (2000), *The Garland Encyclopaedia of World Music: Europe, vol. 8,* New York: Garland Publishing.

Ricoeur, Paul (1981), *Hermeneutics and the Human Sciences: Essays on Language, Action and Interpretation*, ed. and trans. J.B. Thompson, Cambridge: Cambridge University Press.

Risset, Jean-Claude and David Wessel (1999), 'Exploration of Timbre by Analysis and Synthesis', in Diana Deutsch (ed.), *The Psychology of Music,* 2nd edn, San Diego: Academic Press, pp. 113–69.

Robbins, Richard (1973), 'Identity, Culture, and Behavior', in John Honigmann (ed.), *Handbook of Social and Cultural Anthropology*, Chicago: Rand McNally, pp. 1199–222.

Rosaldo, Renato (1993), *Culture and Truth: The Remaking of Social Analysis*, Boston, MA: Beacon Press.

Rouget, Gilbert (1977a), 'Music and Possession Trance', in John Blacking (ed.), *The Anthropology of the Body*, ASA Monographs No. 15, London: Academic Press, pp. 233–39.

—— (1977b), Review of John Blacking's *How Musical is Man? Times Literary Supplement*, p. 410.

—— (1985), *Music and Trance: A Theory of the Relations between Music and Possession*, trans. B. Biebuyck, Chicago: University of Chicago Press.

Rousseau, Jean-Jacques (1767), *Dictionnaire de musique*, Geneva.

Rycroft, David (1961), 'The Guitar Improvisations of Mwenda Jean Bosco', *African Music*, **2**(4), 81–98.

—— (1971), 'Stylistic Evidence in Nguni Song', in Klaus P. Wachsmann (ed.), *Essays on Music and History in Africa*, Evanston: Northwestern University Press, pp. 213–42.

—— (1977), 'Stylistic Continuity in Zulu Town Music', in Lois Anderson *et al.* (eds), *Essays for a Humanist: An Offering to Klaus Wachsmann*, New York: The Town House Press, pp. 216–60.

Sachs, Curt (1929), *Geist und Werden der Musikinstrumente*, Berlin: Dietrich Reimer Verlag.

—— (1943), *The Rise of Music in the Ancient World, East and West*, New York: W.W. Norton & Co.

—— (1962), *The Wellsprings of Music*, The Hague: M. Nijhoff.

Said, Edward W. (1993), *Culture and Imperialism*, London: Vintage Books.

Scarry, Elain (1985), *The Body in Pain*, New York: Oxford University Press.

Scheper-Hughes, Nancy and Margaret Lock (1987), 'The Mindful Body: A Prolegomenon to Future Work in Medical Anthropology', *Medical Anthropology Quartely*, **1**(1), 6–41.

Schneider, Albrecht (1976), *Musikwissenschaft und Kulturkreislehre. Zur Methodik und Geschichte der vergleichenden Musikwissenschaften*, Bonn-Bad Godesberg: Verlag für Systematische Musikwissenschaft.

Schneider, Marius (1968 [1934]), *Geschichte der Mehrstimmigkeit: Historische und phänomenologische Studien. I: Die Naturvölker, II: Die Anfänge in Europa* [1934, reprint 1968 with *III: Die Kompositionsprinzipien und ihre Verbreitung*], Tutzing: Hans Schneider.

Schulenberg, David (2000), 'History of European Art Music', in Timothy Rice, James Porter, and Chris Goertzen (eds), *The Garland Encyclopaedia of World Music: Europe, vol. 8*, New York and London: Garland, pp. 68–88.

Schutz, Alfred (1964), 'Making Music Together: A Study in Social Relationship', in *Collected Papers II*, The Hague: Martinus Nijhoff.

Scott, Cyril (1976 [1933]), *Music: Its Secret Influence through the Ages*, Wellingborough: The Aquarian Press.

Scott, James C. (1993), *Domination and the Arts of Resistance: Hidden Transcripts*, New Haven, CT: Yale University Press.

Shelemay, Kay Kaufmann (1997), 'The Ethnomusicologist, Ethnographic Method, and the Transmission of Tradition', in Gregory Barz and Timothy Cooley (eds), *Shadows in the Field: New Perspectives for Fieldwork in Ethnomusicology*, New York: Oxford University Press, pp. 189–204.

Shiloah, Amnon (1991), 'An Eighteenth-century Critic of Taste and Good Taste', in Steven Blum, Philip V. Bohlman and Daniel M. Neumann, *Ethnomusicology and Modern Music History*, Urbana and Chicago: University of Illinois Press, pp. 181–89.

Slobin, Mark (1993), *Subcultural Sounds: Micromusics of the West*, Hanover and London: Wesleyan University Press.

Slobin, Mark and Jeff Todd Titon (1992), 'The Music Culture as a World of Music', in Jeff Todd Titon (ed.), *The Worlds of Music: An Introduction to the Music of the World's Peoples*, 2nd edn, New York: Schirmer, pp. 1–15.

Small, Christopher (1977), *Music, Society, Education*, London: John Calder.

Smith Brindle, Reginald (1966), *Serial Composition*, London: Oxford University Press.

Stobart, Henry (1996), 'The Llama's Flute: Musical Misunderstandings in the Andes', *Early Music*, **24**(3), 471–82.

Stock, Jonathan P.J. (1993), 'An Ethnomusicological Perspective on Musical Style, with Reference to Music for Chinese Two-stringed Fiddles', *Journal of the Royal Musicological Association*, **118**(2), 276–99.

—— (1998), 'New Musicologies, Old Musicologies: Ethnomusicology and the Study of Western Music', *Current Musicology*, 62, pp. 40–68.

Stone, Ruth M. (1982), *Let the Inside be Sweet: The Interpretation of Music Events among the Kpelle of Liberin*, Bloomington, University of Indiana Press.

Sundberg, Johan (1999), 'The Perception of Singing', in Diana Deutsch (ed.), *The Psychology of Music*, 2nd edn, San Diego: Academic Press, pp. 171–214.

Suppan, Wolfgang (1973), *Deutsches Liedleben zwischen Renaissance and Barock*, Tutzing: Schneider.

Surplus People Project (1983), *Forced Removals in South Africa*, 5 vols, Cape Town: Surplus People Project.

Sweers, Britta (2000), 'Ethnomusicology in Germany', *SEM Newsletter*, **34**(3), 1, 4–5.

Synnott, Anthony (1993), *The Body Social*, London: Routledge.

Tajet-Foxell, Britt and F.D. Rose (1995), 'Pain and Pain-tolerance in Professional Ballet Dancers', *British Journal of Sports Medicine*, **29**(1), 31–34.

Titon, Jeff Todd (1997), 'Knowing Fieldwork', in Gregory Barz and Timothy Cooley (eds), *Shadows in the Field: New Perspectives for Fieldwork in Ethnomusicology*, New York: Oxford University Press, pp. 87–100.

Tomkins, S.S. (1964), *The Polarify Scale*, New York: Springer.

Tomlinson, Gary (1984), 'The Web of Culture: A Context for Musicology', *Nineteenth Century Music*, **7**, 350–62.

Tracey, Andrew (1989), *The West and African Music: South African Traditional Musicians Visit Paris*, press release, Grahamstown: International Library of African Music.

Turner, Bryan S. (1984), *The Body and Society*, Oxford: Basil Blackwell.

Turner, Victor W. (1969), *The Ritual Process: Structure and Anti-Structure*, Chicago: Aldine.

van den Toorn, Pieter (1997), *Music, Politics, and the Academy*, Berkeley: University of California Press.

van Warmelo, N.J. (1935), *Preliminary Survey of the Bantu Tribes of South Africa*, Ethnological Publication No. 5, Pretoria: Government Printers.

—— (1952), *Language Map of South Africa*, Pretoria: Government Printers.

Velichkina, Olga (1998), 'Playing Panpipes in Southern Russia: History, Ethnography and Performance Practices', unpublished PhD thesis, Ohio State University.

Wacquant, Loic (1992), 'The Social Logic of Boxing in Black Chicago: Toward a Sociology of Pugilism', *Sociology of Sport Journal*, **9**, 221–54.

—— (1995a), 'The Pugilist Point of View: How Boxers Think and Feel About Their Trade', *Theory and Society*, **24**(4), 489–535.

—— (1995b), 'Pugs at Work: Bodily Capital and Labour Among Professional Boxers', *Body and Society*, **1**(1), 65–93.

Wainwright, Steve P. and Bryan S. Turner (2003), 'Narratives of Embodiment: Body, Ageing and Career in Royal Ballet Dancers', in Helen Thomas and Jamilah Ahmed (eds), *Cultural Bodies*, Malden, MA: Blackwell.

Waterman, Christopher A. (1990), *Jùjú: A Social History and Ethnography of an African Popular Music*, Chicago: Chicago University Press.

Waterman, Richard A. (1952), 'African influence on the music of the Americas', in Sol Tax (ed.), *Acculturation in the Americas: Proceedings and Selected Papers of the 29th International Congress of Americanists*, Chicago: University of Chicago Press, pp. 207–18.

Whitehouse, Harvey (1995), *Inside the Cult*, Oxford: Clarendon Press.

Widdess, Richard (1996), 'Editorial', *Early Music*, **24**(3), 372–73.

Wilson, John (ed.) (1962), The Faith of an Artist, London: George Allen and Unwin.

Wilson, M. (1982), '"The Nguni People" and "The Sotho, Venda and Tsonga"', in M. Wilson and L. Thompson (eds), *The Oxford History of South Africa*, Cape Town: David Philip.

Witzleben, J. Lawrence (1997), 'Whose Ethnomusicology? Western Ethnomusicology and the Study of Asian Music', *Ethnomusicology*, **41**(2), 220–42.

Wulff, Helena (1995), 'Introducing Youth Culture in its own Right: The State of the Art and New Possibilities', in Vered Amit-Talai and Helena Wulff (eds), *Youth Cultures*, London: Routledge.

—— (1997), 'Studying Ballet as an Ex-native: Dialogues of Life and Field Work', in Anne Clair Groffman, *et al.* (eds), *Kulturanthropologinnen im Dialog*, Königstein: Ulrike Helmer Verlag.

—— (1998), *Ballet across Borders*, Oxford: Berg.

—— (2000), 'Access to a Closed World: Methods for a Multilocale Study on Ballet as a Career', in Vered Amit (ed.), *Constructing the Field,* London: Routledge.

—— (2002), 'Aesthetics at the Ballet: Looking at "National" Style, Body and Clothing in the London Dance World', in Nigel Rapport (ed.), *British Subjects*, Oxford: Berg.

—— (2003), 'The Irish Body in Motion: Moral Politics, National Identity and Dance', in Eduardo P. Archetti and Noel Dyck (eds). *Sport, Dance and Embodied Identities*, Oxford: Berg.

Young, Susan (1995), 'Listening to the Music of Early Childhood', *British Journal of Music Education*, **12**(1), 51–58.

Yung, Bel (1984), 'Choreographic and Kinesthetic Elements in Performance on the Chinese Seven-string Zither,' *Ethnomusicology*, **28**(3), 505–17.

Zemp, Hugo (1971), *Musique Dan: la musique dans la pensée et la vie sociale d'une societé africaine*, Paris: Mouton.

Index